AVID

READER

PRESS

ALSO BY MARGARET HEFFERNAN

Beyond Measure

A Bigger Prize

Willful Blindness

Women on Top

The Naked Truth

UNCHARTED

HOW TO NAVIGATE
THE FUTURE

MARGARET HEFFERNAN

AVID READER PRESS

NEW YORK LONDON TORONTO SYDNEY NEW DELHI

AVID READER PRESS
An Imprint of Simon & Schuster, Inc.
1230 Avenue of the Americas
New York, NY 10020

First Avid Reader Press hardcover edition September 2020

AVID READER PRESS and colophon are
trademarks of Simon & Schuster, Inc.

For information about special discounts for bulk purchases,
please contact Simon & Schuster Special Sales at 1-866-506-1949
or business@simonandschuster.com.

The Simon & Schuster Speakers Bureau can bring authors to
your live event. For more information or to book an event,
contact the Simon & Schuster Speakers Bureau at 1-866-248-3049
or visit our website at www.simonspeakers.com.

Interior design by Kyle Kabel

Manufactured in the United States of America

1 3 5 7 9 10 8 6 4 2

Library of Congress Cataloging-in-Publication Data has been applied for.

ISBN 978-1-9821-1262-2
ISBN 978-1-9821-1264-6 (ebook)

For
Jonathan
Raj
Robert
and
Roger

CONTENTS

PART III
LIFE HAPPENS

INTRODUCTION

We think about the future all day, every day. What time do I need to leave the house? What's for breakfast? Can we picnic on the weekend? Should I change jobs? Move house? Online and offline, the news is mostly speculation: what will happen in Congress, in traffic, in the markets. However much we might aim to live in the present, we can't cross the road without thinking ahead: Will that car reach me before I'm safely across? Our brains have evolved to anticipate whether we'll like this food, this person, that book. Entire industries—property, travel, banks, insurance, pensions, technology—analyze, construct, and sell permutations of the future. So we cannot *not* think about it: neither our brains nor our lives will allow it.

Prospection bestows tremendous evolutionary advantage, alerting me to danger or reassuring me that the noise I hear isn't a burglar but a cat. For the most part, it works so well that we scarcely notice when we get home on time, pack the right clothes, select satisfying homes and holidays. Apps train us to expect accuracy in plotting routes, choosing hotels, restaurants, and lovers with levels of confidence our ancestors never imagined. We have come to expect the future to be minutely and perfectly predictable.

And then it rains after all, the train's late, traffic is held up by a crash, the neighborhood is noisy, the job hateful, and the election doesn't go our way. Trump. Brexit. The end of history. The fall of idols. A new virus. Booms and busts and out of the blue, #MeToo. The predictability of life, on which we've come to depend, seems to fall away and we're left angry, intolerant, fearful.

Our expectations are wrong. The future isn't perfectly knowable and never has been. Our brains may be the single most complex object in the known universe, but they still make mistakes. Today's technology may be the most advanced the world has ever seen but it is imperfect, too: incomplete, biased, and full of error. Google isn't always right. Satnavs can't foresee when a child will run into the road. Artificial intelligence trusts correlations that turn out to be irrelevant, biased, or ill-informed. DNA knows nothing about broken legs or toxic pollution.

Ineradicable uncertainty remains inherent to human life; Hannah Arendt called it the defining characteristic of the future. That this leaves us uncomfortable and anxious is why humans have always searched for ways to see what's coming: oracles, shamans, horoscopes, religions. Longing to reduce uncertainty and doubt has driven much of our progress. The more we noticed, remembered, wrote down, and shared, the more knowledgeable we became and the better able we were to pass our learning on for future generations to increase. This made us better and better estimators, able to plan. The entire construct of management—forecast, plan, execute—hinges on our capacity to make well-informed estimates. The more we practiced it, the more accurate we became.

It makes sense to imagine that progress is infinitely sustainable, but it isn't. Along the way, fundamental change has occurred. We have moved from a complicated world to a complex one. The two aren't the same—and complexity isn't just complication on steroids. Complicated environments are linear, follow rules, and are predictable; like an assembly line, they can be planned, managed, repeated, and controlled. They're maximized by routine and efficiency. But the advent of globalization, coupled with pervasive communications, has made much of life complex: nonlinear and fluid, where very small effects may produce disproportionate impacts. General Stanley McChrystal distinguishes between the First Gulf War (1990–91), which he says was complicated—an intensely planned application of overwhelming force, executed by the book—and the Iraq War (begun in 2003), which was complex: a fluid, volatile environment of shifting opacity where a lone individual with a cell phone could tip the balance. On a more mundane level, the maker of electronic keyboards inhabits a complex world where a single negative review on Amazon can reduce sales by 50 percent.

What this shift means is that, while we can still be generally certain about many things, much remains specifically ambiguous. We know climate change is real but we can't predict when or where wildfires will break out or when extreme weather events will destroy which harvests. The Bank of England acknowledges that there will be future banking busts, but cannot say when or why. Their executives aren't stupid, just candid about navigating daily tsunamis of data and interactions, of which some are meaningful, much is obscure, and quite a lot is pointless. The bank recognizes that much of the financial system—Trump's tweets, corruption trials in Korea, the outbreak of a new virus—lies beyond prediction or influence. We used to ignore these systems but their problems have become ours now, when a bank halfway across the world crashes or a government falls.

Apple's iPhone may have been "designed in California" but making it depends on raw materials and suppliers from Ireland, the Philippines, China, Taiwan, Japan, Austria, Korea, Singapore, Thailand, Germany, the United Kingdom, the Netherlands, Indonesia, Puerto Rico, Brazil, Malaysia, Israel, Czech Republic, Mexico, Vietnam, Morocco, Malta, Belgium, and many of the United States. This complex supply chain is designed to reduce costs and take advantage of labor expertise, employment conditions, currency fluctuations, and tax breaks. But they expose Apple (and similar phone manufacturers) to natural disasters, labor disputes, economic volatility, social turmoil, religious strife, trade wars, and political discontent: all factors over which the company has no control, little influence, and poor foresight. We're so dazzled by such systems, we forget, or prefer to deny, that contingencies have multiplied, fragility has proliferated, and accurate prediction has become harder.

To be able to do and know so much, and yet not to be able to predict what we crave to know, is painful and frustrating. So we perpetuate the age-old search for sources of certainty. That leaves us susceptible to pundits and prophets: experts and forecasters who claim superior knowledge. But the more famous they are, the more likely they are to be wrong. Other models prove unsatisfactory, too. History doesn't always repeat itself but often misleads us with aesthetically pleasing analogies that underweight critical differences. Psychological profiling is flawed by subjective models, attribution errors, and inadequate data. DNA tells only part of our story; the rest is driven by more factors than we see or know. Proponents of each model oversell their promise and each one falls down, defeated by the ineradicable uncertainty of life. Overwhelmed by complexity, we seek simplification and too quickly reach for binary perspectives, just at the moment when we need broader ones.

Technology offers a shiny new model, purporting to solve the problem that it amplifies and accelerates. Big data, analytics, machine learning, and artificial intelligence may help us to see more, to glean patterns previously impenetrable to the human brain alone. But their capacity to assess mountains of data at speed obscures their flaws. A large dataset might describe a group or neighborhood of voters well, but still be unable to forecast with certainty how an individual will decide to vote next time; people change—and not always predictably. Algorithms are, as the mathematician Cathy

O'Neil once said, opinions encoded in numbers. They combine assumptions that are subjective, imposed on data that's skewed and incomplete in complex environments. Unique or rare external events may render what was formerly predictable suddenly unforeseeable, where historical data is irrelevant or useless. (This is frequently true of epidemics.) And finally there is the problem of life itself: the tendency of organisms, atoms, and subatomic particles to behave in nonrandom but fundamentally unpredictable ways.

The utopian fantasy of the tech industry—that all the data in the world will yield perfect predictions—appropriately provokes privacy champions. But that isn't its only challenge. These predictive systems are frequently wrong, as when they recommend to me a book I've written or one I hated. Such flaws are trivial, because the recommendation is cheap to produce and easy to ignore. But when determining who should have access to jobs, social services, or health care, such errors can be dangerous and unjust. All computer code contains bugs, and managers of AI technologies say that every now and then—unpredictably—their systems need to be reset. They don't know why.

But depending on technology incurs a high cost. Every time we use it, we outsource to machines what we could and can do ourselves. The more we use GPS, for example, the more the parts of our brain responsible for navigation and memory shrink.[1] And the less we know our neighborhood. This is known as the automation paradox: the skills you automate, you lose. So the more we depend on machines to think for us, the less good we become at thinking for ourselves. The fewer decisions we make, the less good we become at making them. We risk falling into a trap: more need for certainty, more dependency on technology, less skill, more need. We become addicted to the very source of our anxiety.

That isn't technology's only cost. If companies once expected perfect data to make consumers perfectly predictable, the fundamental uncertainty of life has deprived them of that prize. We aren't machines—but that hasn't stopped tech companies from trying to turn us into them. As the Harvard academic Shoshana Zuboff has so eloquently revealed, they now hope to turn all the tools of behavioral psychology on us to create the predictable creatures they need us to be. "The goal of everything we do," a Silicon Valley data scientist told her, "is to change people's actual behavior at scale." The ambition is to use nudges, rewards, the lure of convenience to reinforce what companies define as good, or to discourage what they define as bad.[2] As digital devices pervade our lives, it becomes easier to solve the so-called problem of human complexity by force-fitting a predetermined model onto human life. The technology that deskills us, together with companies actively attempting to deprive us of human agency, threatens to leave us passive and conformist. But absolute certainty about all aspects of life would be tyranny. So, at a time in our history where we have huge decisions to make—about the climate, about technology, capitalism, democracy—we need our freedom, of thought and action, more than ever. In an age of uncertainty, we have to ask ourselves what we need to be, and what we need to do—and to come up with our own answers.

The first part of this book looks at how our models for knowing the future let us down. It isn't an argument for apathy or resignation. Only when we reject pundits and propagandists can we free ourselves to explore the contours and landscape of possibility. Our choice is not between false certainty or ignorance; it is between surrender or participation. So we need to leave simple solutions behind, to be bolder in our search, more penetrating in our enquiry, more energetic in our quest for discovery.

Accepting that the future is unknowable is where action begins. Experiments are ideal for complex environments because they yield clues about where you are; they are the best thing to do when you can't see where to start. Scenarios expand and explore the terrain, revealing a range of possibilities—good and bad—that also enlarge our capacity to understand ourselves and each other. The work of artists endures because they dare to imagine what they can't see and allow their minds to leave predetermined paths; we may not all be artists, but we need their independence and stamina. Cathedral projects whose ambition defies master plans show how much more can be achieved with a collective sense of meaning.

In existential crises, there is no time to consider the future. But survivors show us what we need, and what we have. When they strike, even in what looks like chaos, they call upon untapped reservoirs of energy, invention, and daring. Even the one certainty in life, death, offers opportunities to influence what goes after us. And just because we don't know the future doesn't mean we're left helpless; there's genius and creativity in preparation. In this complex, nonlinear world, there can be no step-by-step rulebook, no linear model, no simple antidote to uncertainty. Planning, theory, and ideologies break down in the face of unpredictability, leaving us instead with an urgent mandate and multiple methods to explore. This always begins with questions: What can we do right now? What do we need to be now? What must we preserve at all cost?

This is an optimistic book. Not because it promises that all is for the best in the best of all possible worlds. Optimists aren't idiots. They do better in life—live longer, healthier, more successful lives—for the simple reason that they don't ignore problems or give up easily. Psychologists distinguish between two kinds of optimists. Explainers accept that bad news is neither permanent (things can improve) nor universal (good news is happening somewhere else). Expectant optimists, by contrast, see problems but anticipate improvement. Unconstrained by reality, they have a fighting spirit. Both kinds of optimism alert individuals to fresh opportunities and to the resources needed to pursue goals. Where pessimists may avoid problems, optimists cope and solve. They are specially productive because optimists are more likely to reach out for help, to collaborate and trust others. That gives them more capacity and resilience than they could possess alone. At a time when Americans are predominantly pessimistic about the future, and even successful CEOs share their gloom,[3] when we are deluged with propaganda threatening to supplant human talents with the so-called perfection of machines, the sheer creativity of human interaction has never been more critical. We have a huge capacity for invention—if we use it. We have limitless talent for questions and exploration—if we develop it. We can imagine what we've never seen before—if we practice. Lose these gifts and we are adrift. Hone and develop them and we can make any future we choose.

Anyone who tries to tell us they know the future is simply trying to own it: a spurious claim to manifest destiny. The harder, more subtle truth is that the future is uncharted because we aren't there yet. So this book can't provide a map, an app, or any perfect certainty about destination or time of arrival. What it will do is provide the questions to lead you in the direction you choose. Many of the most inspiring people and stories start with uncertainty, are saturated with doubt, yet arrive triumphant at places in life they could not see when they set out. Their successes are deeply human, derived from curiosity, imagination, and not a little bravery. They were prepared to navigate the unknown in pursuit of the ill-defined because they knew that the only way to know the future is to make it.

PART I

PREDICTION ADDICTION

CHAPTER ONE

FALSE PROFITS

The only function of economic forecasting is to make astrology look respectable.

—John Kenneth Galbraith

Who knew what was in the air? Even a breath can be a catalyst. Enjoying the waters just beyond Narragansett Pier, Rhode Island, the economist Irving Fisher kept swimming. A happy marriage, two daughters. The full professorship at Yale was a lifetime appointment and the future seemed as dazzling as the summer ocean. But looking back to the shore, he was surprised how far the current had carried him. It took all his energy to regain the beach. He arrived at last exhausted, unnerved by the speed with which his glorious future had turned precarious.

For the rest of his life, Fisher would wonder whether that episode in the summer of 1898 had been an early warning sign. Was the swim so tough because he was already infected—or did his exhaustion trigger the crisis? Whichever way it happened, by the autumn Fisher scarcely recognized himself. Everything tired him and every afternoon he ran a fever. His doctor was stumped. Not a man to appreciate uncertainty, Fisher demanded a saliva test. When it came back positive, the physician felt too abashed to face his patient. Instead, he quit, never submitting his bill.

It was left to Fisher's wife, Margaret, to deliver the diagnosis: tuberculosis. At the time, TB was the single greatest cause of death in the Western world. Autopsies showed almost every city dweller to be infected. But even without the data, Fisher knew the danger he faced: his father had died from the disease. Now aged thirty-one, what kind of future did he face?

Millions asked themselves the same question. By 1898, educated people knew that tuberculosis was an airborne bacillus, but there was no vaccine and no certain cure. Nor was there any reliable prognosis: the disease could lie latent for years, even a lifetime, or you could be dead in a matter of weeks. So diagnosis was almost worse than useless. Had Fisher received a life sentence—or just experienced some mild discomfort that would never return? As painful as the disease was the doubt.

As with all epidemics, moralists were quick to construct punitive theories to explain its cause. The disease was divine retribution for alcohol or tobacco consumption, sexual "self-abuse," even dancing was suspected. Or perhaps society was to blame: commentators noted that TB thrived in places where urban crowding, pollution, and mixed races proliferated. One surgeon, Ambrose Ranney, insisted that whether the disease killed you could be discerned through analysis of the lines of the brow, the hue and texture of the skin.[1] From causes to cures, everyone searched for predictive patterns.

Fisher turned to diet. He eschewed meat, forswore alcohol, and became an energetic advocate for prolonged mastication. At Yale, he urged athletes to correlate the length of time that they chewed their food with their athletic performance. He endorsed the new breakfast cereal Grape-Nuts, certain its extreme chewiness would make its consumers stronger. Diet became a life-or-death mission for Fisher; but not only for Fisher. Convinced that the health of a nation determined the wealth of the nation, he estimated the annual economic cost to the United States of tuberculosis at $550 million—around $254 billion today.[2]

Although the TB bacillus had been isolated by Robert Koch in 1882, no cure was known until 1944, when Albert Schatz and Selman Waksman discovered streptomycin. Until then, patients remained suspended in crisis: fearful of the future and desperate for any remedies or signs that might foretell their future. For Irving Fisher, uncertainty was not an abstract idea but a visceral reality.

He was not alone. Even a casual scan of events at the start of the twentieth century reveals a concatenation of wars, terrorism, political assassinations, earthquakes, royal suicides, epidemics, and famine. What did these events portend? Did they spell progress or doom? Market crashes, revolutionary movements, new political parties, scientific breakthroughs, radical technological change, and a chaotic cultural scene just barely contained order, anxiety, and mayhem. The old fashioned and the avant-garde—Peter Rabbit, Picasso, Singer Sargent, Munch, Gilbert and Sullivan, Stravinsky, Chekhov, and Ibsen—jostled for attention as consumers marveled at the first plastics, motorbikes, rubber gloves, zippers, telephones, radio programs, x-rays, color photographs, and cinemas. Whole new countries took shape while scientists struggled to understand the impact of four-dimensional geometry, new moons, gases, and the new science of relativity and quantum theory. Whether through fear of the unknown, or hope to capitalize on new trends, a large, eager, and susceptible market arose, desperate to know what the future might hold. And for the first time in history, technology provided tools that promised to make forecasting scientific. The telegraph and telephone enabled the collection of large amounts of up-to-date information. The emergence of statistics as a rigorous mathematical discipline, together with the growing sophistication of economics, facilitated serious data analysis. An ever-expanding railway network could distribute newsletters, newspapers, and magazines to an eager market of punters and pundits.

Astrology became a big commercial business at this time, too, but it was in financial markets that forecasting first became an important industry. Panics in the United States in 1893, 1896, 1901, and 1907 had exposed how little reliable information consumers, investors, and managers had about the health of companies, industries, or the economy at large. Into that vacuum rushed three men : Irving Fisher, Roger Babson, and Warren Persons. All were eager to sell reassurance, inspiration, and advice. All three believed that, through data, they could discern future trends in the markets and hoped to build important businesses doing so. And all three, carrying the diagnosis of TB, viscerally understood the pain of uncertainty and sought to alleviate it. Almanacs had been around for centuries— supplying farmers with information on sunrises and sunsets, tides and weather—and the new forecasting ventures aspired to something similar for investors: business barometers with which to analyze the present and forecast the future.

But the metaphor posed more questions than it answered. With more economic and business data than ever before, how could they tell what was meaningful or trustworthy? It was easy to take the temperature with a thermometer, but in the early days of modern economics, no one quite knew which data was its equivalent. Farmers knew from experience what weather their crops required, but nobody really understood what kinds of economic conditions were needed to temper an overheated market, grow a slow one, or stabilize volatility. Did different industries always thrive in the same market conditions? The density of collective unknowns left it up to the forecasters to choose what mattered to whom, why, and when. And they had a field day.

Each of the forecasters built commercial businesses selling their special take on the future. Fisher, whom Milton Friedman considered the greatest economist the United States has ever produced, was one of the first to try to analyze national economies, seen through the lens of the money supply. His working assumption was that too much money in circulation would produce an inflationary boom, too little a recessionary bust. At the time, government didn't measure money supply, which left Fisher trying to do so. He needed indicators of activity—but none existed. He started tracking prices, only to discover that they didn't always move in lockstep; some went up as others sank. So he created indexes, aggregates of data he hoped would reveal overall patterns in economic activity. It was impossible to collect everything so he needed to be selective. But how could he identify representative data when he didn't know what the whole contained?

Whatever he chose, Fisher's theory required mountains of data. He packed his home with employees collecting it on index cards. What his homemade indices revealed was volatility—in prices and in markets. So Fisher became obsessed by a search for stability: Where did it come from, what influenced it, and what sustained it? How could stable currencies be realized? The more data he collected, the more questions emerged, all needing answers before Fisher could hope to anticipate where the economy was going.

Giddy with new insights, Fisher became one of the world's first economic pundits. His Index Number Institute, syndicating indexes and forecasts through newspapers and newsletters, made Fisher famous for financial commentary, analytical nous, and an immense capacity for data analysis. Competitive, commercial, and publicly spirited, he was easily drawn into commenting on a whole range of topics from Prohibition to simplified spelling and calendar reform. But his fortune was made when he sold his card index system to the Rand Kardex Company for $660,000 (approximately $8 million today). Spread thin and often mocked for his humorlessness, Fisher nonetheless commanded attention and credibility for his mathematical rigor that promised to bring economic forecasting one step closer to a science.

Economics has long suffered from physics envy and nowhere was that more explicit than in the early days of forecasting. One of Fisher's rivals, Roger Babson, believed that almost everything in life could be reduced to Newton's laws of cause and effect. Like Fisher, Babson had contracted TB as a young man and devised his own eccentric, ascetic health routine: freezing air and a strict diet. Pictures of him in the Massachusetts winter, dressed in a long woolen gown as he works in front of a wide-open window, show a man bent on proving that knowledge and determination could beat any odds. In particular, Babson was on a mission to redress a power imbalance. As a young bond salesman, he had discovered that banks held a monopoly on business information; investors knew only what institutions told them.[3] He had seen firsthand the human cost of that exclusivity, too: visiting the stock exchange during the panic of 1907, he saw men actually turn gray.[4] So Babson brought to his new business an evangelical determination to empower individuals with data as sound and thorough as any bank's. Babson wanted people to understand how intricately companies were connected to the economy as a whole and he became famous for his Babsoncharts, spectacularly baroque sheets of graphic design on which he tried to display the full complexity of an economy: stock and commodity prices, manufacturing data, railroad traffic, agricultural production, building construction, business failures, and other indicators of economic output. Onto this data he placed what he called the "normal line," indicating periods of expansion and recession. Ever the fervent Newtonian, he put his trust in the Third Law of Motion: for every action, there is an equal and opposite reaction. He believed that a period of depression was always matched by a period of prosperity and that the steeper the decline, the faster the market would recover.[5]

Like many then and now, Babson imbued economics with morality; cause and effect resonated with crime and punishment. So booms were the product of wasteful exuberance that needed to be purged by sensible self-discipline. These views made him a contrarian: when markets went up, he foresaw extravagance and urged healthy restraint. Profiled as "the man who refused to die," his success and fame conflated his apparent victory over tuberculosis with the moral lessons implicit in his market predictions; excess spelled danger and health demanded moderation. Each piece of data contained some meaning and Babson maintained a boosterish faith that everything—health, behavior, food, parenting, handwriting—was predictive of something and that he was the man to decode them all. By 1910, he, too, had become a national pundit, called on to pronounce on everything from markets to medicine, education, diet, and religion. No matter the topic, whenever Babson made predictions, he always looked for excess that needed reining in, or restraint that demanded a bigger push.

Both Fisher and Babson became irrepressible entrepreneurs, financing their forecasting businesses with their own money and running them from home. They both worked through deduction, applying their theories to mountains of data in the belief that their efforts would elucidate patterns that predicted the future. By stark contrast, Warren Persons built his forecasting business, the Harvard Economic Service, right inside the university that funded it, hoping that, far from Wall Street, it could remain aloof from punditry and secure a solid reputation for scholarship and objectivity. A masterful statistician, he took an inductive approach, skeptical that any theories fully captured the complexity of economic markets. The best you could do was watch and measure what was in front of you, and ask if you had seen such correlations and patterns before. In essence, he forecasted by analogy, believing that history repeated itself, albeit imperfectly. The Harvard Economic Service was the world's first economic advisory business to serve a worldwide market of the elite. In the 1920s, the Service began to collaborate with Keynes and Beveridge's London & Cambridge Economic Service, but for all these academic credentials, a problem lay at the heart of Persons's approach. Even if he believed himself immune to theory, didn't his attention to some trends over others imply a theory? In denying his assumptions, did he risk being blind to them?

All three men were personally invested in their competing theories and methods; their businesses and professional reputations depended on them—as, to a large degree, did the future of the forecasting industry as a whole. There were fortunes to be made in prophecy and their large, aggressive sales teams competed in a torrid market, each disparaging the others. Persons compared Babson's ideas to astrology and said that Fisher's data was unreliable. Where both men's methods were opaque and easily castigated as pseudo-science, Persons published hundreds of pages explaining how he worked—which just left him open to intense, methodological criticism from rivals and colleagues alike. Across the industry, rivals sniped at each other, trying to prove that they, and they alone, held the key to the future.

The test came in October 1929. At the beginning of the month, Fisher had been buoyant, claiming that stocks had "reached a permanently high plateau." Stability at last! When the market collapsed on October 24, while conceding there might be a slight price retreat, he saw nothing "in the nature of a crash." For months afterward, he insisted that a rapid recovery was imminent. His faith cost him dear, his son later commenting that "his eagerness to promote his cause sometimes had a bad influence on his scientific attitude. It distorted his judgement."[6] Holding on to his shares in Rand Kardex, it also meant that he lost his fortune.

Persons's Harvard Economic Service was equally blindsided. He later maintained that, with no historic precedent for the crash, a normal and swift recovery must follow. Month after month, the Service kept predicting a recovery that failed to arrive. Cleaving to his big idea—that the economy always moved in cycles like the tides—proved too rigid in the new environment. The Service closed in 1931. That so prestigious a group had failed so dismally soon gave rise to more disturbing questions: Did such a commercial venture belong in an academic setting? Had the elite nature of the Service and its clients influenced their predictions? Was the Harvard

Economic Service unwilling to deliver bad news or, even worse, had its optimism contributed to the crash?

Only Babson, the least scientific of the three men, came out with his reputation enhanced. The reason was simple. Ever the contrarian, he had been predicting a crash every year for the past three years. "I shall repeat what I said at this time last year and the year before; namely that sooner or later a crash is coming. . . . Fair weather cannot always continue." He basked in his triumph, snapping up some of his failing competitors and blaming his rivals for encouraging speculation. But in May 1931, he announced that the market had bottomed out and that it was time to get back into the stock market. He was wrong: the U.S. economy wouldn't recover for a decade.

Persons moved on to consulting, where his statistical punctilious-ness was said to dismay clients. Fisher, his reputation in ruins, died broke; his investments had all gone bust. Though Babson was the forecaster who left behind a fortune and a college that still bears his name, his ideas—about markets and medicine—are now discredited. His "normal line" wasn't brilliant, but random.

Not one of these three men had accurately foreseen his own leg-acy. While they had seen themselves as wildly differentiated rivals, in fact these three pioneers had much in common. Beset by per-sonal uncertainty, they believed that deciphering patterns in their data would give them control over their lives. They had more faith than skill, imbuing their theories and data with the certainty and consolation they and their readers craved for their own lives. They imagined themselves objective scientists uncovering laws about mar-kets as absolute and reliable as the laws of physics. They believed that financial numbers unambiguously revealed immutable scientific truths. In all of these shared beliefs they were wrong.

What they left behind was the commercialization of a fantasy: the belief that the future is knowable, that all life is susceptible to certain laws if we could only figure out what they are, and that there are some special people or processes that can reveal what the future holds. They both ratified our addiction to prediction and proved that fame and fortune could be made from it. But these early pioneers also uncovered three profound problems endemic to forecasts that dog them still today: they are incomplete, ideological, and self-interested.

The first problem is models. Fisher and Babson relied on simplified versions of the markets they sought to understand. They didn't have the resources or the means to capture all the data on the economy—and even if they had, they lacked the tools to handle it. So they had to make choices about what to leave in and what to leave out. All economists do this kind of editing, in an effort to see more clearly what is really going on. Today's technology accommodates far more data but the intrinsic difficulty of models remains: the more data is compressed, the more its predictive power is compromised. Paul Krugman, who won the Nobel Prize for economics at least in part due to the beauty of his models, once quipped that he thought the data left out of his models might be more important than the data that went in.[7] It's an explosive and challenging remark, revealing the intrinsic difficulty of models: they will always be subjective and incomplete representations of complex reality.

The second problem lay in agendas. However much the early forecasters believed themselves to be men of pure, scientific inquiry, they all held cherished, implicit beliefs about how the world worked, about what mattered and what did not. Alan Greenspan later called these ideologies. Testifying before Congress, after his failure to foresee the banking crisis of 2008, he said, "ideology is a conceptual framework with the way people deal with reality, everyone has one. You have to."[8] Between 1994 and 2008, his own belief—that deregulated markets are safe—had caused him to ignore a whole series of failures in the unregulated derivatives market, right up to the crash in 2008. He hasn't changed his mind about regulation, but what he has done, as many others have not, is acknowledge that his mental model is an ideology, that forecasts always contain an agenda.

Moreover, all of these early forecasting businesses were commercial enterprises. They depended on customers who themselves had preferences and priorities. How far were forecasters driven to please their payers? The first person to raise this question had been John Maynard Keynes, whose early interest in business barometers had led him to work with Persons. But writing to colleagues at the Harvard Economic Service in 1925, he had wondered whether there wasn't a conflict of interest in the very nature of the business. Didn't these men, and their companies, *depend* on boom and bust? The drama of market cycles, the promise of riches and the tantalizing promise that, with special information, you could win: Didn't this lure create an implicitly corrupt relationship with clients? With elegant tact, Keynes wondered at the position in which the Harvard Service (and, by implication all forecasters) put themselves. "I feel it would be a great pity if the Service were to get into the state of mind of having, so to speak a vested interest in the due recurrence of the boom and slump."[9] In this one casual question, Keynes opened up a question that resonates to this day. If boom and bust was good for the forecasting business, how easily might the industry itself, instead of reporting data, start trying to influence events instead?

According to Robert Skidelsky, Keynes's biographer, the economist was always alert to vested interests; they were a big and frequent idea for him. He appreciated that economics was a complex system—but also recognized that it was a human one, inhabited and influenced by those who studied it. Economists could never be impartial observers. Their models are profoundly susceptible to the human beings who design and run them; they aren't and cannot be morally neutral. Because economics always requires moral choices, Keynes believed, it could never be a science.[10]

Rejecting the hope that economics might one day be like physics—as forecastable as the tides—Keynes was far more comfortable seeing uncertainty and discontinuity as sources of hope. These meant that policy makers were not passive bystanders but could intervene and influence what happened next. But perhaps his shrewdest insight was that the prediction business had a commercial interest in giving forecasting more precision than it legitimately possessed.

"The problem with precision," Skidelsky explained, "is that where there's more precision, there's more drama. And if there's more drama, there's more money."

What Babson, Fisher, and Persons had discovered, and Keynes had identified, was that forecasters gained bigger reputations and could make more money by being bold; they had a vested interest in exploiting our hopes and our fears. What none imagined was that the drama of the markets would evolve so spectacularly from drama to showbiz to hype to propaganda and the manipulation of consumer behavior. Human discomfort with uncertainty, together with a craving for reassurance, has fueled an industry that enriches itself by terrorizing us with uncertainty and taunting us with certainty. Master of the genre, a kind of bastard grandchild of Babson, Fisher, and Persons, is *Mad Money*'s Jim Cramer, who boomerangs around his TV studio to the dramatic cacophony of bullhorns, cash registers, and bowling pins as he celebrates or mourns flourishing or decaying businesses. Predictions are the candy of his sweet shop, and viewers eagerly swallow his advice, with prices on his picks visibly rising as the show airs.

What happens next is off air: investors in Cramer's picks don't make money. Academic analysis of his advice showed that over time his believers either made no profit or incurred losses. If you slavishly followed his tips, you could lose a third of your money in under two months. The analysts conclude: "Because there is scant evidence that Cramer has skill in selecting underpriced stocks, it is puzzling why viewers act on the recommendations at all."[11] The chief beneficiary of Cramer's drama is Cramer.

In reality, without inside information, it is impossible to beat the market consistently.[12] This is one reason why the market is increasingly dominated by passive investment funds that promise only to match market indexes, not beat them. But when we fall for exuberant forecasters, we collude in their fiction. Our desire for certainty leaves us susceptible to other people's agendas and business imperatives. This is never more true than in competitive and turbulent times when the difference between winning and losing is so marked.

On the face of it, the fame of pundits ought to subject them to more scrutiny, making them more accountable for what they predict, not less. But according to the academic Philip Tetlock, that isn't the way it works. Decades of studying forecasters revealed a perverse trend: the more famous the pundit, the *less* reliable they appeared to be. They survive because almost nobody follows up to see what happened afterward. If prediction were a science, you'd demand proof; even the Greeks trusted most only those oracles with a solid track record of success. But, for the most part, we don't check.

But Tetlock did, crunching twenty years of data. And he concluded that big names were held hostage by their big ideas, driven to see consistency where it didn't exist. Tom Friedman, Paul Krugman, and Niall Ferguson may once have started as objective seekers after truth but, over time, just like Alan Greenspan, they developed their own ideologies: mental models of how the world works. They cleave to what they know and are loyal to the grandeur and power of their big ideas—sticking to them, often in the face of overwhelming evidence. In a crowded, noisy, competitive market, their followers and personal brands lock them into conceptual boxes, where they remain captive to consistency.

Tetlock relishes taking pot shots at illustrious commentators captive to big ideas, none more so than the CNBC pundit (and Jim Cramer's frequent co-presenter) Larry Kudlow. An economist in the Reagan administration, Kudlow has no economics qualification, but his big idea was supply-side economics: a theory that economic growth is best created by reducing taxes and regulation.

When President George W. Bush instigated tax cuts, Kudlow predicted a boom. With each year that passed, Kudlow continued to insist the economy was booming—even if nobody else could see it. In 1993, he predicted that Clinton's tax increases would squash economic growth—and when the late 1990s boom ensued, attributed it to Reagan's tax cuts back in the early 1980s. Ten years later, he was rewarded for his intellectual intransigence when President Trump made him director of the National Economic Council.[13]

Incomplete, ideological, and self-interested: the harder economists try to identify surefire methods of predicting markets, the more such insight eludes them. The rise of big data and artificial intelligence enables firms to analyze quantities of information far beyond the dreams of earlier forecasters: not just prices, money supply, and national economies but satellite images tracking the number of oil tankers on the seas or cars at shopping malls. Uncertainty remains endemic and the growth of passive investors (hoping only to match market indices) testifies to the gradual acceptance that there are no magic formulae that accurately anticipate financial markets. Few organizations or investment managers are willing to have their results analyzed to determined whether they have a smart approach—or have just been lucky.[14] In the competitive market for analysis and advice, when winning models do emerge, they are so quickly copied that any advantage evaporates. The only true source of advantage is new knowledge, but that is, by definition, unpredictable—because if it were predictable, it wouldn't be new.

But the power of prophecy to make reputations has not abated. When two researchers at the Oxford Martin School announced, in 2013, that 47 percent of U.S. jobs would disappear to automation by 2035, they hit the bull's-eye. The research offered ample drama—a big number of disappearing jobs—while the sheer precision of it—*exactly* 47 percent—sounded like certainty. When I read it, I was instantly puzzled. Twenty-three years hence, *exactly* 47 percent of jobs could be *known* to disappear? But it was the very grittiness and size of the numbers that made them sound like fact and seized the world's attention. Soon the numbers were embedded in PowerPoint presentations and newspaper and magazine articles. Bill Gates talked about them. The World Economic Forum at Davos discussed them. *The Economist* wrote about them. Striking workers quoted them. Radio and television programs gasped at them. It was possible the report was correct, but it was impossible—and still is—to know. But everyone from government officials to philosophical pundits projected onto what was a hypothesis the appearance of inevitability.

The authors of the original paper had disclosed, from the outset, their "novel methodology" but that didn't seem to prompt any skepticism about an untested, unproven approach. Nobody I talked to about it had read the paper itself (cosponsored by Citibank), so they couldn't explain how the number had been derived. Subsequent studies, from the Organisation for Economic Co-operation and Development (OECD), concluded that just 9 percent of jobs were automatable.[15] A PWC report in 2017 plumped for 30 percent of jobs at risk in the United Kingdom, 38 percent in the United States, and just 21 percent in Japan. McKinsey estimated that 60 percent of occupations were at risk.[16] A subsequent report from the World Economic Forum predicted that, while 75 million jobs globally would be destroyed, 133 million would be created.[17] Among the cacophony of guesses, the only idea established without doubt was that these forecasts were guaranteed media attention.

But the gritty Oxford Martin numbers performed mightily for their authors. Such exposure *is* currency in universities today. Academics need people to talk and write about their work; that is how they rack up citations that help determine career prospects. Their institutions need the attention, too, as those citations also help push up the rankings of British universities. There are big personal and institutional incentives to produce headline numbers like these. As Babson and his contemporaries proved, in the forecasting market, everyone competes for attention.

An inescapable quality of forecasting lies within that word: it can be about *casting forward*: seeking to shape, to cast a mold, for what lies ahead. The forecast in Shakespeare's *Macbeth* is a classic example. When predicting that he will be king, are the witches telling Macbeth what they know will happen, or are they priming him, dropping into his mind an idea he cannot shake off? In the prediction business, it's but a small step from selling forecasts as a business to using prophecy as a sales technique to shape or accelerate a future you seek to dominate.

Nowhere has this subtle shift from prediction to propaganda been more prominent than in the marketing of autonomous vehicles. The driverless car, we have been told for over ten years now, is inevitable. There's no point even learning to drive anymore, so immediately will the liberating technology be upon us. Big public events announcing supportive legislation purport to give marketing the status of fact, as when Governor Jerry Brown signed a bill facilitating the new technology in California. A close observer would have noticed how the event exuded irony, as Brown celebrated California as the home of the gold rush—an epic of exploiting hopes and dreams if there ever was one—and Google's Sergey Brin sported Google Glass, a failed but one-time inevitable product.

The real drama was the one nobody wrote about: the absence of questions. It was hard to see how the blind would use driverless cars if safety requires that the driver remain capable of last-minute intervention. It remained unclear why, if drivers already on the road were joined by those who couldn't drive, the streets would be clearer. More cars in use sits oddly with the notion of needing fewer parking spaces, while promises of 100 percent safety left thoughtful consumers wondering if there had ever, in history, been a 100 percent safe product. Since any obstacle automatically stopped these cars, couldn't any pedestrian merely step in front of them—and would that risk require that pedestrians be caged in, so as not to impede traffic? Where would all the cars go at night and what would happen in snow or fog when sensors don't work? That the cars were all connected and might therefore be able to drive in convoy more efficiently was cool, but this was also a hacker's dream. The forecasts were so dazzling, the rhetoric of inevitability so dramatic and so confident, everyone stopped thinking about implications but was seduced into submission by the beautiful, frictionless fantasy. We call it salesmanship because there are products and money attached—automobiles are the largest manufacturing business in the world—but if the technology were correctly seen as a campaign, we'd recognize it as propaganda: we are being recruited into an army of believers.[18]

Quashing pragmatic questions is not the only consequence of such grandstanding. It also discourages policy questions, about the impact of AVs on the labor market, on civil liberties, and on other, possibly better solutions, like public transportation.[19] Google's Chris Urmson suggested that the autonomous vehicle "has the potential to reduce current Federal spending pressures for roadways, parking and public transit." In a perfect world where everyone has easy access to a driverless car, there's apparently no need to invest in public transportation or to address the geographic segregation that plagues so many cities. The more we believe, the less we question, the more probable the forecast becomes. A simplistic commercial view of the future is being forced onto a world as though there are no alternatives possibilities, when in fact there are many.

The same sleight of hand is intrinsic to almost all discussions of artificial intelligence. Wild promises are made about the capacity of AI to predict disease, crime, recidivism, career trajectories, life span. Inevitablism discourages practical questions. Even data scientists acknowledge that the sheer scale of information may impart an exaggerated level of confidence, that it may cut them off from underlying problems and provide so-called answers that are devoid of meaning.[20] With a large enough dataset, projecting trends with gross accuracy is easy, but it's near impossible to reduce from that to pinpoint accuracy for an individual. Philosophical problems abound, not only about who owns the data and for what purposes. The rhetoric flowing from Silicon Valley casually assumes that a person is simply an aggregation of data. Accepting this begs questions of what aspects of existence can't be standardized and measured, and therefore the value and importance of what gets left out. Does anyone seriously propose a standardized measurement of how much I love my partner or my child? But omit that and an individual profile full of data still is not me. Which means that when artificial intelligence assumes that I am the sum of the data available about me, it will make mistakes.

The aim of propaganda is to disarm critical, independent thinking. Imbuing these new technologies with an aura of inevitability distracts from important questions about who controls them, and to what ends.[21] These early implementations of AI resemble nothing so much as public drug trials on an unsuspecting public in a market with no oversight. Such questions cry out for public debate and the difficult, slow task of crafting consensus and rules. But businesses are advised to avoid that; doubt doesn't sell. If consumers balk at technologies that track where they go or how they drive, the advisory firm Deloitte recommends that they be worn down with the argument that "enhanced surveillance and/or geo-location capabilities are part of the world we live in now, for better or for worse. . . . The genie is out of the bottle."[22] If it's inevitable everywhere, why bother having the argument? Promising improbable benefits, the propagandists exploit one enormous advantage: ignorance. The future hasn't happened yet, so we can't be completely certain that they are wrong. Just as surely as the witches left Macbeth tantalized and confused, so the propagandists and marketers of Silicon Valley hope to disarm rational questioning. But we do better to remember that a prediction is really just a hypothesis.

As chief of research at Gartner, a technology advisory firm, Daryl Plummer wants his forecasts to provide an antidote to the overheated rhetoric of tech inevitablism. His customers are companies making decisions about what kind of technology to use, and his aim is to help them distinguish hype from reality. When it comes to prediction, Gartner's analysts engage in a great deal of debate and what Plummer calls "a bit of a slugging match" and a lot of challenge. Ninety-five percent of predictions get changed along the way. That doesn't mean Gartner always gets it right, but, in striking contrast to popular pundits, it is a routine part of Plummer's work to scrutinize their final predictions and compare them with what, in fact, happened next. Prediction accuracy reports give Gartner analysts feedback that impossibly long-term speculations seek to avoid. At conferences, the company proudly broadcasts the many areas in which the company has been right—but it also shares the topics on which it's been proved wrong.

"We predicted that Windows 8 would be the last release of an operating system by Microsoft," Plummer recalled. "It was wrong because of how we defined what an OS was—and Microsoft redefined it. But if you're not wrong, you're not trying hard enough. Sixty percent accuracy is optimal; if you are right more than that, you're diluting what you're predicting. Nobody here is hired because they're psychic; they're hired to generate insights that are useful— even if they turn out to be wrong. It's useful if it gets you thinking."

Plummer is making a provocative and important point: that what matters most isn't the predictions themselves—but how we respond to them, and whether we respond to them at all. The forecast that stupefies isn't helpful, but the one that provokes fresh thinking can be. The point of prediction should not be to surrender to them but to use them to broaden and navigate your conceptual, imaginative horizons. Don't fall for them—challenge them.

"Inevitability," Plummer said laughing, "is just a statement seeking a reaction. You're putting a stake in the ground: this is the faith I have and you should believe what I believe—because if we *all* believe, well then, angels get their wings!"

More than a century of modern forecasting has revealed and exacerbated intrinsic problems that remain unsolved. Even the newest technology leaves models incomplete, their designers unable to see what's missing until it presents problems. All interpretations of the present are rife with assumptions, ideologies, and big ideas that organize, but also influence, prediction. The self-interest of forecasters, be they pundits, academics, technologists, or companies, cannot but motivate what is seen and sold. But those problems won't, and can't, stop human beings from thinking about the future. So if we can't be perfect, could we at least do better? Is there any chance that self-interest and ideology could be removed, or at least reduced?

Those questions lay at the heart of Tetlock's Good Judgment Project, a tournament sponsored by IARPA, the U.S. Intelligence Advanced Research Projects Activity. With billions of dollars invested in intelligence that informs decisions about security, terrorism, energy, environmental, and social and political policy, IARPA's work is neither a commercial venture nor entertainment; the government has a clear and urgent need for objective, accurate insight. Tetlock knew how unreliable pundits could be, so this project offered to test the standards that could be achieved, absent fame and fortune. Five teams of researchers chose their own people and methods to tackle nearly five hundred questions about world affairs in a prediction tournament designed to compare results: Which, if any, could sustainably achieve significant levels of accuracy?

In the Good Judgment Project, Tetlock recruited volunteers who weren't in it for the money, out to build personal reputations, or on ideological crusades. At the end of each season's work, they received a $250 gift certificate; that's all. The collective intelligence of the teams mitigated individual biases and ideological differences. Each participant drew on a very broad range of information sources and constantly revised their assessments. Their forecasts—individually and in aggregate—were logged and subsequently compared to what happened. In the first year of the tournament, Tetlock's team proved 60 percent more accurate than the control group—superior to university teams at the Massachusetts Institute of Technology and the University of Michigan. The following year, they did 78 percent better, outperforming professional intelligence analysts who had access to classified information. Confronted by that margin of success, IARPA saw no point in continuing the contest and stopped it. Tetlock's process had won.

The Good Judgers didn't make binary forecasts; they almost never gave an absolute yes or no to any question. Instead, they assessed probabilities: How likely was it that an event would occur or not? Probabilities changed the way that they thought about the future, allowing them to accept uncertainty and to reject the dramatic absolutism so beloved of popular audiences. It made them more thoughtful and more accurate. Measuring the results of their work showed Tetlock that yes, some individuals—he calls them super-forecasters—are better than others. But depending on any single voice or loud opinion is folly.

There is much that is hopeful in this outcome. The Project showed that ordinary people who were open-minded, educated, prepared to change their minds, humble, and attentive could gain real insight and awareness into what might happen in the next year or so. These were people who were prepared to see multiple, not single, causes of events and who were comfortable updating or changing their initial expectations. They weren't beguiled by consistency but, like the analysts at Gartner, learned from their mistakes and got better over time. They appreciated that all forecasts are probabilities, not absolutes. And working in teams, they did even better.

Tetlock believes in doubt but isn't paralyzed by it. Few things, he says, are absolutely certain or completely impossible. Lacking the evangelical salesmanship of a Babson or Fisher, he has put the Good Judgment Fundamentals curriculum online to share what he learned. Calibrating my confidence against my accuracy, I found that, in areas where I had expertise, I was overconfident and estimated probabilities too narrowly. In areas where I knew I knew little, I was underconfident, assessing probabilities so broadly as to be meaningless; a 50 percent probability, after all, tells you nothing. Implicitly, the training moves you away from purely wishful thinking because predicting what you want to happen just produces poor results. Instead, it starts to make you ask better questions—of yourself and others—and to be more comfortable with the suggestion that you could be wrong.

But the time horizon for accurate forecasts is dauntingly small: the Good Judgment Project found that, while many forecasters were accurate within only about 150 days, its own super-forecasters weren't confident beyond 400 days.[23] That number should give anyone pause when confronted by loud pontification about life and events far into the future. Organizations that invest time and effort into intricate five-year plans or thirty-year plans can't believe that they represent any kind of absolute truth. They shouldn't mistake the gritty realism of numbers for anything more than informed guesswork, rife with assumptions, ideology, and bias.

When you assess a forecast can make a decisive difference to seeing it as true or false. The future doesn't unfold evenly but often reveals new information long after it looks like the story's over. When, in the days and weeks following the Brexit referendum, the British economy appeared to defy the predictions of imminent decline, it was easy to conclude that dire warnings from those campaigning to remain in Europe had been bad, stupid, and wrong. After all, in the days and weeks after the 2016 referendum, the United Kingdom had remained the fastest-growing economy in the G7. But then, in the first three months of 2017 and on into the first six months of 2018, it had become one of the slowest, having missed out on a boom enjoyed by the rest. Neither forecast—of utter resilience or total disaster—had proved right, but either could be validated in different time frames.

Sooner or later, everyone, even the best of the best, gets it wrong. The Good Judgment Project itself is no exception: it called the Scottish referendum correctly in 2016 but got Brexit and Trump wrong. There is no one person, process, or prophet who gets it right every time. But that message is hard to hear against a noisy backdrop of daily prophecy. Listen carefully to the news: today, just over half of the items weren't reported events but speculation about the future. It's tempting to dismiss most of it as guesswork, posturing, propaganda, lobbying, marketing, or hot air, but that doesn't mean it is without impact. I'm haunted by the headline about 47 percent of jobs vanishing by 2035, not just because nobody can make reliable forecasts that far out. Not just because it feels more like PR than anything else. But because it was so quickly absorbed as fact. Instead of appearing unknown, debatable, and uncertain, suddenly the future looked foreclosed. In that guise, it becomes propaganda. When we trade the effort of doubt and debate for the ease of blind faith, we become gullible and exposed, passive and irresponsible observers of our own lives. Worse still, we leave ourselves wide open to those who profit by influencing our behavior, our thinking, and our choices. At that moment, our agency in our own lives is in jeopardy.

At Davos, queried as to how forecasters had got both Brexit and the Trump election so wrong, Tetlock was laconic and relaxed. He has, he told me, an existential comfort with uncertainty. Public hunger for certainty had misinterpreted probabilities; expectations of forecasters, he said, were simply misplaced.

"The very best forecasters are wrong a lot. We live in a world where there is a lot of irreducible uncertainty. And the very best forecasting systems, even systems that are very well calibrated, there are going to be conspicuous cases where they look wrong. It is in the nature of the political world that there is uncertainty. . . ."[24]

Because the future is unknowable, the best we can hope for are probabilities—which themselves may be incorrect. Even professional statisticians and mathematicians find probabilities counterintuitive and difficult, at odds with gut instinct.[25] For those of us who are not super-forecasters, this leaves us with a dilemma. What forecasters should we trust? If by trust we infer absolute belief that we'd stake our lives on, the answer is: nobody. Not our neighbors. Not our boss. Not our financial advisor. Not corporate propagandists. And not ourselves. We could and should treat predictions as hypotheses and ask better questions of ourselves, about where the vested interests lie, what's at stake, and what is being sold. Distinguishing propaganda from bad science, careerism, or entertainment robs prediction of its suggestive power. It's important to ask questions about how forecasts are formulated, how long their horizon is, and what the counter-forecasts might be. What's the agenda? Only when we kick our addiction to prediction do we stop being spectators and become creative participants in our own future.

The future is uncharted and life remains uncertain. But doubt is so uncomfortable that people will invest a great deal to eliminate it, as the founding fathers of forecasting discovered. They themselves tried and failed to map the unknown, and uncertainty persists throughout their story even to this day. While Fisher lived until he was eighty, Babson to ninety-one, and Persons to fifty-nine, neither they nor we will ever know whether their cold air or chewing regimens extended their lives. We don't even know, after all this time, whether they had TB at all, because no reliable test for the disease was commercially available at the time each received the terrifying diagnosis. We know that there's a high probability that they were infected, and we know that they thought they were. That belief is a powerful motivator and is what gives prediction its power.

CHAPTER TWO

DOES HISTORY REPEAT ITSELF?

To remember this world is to create it.

—Toni Morrison

Eleanor Maguire gets lost a lot. Her sense of direction is so poor, she says, that she doesn't even bother trying to drive. As professor of cognitive neuroscience at University College London, she understands better than many that if navigation absorbs most of her attention, she'll have little capacity left to think about traffic. Far safer to walk.

Geneticists might see her lack of spatial awareness as a flaw but Maguire has transformed it into a formidable strength. The difficulty she had finding her way around London made her curious about people for whom this ability has become second nature: London taxi drivers.

"Even GPS doesn't help me, so I was really trying to cure myself!" she said with a laugh. "I could see that there were huge differences in human navigation and I was trying to understand why some people can learn this stuff well and others, well, they just can't do it."

To qualify as a licensed London cabdriver, candidates must do the Knowledge: a series of tests that requires learning to navigate 25,000 streets within a six-mile radius of Charing Cross station. Typically, candidates spend three or four years riding around on a scooter with a map, wandering and memorizing the spatial relationship between streets, landmarks, and popular destinations. At the beginning of their training, Maguire scanned the brains of seventy-nine male taxi drivers and could identify nothing that might indicate who might succeed or fail: she found no general intellectual, mnemonic, or structural differences between the candidates' brains. The candidates started their training, therefore, on equal terms.

During the course of their training, many drivers dropped out; hours crisscrossing London on a scooter in traffic with rain and snow takes commitment. Thirty-nine drivers qualified in the end and Maguire noted that the successful drivers had put in far more hours than those who failed. She gave all candidates memory tests about the spatial relationships between landmarks and found, unsurprisingly, that the successful cabdrivers were better at this. But they weren't better at other kinds of memory tests. What Maguire discovered when she did MRI brain scans was that the successful cabdrivers now showed a visible increase in gray matter in the hippocampus—where no such physical change was visible in those who failed to qualify.[1]

Hailed as a dazzling demonstration of neuroplasticity and neurogenesis, the results stimulated in Maguire an abiding curiosity about the nature of memory: how it works, how it changes, what parts of the brain it recruits and what those parts are used for. Her next finding excited the press less but was just as profound. In 2007, in what was deemed a runner-up for "Breakthrough of the Year" in science, Maguire and her colleagues reported five people with amnesia caused by damage to the hippocampus were less able to imagine future events. Memory, they found, serves many functions—but one of them is to allow us to simulate the future. The idea—that without a sense of past we can't have a sense of the future—isn't metaphorical. It is the physical reality of how our brains operate. We draw from the past in order to imagine what lies ahead.[2]

"The whole point of the brain," Maguire told me, "is future planning. You need to survive and think about what happened when I was last here; is there a scary monster that will come out and eat me? We create models of the future by recruiting our memories of the past."

Mentally, we are all time travelers. We might exhort one another to live in the moment, but the truth is that we can't, we don't—and wouldn't want to. What gives life meaning is the rich and constant interplay between past, present, and future. In taxi drivers, Maguire now saw, a new address generated the live construction of a map, drawn from memories of landmarks and past routes, and updated with current knowledge of driving conditions. Old materials, combined with the present, were required for a vision of the future route. But her work with amnesiacs added a twist: people who didn't have, or couldn't find, memories lacked material with which to map the future.

But to have memories requires being alert and attentive, aware of where we are and what we're doing. Distraction and overload, Maguire says, impede this, reducing our ability to create memories for future use. So, too, do some forms of technology. Whenever we drive to a destination, just like a taxi driver, our mind is drawing and storing a mental map of the environment, logging landmarks and making memories. But using GPS displaces this activity. We pay less attention to our surroundings and more attention to our phones or satnav. Less awareness, fewer memories—and as a result, the brain area responsible for navigation is less used and tends to shrink.[3] The less we engage with the here and now, the more impoverished our scenarios of the future become.

But when we pay attention, reading a book or listening to a piece of music provides memories just as rich and pliable as physical experience. Memory also contains feelings: I remember that place was cold, this kind of food was revolting, that person cheered me up. How I use these memories of the past depends on my situation in the present. If I have painful memories of the dentist and today I feel fine, the prospect of going to the dentist this afternoon feels grim. On the other hand, if today I have a terrible toothache, then my present may create a future scenario of relief.[4]

We create a multiplicity of these kinds of scenarios because context keeps changing and because our memories are unreliable, subject to bias and editing. We tend to pay more attention to the way that events finish than to how they start or unfold. A gruesomely painful event (like childbirth) may be remembered as more joyful than it actually was because the outcome was happy (a healthy child). Big events are more readily recalled than trivial ones, many of which are lost. Maguire was at pains to point out that the fluidity of our memory isn't always negative; it is what makes us flexible, adaptable, and creative in our thinking.

Like many neuroscientists, Maguire is wary of analogies. The brain isn't like a computer and memory isn't like a video player. We don't retrieve a memory, we don't replay the event, we reconstruct it on the fly, assembling each time a new picture, a fresh sensation. It's unhelpful to think of these as flaws or bugs, because the very fact that memory comes to us freshly assembled is why we can use it to come up with new ideas. Memory does not repeat itself. These additions, subtractions, and rearrangements may play havoc with our legal system, but they also propel us into new and unexpected creations and experiences, and prevent us from becoming trapped or static. Our capacity to generate a vast range of scenarios is what gives us the capacity for change.

What Maguire and her colleagues are discovering pushes far beyond mechanical descriptions of our brain as simple sources of crude cause and effect. The emerging view of our brain (and, by extension, of our mental, emotional, and physical lives) shows that we routinely create, assemble, and discover a vast array of possibilities not only at big dramatic crossroads but throughout our lives. Like London cabdrivers, we can navigate thousands of possibilities with a lively, free combination of routine and creativity, knowledge and improvisation. How rich or poor the results are depends on how much attention we bring to our surroundings and to ourselves. But there is nothing predictable or predetermined about what we will produce with the ingredients of our minds. We neither forsake our past nor are we mired in it.

So an open-ended approach to life defies the narrative view that sees each of us as merely playing out a part in the preordained plot of our lives. In the same way that forecasters persuade by constructing a compelling story, strong narratives can become a trap, too, constraining and limiting how we see ourselves and other people. Instead of illuminating freedoms, choices, and imagination, narrative proposes that we are slaves to plots we can't know and didn't write. The fallacy of narrative lies in the fact that human beings don't experience themselves in just one way, but in a wide variety of ways over time. Our history is not static but fluid. Yesterday's cab route won't necessarily be today's, because of road work, a colleague's tip, the overnight appearance of a crime scene, or just a moment's lapse in attention. A career choice early in life need not be deemed an error in the light of a change of profession decades later. People change, events change them, and their own choices move them to places where they see more of life differently. These contingencies, accidents, or flukes aren't errors or bugs; however uncertain, they are an infinite source of life's richness, opportunity, and freedom. That the past is a very poor predictor of the future is not true only of financial markets. It is a source of hope and redemption for anyone with a poor start in life.

"Whenever I failed at something, I gave up. I blamed other people. That's just what I did, it's what everyone around me did."

Today Jacob Dunne is a solid student, flourishing in his last year at university. But nothing in his history predicted that this would be his life. He'd grown up in a single-parent family and done all right in primary school. But secondary school and adolescence proved

typically challenging for a young man in a tough Nottingham project. Kicked out of two schools and routinely told he was stupid, he
saw nothing that gave him hope or ambition. He became, he said,
a ticking time bomb. Abusing drugs and alcohol, he depended on
gang life to give him a sense of belonging. The test of loyalty was
violence.

"It started to become normal to go out and fight for an adrenaline
rush," Dunne recalled. "And we used to do it to show each other
that we are there for each other."

One night, Jacob got separated from his friends but got a call
from them asking for help. When he arrived, he threw a punch and
felled James Hodgkinson, a paramedic visiting Nottingham for a
cricket match. Jacob ran away and thought no more of it until, nine
days later, he learned that Hodgkinson had died. He turned himself
into the police and, pleading guilty, received a reduced sentence
of thirty months for manslaughter. At this point, there is nothing
notable in his history but crime and failure. He is racked with guilt,
for what he's done to his mother, for what he hasn't done for himself.
He's crying, frustrated that nobody helps him. He's angry that his
friends snitched on him. He has an overwhelming sense that he
deserved more from life but that now the only identity available is
that of a victim. He feels unlucky, alone, and doomed.

On release, Jacob is homeless and can't access benefits. He doesn't
think he stands any chance of getting a job. He feels bound to retrace
the same steps, over and over again. But then something unexpected
happens. A fluke. One of his probation officers asks if he will see two
women who work in restorative justice. Jacob doesn't know what
that is. They've been in contact with James Hodgkinson's parents,
who have questions about what happened that night. But there's
no pressure; it's Jacob's choice to make.

"My initial response was to say no. Then I felt obliged to do it.
I felt so bad about myself, I thought at least I can answer some of
their questions and they can move forward in a more positive way.

I heard horrible things about them sitting by their son's life support machine, arranging the funeral, what kind of person James was. He became real. How can I ever appreciate the harm caused without hearing it from those closest to him?"

Nothing about the exchange makes Jacob think he can change. The probation officers keep bringing questions and go back to Hodgkinson's parents with Jacob's replies. A correspondence begins. Hodgkinson's parents ask what he will do with his life, but Dunne has no idea. He wants to tell them something so he mentions going back to school. In the past, he'd found education meaningless, but now he feels a strong urge to develop himself as a human being. At the age of twenty-two, sitting in a classroom of sixteen- and seventeen-year-olds, he feels embarrassed, knowing the kids he'd gone to school with would have degrees by now. He is also driven by shame, a deep desire to repair the harm he'd done. But on their own, those feelings would never be enough to keep him going.

Studying English, math, and psychology, Dunne learned about memories and how we constantly reconstruct them. The learning prompts questions: How had he been interpreting what had happened to him? How far had he constructed a story that trapped him in an identity that felt doomed and led nowhere? What different story might help him grow?

Jacob meets a man he remembers having seen at church with his mother. Another fluke. At first he fears the man might try to convert him to Christianity, but the request is more modest: Would Jacob come and talk to some of the volunteers on the young offenders team the next day? At first, he's petrified, too scared to come up with a good reason to refuse. To his own surprise, he turns out to be good at describing what happened to him: direct, no bullshit, straight from the heart. He speaks again, at a conference about restorative justice. He is starting to feel like a citizen.

Jacob's narrative wanders; he is looking around for different ways to think about himself, different ways of seeing the world.

His mother dies and she becomes a memory of someone he could have helped and loved more. This is a new thought for him. He now remembers that she had never washed her hands of him, had always believed in him. When she died, he can see that now he has a fresh excuse to feel sorry for himself again—but this time, he doesn't take it. His own bereavement helps him appreciate what James Hodgkinson's parents had endured.

"Hurt people hurt people. That's what they do. That's what I didn't want to do. What helped me were David and Joan Hodgkinson. If ever I gave up, or failed my exams, what could I say to them? It was only when I got my place at university that they felt comfortable meeting me because they realized I meant it when I said I was going to change. What was extraordinary is that after that, they said: you don't have to go to university just for us! But by then it wasn't just for them; it was for me. They set me free."

Jacob's story doesn't have a tidy end. He's currently finishing university—a degree in criminology—and isn't quite sure what he will do next. Jacob's story is neither predetermined nor is it ahistorical. What he senses is that he has possibilities.

Although Jacob's story is dramatic, and moving, it isn't unique. Most of us can find times in our lives when we might have turned one way but went another. These are when we feel we have freedom, but we need skill to notice it and valor to use it. The act of imagination required to see choices and imagine better ones is how we craft the lives that are our own. When George Santayana wrote, "Those who cannot remember the past are condemned to repeat it," he was writing specifically about the development of young people, from childhood to old age.[5] Progress, he argues, depends on retentiveness; if, every day, we had to learn from scratch, we would remain infantile. Instead, new learning creates new perspectives and memories, which themselves prompt the creation, or identification, of new possibilities. Just as Eleanor Maguire found that memories are constantly being reconstructed, so our lives are reconfigured by what we do and see and feel. Our capacity for learning means that the past doesn't foretell our future—because we keep integrating new experiences and creating new memories.

In much the same way, the Austrian philosopher Karl Popper argued that the fundamental driver of all human history is the growth of knowledge. We obviously can't predict what we don't know yet and don't know how, in what directions, or at what speed, human knowledge will develop. And therefore, Popper concludes, we can't predict history, because we can never know what those who come after us will know and what they will believe. Neither can history itself be a predictor, because it can't possibly take into account what is yet to be learned. There are, he argued, no laws, tantamount to the laws of physics, that determine what happens next. Popper was refuting Marx's famous edict that history repeats itself, seeing in Marx's determinism the heart and soul of authoritarianism. Eliminating the power of choice and action, Popper believed, is what autocrats seek to do. Identifying choices for ourselves is how we remain free.

Our memories of the past don't determine the future because they keep changing and because we add to them. In the same way, history does not predict the future because we bring to each event knowledge that those in the past did not have. Yet belief in the cliché—that history repeats itself—is stubborn. It's so tempting to think that when the past and the present look the same, they must somehow be the same—and play out in the same ways. But what we have instead are any number of examples where not only did history fail to repeat itself but believing that it did led to blindness and blunder.

The poster child for this error is the Maginot Line: fifty-eight underground fortresses, built in the 1930s along nine hundred miles of the French border with Italy, Switzerland, Germany, and

Luxembourg, they represented the largest single fortification in the world after the Great Wall of China. These massive and elaborate installations, complete with underground trains, kitchens, and operating theaters, were impregnable to tanks and aerial attack—but their location assumed that the Germans would repeat their strategy in World War I and launch any new attack along exactly the same geographical axis. But at such a vast scale, the Germans could watch the line being built and changed their plans accordingly. Instead of repeating the 1914 battle plan, they attacked through Belgium and the Netherlands. Within five days, Germany had successfully invaded France. Its ruins stand today as a vivid reminder of the dangers of believing in the past as a predictor of the future.

In believing that the future would be like the past, the British and the French succumbed to the power of similarity. When two things looks similar, we assume that they are the same and therefore predict that they will behave in the same ways.[6] It's a different form of narrative fallacy that feels logical but is so often wrong. The difficulty posed specifically by historical analogies is that they overweight parallels and leave us blind to crucial differences. History doesn't repeat itself, but thinking that it does makes forecasting flawed.[7]

The most routine historical analogy deployed by politicians is Munich: the archetype of the failure to stand up to a brutal dictator. Prime Minister Harold Macmillan used it, to disastrous effect, to guide his strategy during the Suez Crisis. President Dwight Eisenhower relied on it during the Korean War and he and Lyndon Johnson both used it at the beginning of the Vietnam War. In 1965, while Prime Minister Harold Wilson and the British urged negotiation, Eisenhower weighed in, urging Johnson, "We, however, have learned that Munichs win nothing." Later, urging negotiation again, Johnson insisted, "To give in = another Munich. If not here—then Thailand."

By all accounts, Johnson wanted to find a way to stop the bombing, but his fear of history repeating itself stopped him from trying a different path. Once he started equating the North Vietnamese with the Nazis, Johnson feared that the South Vietnamese president, Ngo Dinh Diem, might prove another Chamberlain: an appeaser whose failure would provoke another global war. Channelling Churchill's rhetoric, Johnson insisted that, to withstand the North Vietnamese, President Diem would "have to meet them in the bushes, and you're going to have to meet them in the mountains, and you're going to have to have to meet them in the forests."[8] Meanwhile, William Bundy, assistant secretary of state for East Asia and the Pacific, insisted that "aggression of any sort must be met early and head-on or it will have to be met later and in tougher circumstances. We have relearned the lessons of the 1930s—Manchuria, Ethiopia, the Rhineland, Czechoslovakia."[9]

The problem here is that the belief that history would repeat itself inhibited fresh thinking about how to deal with the threat they believed they faced. They saw the South Vietnamese as similar to themselves, thirsting for democracy. And they saw North Vietnam as a fascist aggressor, set on world domination. In his memoir, *In Retrospect*, Secretary of Defense Robert McNamara discusses how the cabinet arrived at what he called "our misjudgments of friend and foe alike." He describes how busy everyone is, how rushed the deliberations, how little time there was available for detailed exploration or even understanding of societies so different from Europe in the 1930s. Had they abandoned that shortcut for open-minded inquiry or even for different comparisons, they might have seen that they were relying on the wrong history, trusting to the wrong analogy. Choosing familiar parallels made the American government overconfident that they were operating in familiar territory when, in fact, they were not. Since then, of course, Vietnam has become an analogy of its own.[10]

Analogies are dangerous, the historian Margaret MacMillan argues, because they fail to take into account both the differences between events and open exposure to accident and contingency. No two events are ever exactly the same, not just because of changes over time. Countries are different, personalities are different, and everyone in the present already knows what happened in the past. So they get to make decisions with information that their predecessors did not possess.

But when the Arab Spring began in Tunisia in December 2010, analogies popped up like daisies. Just the term "Arab Spring" evoked comparisons with the European revolutions of 1848 and the Prague Spring of 1968. Even more common were references to the fall of the Berlin Wall, another event that had defied prediction.

"The Arab Spring is truly historic," a nongovernmental organization commentator wrote. "People are standing up in a region where customs have required deference to the wise and elder. This is nothing short of a socio-cultural quake. Today's mostly youth-led revolt is new for the Middle East but not for the world. In 1989 and 1990, young activists saw the culmination of their *Leipziger Montagsdemonstrationen* as they peacefully challenged the status quo and proved to be smarter than the Communist East German state."[11]

The belief that history repeats itself often leads people to think that it is *their own* history that is being repeated—not someone else's. The Russians saw Russian history in the Arab Spring, with Prime Minister Dmitry Medvedev fearing that, like the fall of the Berlin Wall, these demonstrations would prove destabilizing for Russia.[12] Meanwhile President Obama likened it to the Boston Tea Party and the beginning of American's war for independence, drawing analogies, too, with the civil rights protest of Rosa Parks.[13]

Everyone saw themselves in these events. So they felt confident they knew where they would lead and how they would end. The reliance on analogies implied inevitability: just like the fall of the Berlin Wall or the Boston Tea Party, the demonstrations would usher in a new era of democratic freedoms. But history proved a poor forecaster and today most commentators see the uprisings in Tunisia, Egypt, Libya, Bahrain, and Syria as more different than they were similar to each other and these countries as more complex than the simple narratives that were so quickly, and easily, attached to them.[14]

It's a very human error to assume that countries, peoples, and histories we don't know very well must be similar to our own, to conflate their history with ours. But historical analogies can be just as forceful, and just as flawed, when applied to homegrown events. In peacetime, there is probably no historical event that strikes such fear as the flu pandemic of 1918. Globally it infected 500 million people, of which 50 to 100 million died. That the flu killed young adults within twenty-four hours, and that it particularly struck the lucky survivors of World War I, made it poignant and horrifying. The stories of such swift and sudden deaths has left an indelible mark on the psyche of every health professional ever since.

So when, in January 1976, doctors diagnosed thirteen soldiers at Fort Dix with flu, no one took their illness lightly. Tests revealed that most suffered from A Victoria or A Port Chalmers virus—not the strain responsible for 1918. But with about seven samples some uncertainty remained. After retesting, just two contained swine flu type hemagglutinin, closely related to the cause of the 1918 pandemic. But meanwhile, one of the flu-ridden soldiers went on a five-mile march against doctor's orders and died. After an emergency medical meeting at Fort Dix with the Centers for Disease Control and Prevention, labs were mobilized to produce a swine flu vaccine.

The United States had experienced flu outbreaks in the intervening years between 1918 and 1976. The 1968 flu outbreak, known as Hong Kong flu, killed 33,800 Americans and provoked a generalized sense that the national response had been too little, too late. In 1976, therefore, two analogies ran together: the abject horror of 1918 and the administrative failures of 1968. That fear set the agenda for the mobilization of the full force of all health-care institutions and of the federal government to ensure that this time history did not repeat itself.

The head of the CDC, David Sencer, argued and gained support for the mass inoculations of the American population. At this
scale, no insurance company would indemnify the makers of the
vaccine, so Congress rushed to pass legislation providing federal
cover. On July 1, Bruce Dull, assistant director for programs at the
CDC, attended a flu forum in New York where he said that he
could see no parallels with the 1918 pandemic. But his reassurances
went unheeded; a mood of sublimated panic prevailed. Any unexpected death caused alarm; an outbreak of illness in Philadelphia,
thought to be swine flu, turned out to be Legionnaire's disease.
On October 1, with inoculation under way, two men died of heart
attacks following their jabs. Those deaths turned out to be pure
coincidence. Within ten weeks, more than 40 million people had
been immunized, without a single case of the disease having been
identified since the first findings at Fort Dix.

The mistaken application of an analogy proved costly in more
ways than one. In the years that followed, it transpired that those
who had been inoculated were four times more likely to develop
Guillain-Barré syndrome, a life-threatening condition that can lead
to respiratory arrest and paralysis; at least twenty people died. The
CDC was accused of using scare tactics to promote its own agenda
and importance, leaving a legacy of cynicism and skepticism about
vaccines and nationwide health programs. Forced to leave the CDC,
David Sencer, the evangelist for mass inoculations, moved to New
York City, where he became the city's health commissioner. And
that's where he was working when a new disease arrived: AIDS.
Sencer seemed now to think that history was repeating itself, but
this time the 1978 analogy guided his thinking and his response. So,
determined not to be alarmed, he didn't rush into action. Only this
time what he saw *was* a pandemic and the gay community rounded
on him for failing to appreciate the scale of an unfolding tragedy.

When we expect history to guide us, we overweight continuity
and narrative, underweighting change and contingency. Aesthetic

similarities often turn out to be no more than skin deep, their appearances masking important variation that could spark better questions and more illuminating debate. History could provide a richer array of components with which to construct images of the future, but we lose that richness when we reach for analogies.

But just because parallels are misleading doesn't render history useless. It means we have to use it differently. The great British military historian Michael Howard considers the comforting stories and patterns that we cherish to be "nursery history." But he also suggests that a mark of maturity is to use history to challenge, not confirm, comfortable assumptions about ourselves and about others. Nursery histories aren't only simplistic, they're also selective. Which history do we attend to: The history of institutions or of protest? Of the powerful or the powerless? Each tells a different story with its own agenda, every bit as much as the models preferred by financial forecasters.

But if the traditional study of history hasn't produced predictive patterns, might our increasing ability to interrogate vast datasets yield more insight than analogies? Could models help? The question is more than academic; predicting outbreaks of violence could save lives. But academic researchers working with massive datasets from history, together with machine learning and neural networks to try to identify predictive patterns, found that people, states, and political causes have changed shape too frequently to be subject to any stable definition. The onset, location, and timing of conflict remain too ambiguous and uncertain to generate a reliable model and violence has too many predictors to know in what circumstance which one of them will become pertinent.[15] Try as they might, they could not identify a series of narratives that could do much more than point out obvious sources of trouble.

It's when we challenge the narrative fallacy that we start to unlock new possibilities, not just in the past but in our own future. In the 1980s the Irish historian Roy Foster was one of a generation of historians who, like Macmillan, probed and challenged simple narratives. For centuries, the history of Ireland had been one of perpetual victimhood, a story that gave the Irish themselves only a small role in their own past. When Foster wrote his *Modern Ireland,* and later *Vivid Faces,* he examined the intimate lives and choices of individuals caught up in events. These weren't tidy or simple, and nothing about the narrative was inevitable. Manifest destiny, he reminded me gently, was propaganda.

"The great stately rolling narrative, people coming out of bondage feeling their way up to the light," Foster recalled. "That was the way that history had been written. But it wasn't the way that people lived. It isn't the way that people do live. I just got so tired of reading moralizing history. There *was* no enormous flow of continuity."

The fissile nature of Irish society, convulsive events like the Famine, could not be described adequately, understood, or honored if portrayed as though they had been just episodes along an inevitable path. Foster became determined to show how much *dis*continuity there was in the story. He took on the immense challenge of writing history as though he didn't know what would happen next—because that's how the people living through these events had experienced them. They did not, could not, know what we know now. Drawing on published and unpublished sources, tracing minute details of individual lives, viewing events through a wide variety of people and places, Foster succeeded in portraying Ireland's history as a series of choices and contingencies that, with no grand plan, shoved one event to the next. The best history, Foster told me, is written when we understand the past in the light of a future that never happened. But it's much harder to write that way, because the narrative is so complex and contingent.

What was difficult but thrilling about Foster's history was that it seemed to be saying: at any moment, it could have been, could be, different. Outcomes weren't inevitable; history wasn't about manifest destinies but unexpected and unforeseen futures. What happened next took place because of choices people made, people without the information we have today and with information perhaps now lost. History wasn't the runaway train on which we all sat like helpless, terrified children. This different view of history quivered with possibilities—some good, some bad, some seized, others overlooked—but all alive and human.

Think about what happens when you apply that mind-set to the future: at any moment, it could be different. Outcomes aren't inevitable. What happens next is a choice. Foster was both reflecting and influencing his generation as it reconsidered its relationship with the past *and* the future. When the Good Friday peace accord was signed in 1998, it wasn't history repeating itself and neither was it some miraculous deus ex machina. It was the result of human beings making decisions very different from those that had gone before.

Knowing that history doesn't repeat itself is what makes it useful. We may glean what appear to be themes—humiliation provokes tyranny, for example—that make us pay attention to new information we might otherwise ignore or marginalize. Like Babson, we can use Newtonian physics to expect equal and opposite reactions—but use history to question whether, this time, it's true. Like Warren Persons, we can search for patterns but instead of focusing on similarities, identify salient differences.

Just as the super-forecasters have to keep their minds open to change, or as London cabdrivers have to know enough to change routes in the face of sudden obstacles, just as Jacob Dunne responded to lucky flukes and was willing to try different ways of being, history offers us a rich inventory of ideas and ingredients with which to interrogate, explore, and craft not old but new narratives of our own making. History doesn't repeat itself because we keep changing and it keeps changing us. It can't offer recipes but it can provide raw material with which to construct fresh combinations, drawn from where we have been, where we are today, and where we wish to be tomorrow. That it offers neither inevitability nor guarantees isn't its weakness but its greatest power.

CHAPTER THREE

FLUKES AND MUTATIONS

"When I was pregnant with Johanna, all I wanted was a normal, healthy baby," Julia recalled. "I had every genetic test I could, but that was it. I was against birth plans, because really you never know what's going to happen. I didn't want to know whether it was a boy or a girl. You're having your first baby, even your doctors don't really know what's going to happen."

Remembering the birth of their daughter, Julia and Mario both chortle. It feels so long ago, they were so innocent. Both approached parenthood as an adventure. With no particular desire to know or predict the future of their family, they were content to make it up as they went along. Young as they were, they understood that life is complex, full of contingencies, the unexpected and the unwonted. They accepted that no plan or research could foresee who or what their children would become.

Julia got her wish. Johanna was a pretty girl, sociable, amiable, with the bubbly personality she inherited from her Welsh parents. She loved primary school, although she detested being asked what she'd be when she grew up. When she was three, her brother, Luca, was born. Being told she was getting a brother is, Johanna says, her first memory. With neat bobbed hair and bright brown eyes, the two children looked almost identical. Warm and affectionate, their parents had no particular ambitions for their children; they just wanted them to be able to choose their own paths in life. For Mario, this goal was paramount. He didn't want his history to repeat itself with his children. As a boy, he had resisted pressure to work in the family chip shop. Thrown out of the house when he refused, he'd run away to Julia's house, returning home only because her mother couldn't cook Italian food. Freedom, happiness, health was all they wanted for their young family.

But when Jo moved to secondary school, her easy wide-eyed charm began to evaporate. She rarely went to classes and when she did, she was bullied. No teacher sparked her interest and neither did most of the kids in her year. After a while, she didn't bother going to school and didn't see why she should. Her parents tried everything—promises, threats, ignoring her, cajoling her, anger, patience. Nothing seemed to work. Then she started vomiting and having seizures. That meant being in the hospital, more time at home, less at school. Years went by. Friends wondered: Was the problem with the girl, with the family, the school? Was it physical or emotional?

"Sometimes it would last a few weeks and then she'd be okay," Julia recalled. "Then something would trigger it again—any kind of stress. Johanna just got completely out of the loop as far as school was concerned. She was missing out on a social life, too; to be so ill, separated from her peer group, the psychological impact, depression: those were huge worries."

One of Julia's colleagues suggested the problem might be CVS, cyclical vomiting syndrome. When the diagnosis was confirmed, being able to name the disease brought some relief, as did talking to other parents whose children struggled with the same condition. But CVS has no known cause or treatment and some sufferers died. Jo's parents felt mired in uncertainty, anxious that their daughter's lack of academic qualifications would shrink her life chances. Not knowing what to do, they remained calm, supportive, and encouraging.

Being at home so much, Jo took up art and eventually developed a strong enough portfolio to gain admission to an arts foundation course at the London College of Fashion. She did well, but then got ill again and had to withdraw.

"She has no exams! She's so ill!" Julia recalled. "But I'd tell myself, she's reading, she's curious, she will come through it in the end. You have to have faith that good enough parenting, a good home, she'll figure it out. . . ."

Tentatively, Jo started to explore jobs: working in a library, reviewing restaurants, then copywriting at an ad agency. She took to social media, teaching herself how it worked, and quickly stood out as an expert, writing digital strategy for the firm. Three years later, she left to run digital media for De Beers, the diamond company. She had no academic qualifications but it was her online expertise they wanted. For a while it was fun but Jo found the company stultifying and left. Unexpectedly she heard from a company interested in her social media savvy; a few weeks later she was working for the British government, tackling radicalism and extremism online. To her surprise, she enjoyed the urgency of the work and the camaraderie of leading a team.

Nothing about this trajectory yielded a coherent narrative. Jo was finding her way through life, little by little, experimenting with what suited her and attracted employers. Every step she took revealed more of who she was and what she wanted from life. There was no map; she just explored.

Her brother Luca's route was just as meandering. His father's history certainly provided no path. Mario had enjoyed a successful career as an animator and artist, well known for a dazzling, inventive style that merges drawing, live action, choreography, and classic animation techniques. The aesthetic of his son's favorite toys—Power Rangers—made him wince but the little boy would spend hours in his bedroom, fighting pretend air battles, shouting coordinates. He showed all the academic disinterest of many young boys at school, until mediocre exam results at school and the failure to get into the university of his choice brought him up short. To his parents' amazement, he graduated with a first-class degree in physics and went to Cambridge to start a PhD. But what his parents didn't realize for a long time was what he yearned for: to be a test pilot.

Nobody took Luca's ambition seriously. It looked like a childish fantasy, doomed by the requirement for perfect and uncorrected eyesight, which he didn't have. But when the criteria changed to allow for corrected vision, Luca was on it: getting the Lasek surgery that would, a year later, make him eligible to apply for pilot training with the Royal Navy. As the possibility of Luca enlisting improved, family discussions became heated. Mario was a lifelong pacifist and both parents describe themselves as anti-authoritarian. What had their son become? They feared for him and were mystified by an ambition so alien to their family.

"You have to have faith," Mario decided. "But it isn't faith that they'll do the right thing. It's faith that they'll notice quickly if what they're doing doesn't work. So they'll be unafraid, not because they *know* what happens next but because they'll figure it out. . . ."

By the time Luca left Cambridge to train as a test pilot, Julia had become equally sanguine. An educational psychologist, she had seen too many kids who had grown up believing their lives would best be determined by following the rules and getting great grades. She'd worked with parents who brought huge files of reports on their children, desperate for reassurance of their future success, eager to impose a conventional model of success. But life, she argued, doesn't follow rules; that's what makes it life. There were no surefire tests or profiles that could guarantee what they wanted. History couldn't predict their children's future and neither would she. She counseled the parents to spend more time with their kids and worry less.

But worrying is what parents do. The positive function of worry is that it encourages horizon scanning: Where are the people, activities, opportunities that might appeal to my kids? How could I broaden their horizons? Worry also makes parents more attentive, tuning in to change and danger. But worry becomes destructive and limiting when it demands instant alleviation—which is what most parenting products purport to offer. The worldwide market for parental advice, reassurance, and certainty is so vast that it is impossible to quantify. What's obvious is that selling certainty to anxious parents is tantamount to selling sweets to their children.

"It doesn't matter if a child is heading for the Nobel Prize or falling behind in 5th grade," runs the promotional material for the MUSE parenting app. "Our deep cognitive modeling and patented machine learning technology allows us to predict life outcomes and to show you what you can do today to maximize the lifelong potential of your child."[1]

The app was developed by Socos Labs, founded by CEO Vivienne Ming, who seems fuzzy about how deterministic life really is. She says of herself that she was "supposed to win a Nobel Prize" but gender dysmorphia, depression, insomnia, and an eating disorder derailed her.[2] Which, if any of these, was predicted or predictable, she doesn't say, nor does she reveal what the appropriate response would be for a parent who could see those in their child's future. (You might even question what it is that makes Ming so certain she will not win a Nobel Prize; there's still time.)

The promise made for the MUSE app could be every parent's dream—or every parent's nightmare. If you could be certain your child would win that Nobel Prize, then knowing the future might be fabulous; since she's bound for a Nobel Prize, no need to worry about her drug habit. But if the future held drugs and a jail sentence, perhaps parents would decide there was no point investing in the education of a deadbeat. All the ethical issues intrinsic to predicting the future are alive and oversimplified here. How MUSE predicts your child's outcome is opaque since, thanks to "patented machine learning," it's a trade secret. So all the app will really do is tell you where or when improvement is seen. It is, in effect, conditioning you to behave like a good parent. But whose idea of good parenting is being promoted? The definitions of progress and success are all Ming's own, and whether her ideas, or your ideas, of improvement are the same, or even compatible or trustworthy, you will never know.

Ming makes great claims for her technology, saying of her infant clients, "We want to change the person you're going to become. It's not the same you but a non-smoker—*it's a different person.* I don't mean this in any spiritual sense. It's the person you were meant to be." How she knows who or what your child is supposed to be (since you don't) is opaque, but she insists that her app's assessment of social skills, emotional intelligence, strategic thinking, and creativity can determine life outcomes.[3] She believes her analysis of historic leaders proves it. But this is a logical fudge: when you look at very successful people in the past, of course their positive qualities are what you notice first. But assessing leadership is rife with attribution errors, which suggest but can't prove that exceptional leaders succeeded purely because of those individual qualities, conveniently discounting good luck, the era they lived in, the people who helped them, the weaknesses and bad luck of adversaries. It's common also to overlook, marginalize, and trivialize all the areas where they failed. Despite the overwhelming amount of data showing that the best predictor of educational achievement is parental income, Ming's assessment doesn't include that.

If it were possible to so simply concoct a recipe for success, absent time and context, we would all be great leaders by now. But then who would the followers be? Using the historic record is problematic because the data is patchy (the leaders we know about) and a product of the past, so the examples we have are mostly white males. There's no reason to believe that what created success in the last century will do so again in this one. How is success defined? If money, power, or life span, Mussolini beats Mozart. Ming's model of achievement may be subjective but it is what users of the app buy into when they adopt it. Just like financial forecasts, these heuristics contain an agenda; they might purport to be objective or scientific, but they can't be. Are you willing to sign up for Ming's definition of success, without knowing what it is or where it comes from?

MUSE could be dismissed as just another example of Silicon Valley hype, saying whatever will attract investors and customers. But the hype isn't cost-free. Users of the app made a surprising discovery. The app distracted them from their children.[4] Parents ended up feeling a slave to it, rather than learning firsthand about their own child. The more anxious they became and the more time they spent on the app, the less they could read their own kids. In effect, using the product meant that parents were being conditioned to condition their children to behave according to Ming's vague and personal concept of excellence. Apps like MUSE come *between* parent and child at a time when the child would benefit most from attention, time together, eye contact, developing mutual understanding. It's no wonder Julia and Mario were aghast at MUSE; it couldn't have helped them with their children, but might have made a difficult situation worse.

Apps aren't neutral. All technology effectively outsources work from humans to machines, promising purported efficiency gains at the expense of individual knowledge and learning. In the case of MUSE, the rich, if stressful, experience of parenting is delegated to a piece of software. But the automation paradox shows that the less we do something, the worse we get at it. The loss is twofold: it isn't just that the child gets computer-generated parenting; it's also that the parents lose the complex lessons of uncertainty, delight, anxiety, growth, and wisdom that are the rewards of family life. What's the point of having children if they're raised by other people's products?

The failure here isn't just exploiting anxious parents; that's been a gold mine for decades. It is treating the child as an object to be efficiently programmed: in other words, to relate to the child as a nascent machine. Implicitly, the app perpetuates a myth: that each individual is no more than an aggregation of data and, with enough data, profiles can be drawn up that can fully describe what they are and what they can be in the future. This is what astrology always promised and what personality tests have offered for nearly a century.

Of these, the most popular, taken by some two million people a year, is the Myers-Briggs Type Indicator, developed by Katharine Briggs and her daughter, Isabel Myers. Briggs, an ardent Jungian, had been captivated by Jung's concept of types and used them for experiments to study her daughter. Briggs pioneered what Ming adopted with MUSE: she looked to historic leaders to define her frame of reference—incurring, of course, all the same biases. Initially, Briggs had designed her questionnaire to identify solid marriage partners. But after World War II, her daughter repositioned it to place people in the right jobs. The MBTI does what all profiling systems do: asks batteries of questions and organizes the answers into types that are supposed to define your personality.

The test itself has no basis in clinical psychology. Deployed by most Fortune 500 companies, many universities, schools, churches, consulting companies, the CIA, army, and navy, its test-retest validity lies below statistical significance, meaning that if you test someone more than once, you are likely to get different results.[5] More worrying, the questionnaire poses binary questions, asking, for example, whether you value sentiment more than logic or vice versa. The question assumes that there is a simple answer to this question, absent context. Yet in real life, preference is highly contextual: I value logic when purchasing car insurance; I may value sentiment more when choosing to play with my son. Binaries always simplify, often to the point of absurdity, and they polarize what are often complements.

More worrying, however, is the underlying assumption that people neatly fall into one of sixteen types—and that this never changes. In her eye-opening biography of Myers, Briggs, and their test, author Merve Emre describes attending an MBTI official accreditation session that is eerily reminiscent of evangelical prayer meetings. Personality, her fellow participants insist, is innate and immutable, like left-handedness or blue eyes, and they urge her to join in chanting: "Type never changes! Type never changes!"[6] This is narrative essentialism at its most crude and static—because we do change over time, just as Jo and Luca did, just as Jacob Dunne did. Experience changes us; flukes, imagination, and accidents change us. The complex interplay of personality, work, illness, education, friends, family, history, success, and failure change who we are.[7] We play with, and add to, our memories and experiences all the time, constructing a myriad of different permutations from them. Most people become significantly more agreeable, conscientious, and emotionally stable as they age. But a Myers-Briggs profile encourages us to think of ourselves as defined for all time along a mere four dimensions. "I'm an ENTJ," the name badge says, meaning I am an extroverted, intuitive, thinking, judging individual. That is my fate, all I will ever be. I may as well forget about developing whatever other qualities I might have. Small wonder that, after her immersion in the history of Myers-Briggs, Emre concluded that personality typing was "among the silliest, shallowest, cultural products of late capitalism."[8]

That there are powerful commercial motives for profiling people is obvious: worth some $2 billion annually, the marketplace for personality assessment is swollen with contenders. After making its name with forecasting polls, the Gallup organization moved into profiling with its CliftonStrengths report. Like the MBTI, this test also asks an array of binary questions (routine vs. variety, heart vs. head) and then algorithmically generates an analysis of thirty-four strengths. If one of your strengths is that you're a learner, you get to learn that "It's very likely that you might have a particular desire for knowledge." The report is more subtle and less rigid than the MBTI, with qualities ranked in order of strength, but few people can resist the implication that those at the bottom are weaknesses.

When pushed on issues of validity, most profilers concede that these tools don't have much in the way of predictive power; they're just useful as conversation starters or to build a sense of community among common types. In itself, that might not be so bad, were it not for the evidence that people tend to believe what they are told about themselves. Telling a parent, or a teacher, that a child is destined for greatness—or not—is not a neutral action; it can influence how they see and respond to their children and what they expect of them. Well understood as the Pygmalion effect, the insight derives from an early experiment where primary school teachers in California were told that a few, named pupils were especially talented. At the end of a year, when the researchers returned to the school they found that, indeed, these children had achieved high marks. The catch was that those children had been chosen at random.[9] The prediction had changed the way the teachers treated the children more subtly than the teachers themselves noticed. (A later experiment with Israeli military platoons showed the same effect.) How people are described changes the way others relate to them and may create expectations that are unfair, irrelevant, or inaccurate. Tell someone that they're bad at math, lazy, or uncreative, and it's amazing how quickly that child conforms to those expectations. Tell an adult that they're punctual, and they start turning up on time. Profiling subtly merges into influence or conditioning, nudging a person's behavior and self-image in one direction or another.

Or consider the Forer effect. This is the strong tendency that subjects show to *believe* feedback from personality tests, regardless of whether those results are bogus. It is sometimes also known as the Barnum effect because it explains why descriptions that offer "something for everyone" are nevertheless taken seriously. The Forer effect is regularly cited when discussing why people believe in astrology, infamous for its nonspecific descriptions and predictions, so bland that they mean almost anything.

Astrological profiles at the back of fashion magazines may not matter much but psychographic profiles do. It's bad enough when we invest them with authority; it can be worse when employers do likewise. Increasingly companies turn to profiling software to facilitate their recruiting: to sift through resumes and match individual characteristics with job requirements. This form of matching is not wildly different from online dating: matching the profile of a job with the profile of a person, derived from job applications and sometimes also psychographic tests. It's fast and cheap and up to 90 percent of employers depend on such algorithms to produce their candidate short lists.[10] But it's wildly problematic.

Between 2014 and 2018, engineering teams at Amazon attempted to develop artificial intelligence that could sort through job applications, hoping to meet the furious demand for new hires. By 2018 they gave up. The AI demonstrated a pronounced preference for men, not surprising since the software drew its profile of a successful hire from a historic dataset. But what defines a successful employee changes over time. Qualities that might have been highly prized last year could be marginal today and irrelevant tomorrow, but neither the employers nor the AI knows in what ways. After several years of trying, the Amazon engineers gave up trying to derive the perfect employee profile from their data and abandoned the project.

Interpreting behavior is rife with value judgments that are invisible to those making them. According to the tech hiring platform Gilt, frequenting a Japanese manga site is predictive of strong coding skills. This could be a correlation but it overlooks the fact that women have less leisure time and that manga is mostly a male-dominated pastime. So even the algorithmic scanning of CVs has its problems.[11]

Profiling may also be illegal. As Cathy O'Neil revealed in *Weapons of Math Destruction*, some software implicitly detects whether job applicants may have had a history of mental illness—and, if they do, the system rejects them. Asking this question and discriminating on the basis of it is illegal under the Americans with Disabilities Act. You could not ask this question in a face-to-face interview. However, bringing a legal challenge is difficult because the algorithm is protected as a trade secret. *What* is being assessed within the programs, and what might be determined by implicit or explicit responses, is legally and ethically ambiguous. You may never know what your answers mean or why you were, or were not, hired. Power lies with those who design and interpret profiles, not those who provide their data.

The more that avid cost-cutters look to this technology, the more problems surface. First, the belief that your capability and capacity can be deduced from data ignores everything else about you. You are more than data. What data is available is always inadequate, a selective subset of a complex human being. Inferences about you are kept secret and may be incorrect, inadequate, or illegal. The dynamic nature of the job or environment isn't encoded in the profile. Moreover, results can't be evaluated against outcomes, because one large dataset will always be absent: employers never follow up with the applicants who *weren't* selected and so never know how many superstars the system mistakenly spat out. This is one reason why even some tech companies, including Google, have rejected such systems.[12] Predicting future performance is impossible, but automating it merely speeds up bias, errors, short-term thinking, and flaky assumptions.[13]

Nor does talent exist in a vacuum. Outstanding performers in one part of a company may, when transferred, suddenly fail. At the pharmaceutical company Roche, in a quest for diversity, a "high potential" executive was moved from Hong Kong to corporate headquarters in Basel. But in Switzerland, he could achieve almost nothing. His bosses considered letting him go but, at the last minute, decided to send him back to Hong Kong—where he flourished once again. Was the cultural difference too great? Had he proved unwilling to adapt? The Roche CEO blamed the firm's culture for being insufficiently inclusive. Hypotheses abounded but what everyone learned is that ability and environment are inextricably linked. As anyone who's suffered a terrible boss will recognize: given the right circumstances, everybody can be made to fail. Because achievement derives in part from context, forecasting individual talent omits half the picture.

Just like economic models, the reductive nature of profiling simplifies what is inherently complex. You need only consider careers like Johanna's and Luca's to appreciate how much hinged on small events and contingencies that neither they nor their parents nor their friends predicted or imagined. Life happened to these children, in the light of which they changed in ways that brought new experiences and perspectives that in turn drove different decisions. Johanna and Luca, like the rest of us, are neither static nor isolated. We live among people, moving across contexts, subject to a vast array of influences, experiences, and data, some of which we choose and much of which we don't. In short, we are more than our data.

Profiling and assessment technologies are a cheap, fast way to weed through thousands of resumes. But they pose psychological and social risks. They feed off stereotypes: simplistic, reductive versions of whole people. As such, they constrain the possibilities and potential of individuals and groups. Stereotyping myself as a Myers-Briggs introvert may make me reluctant to experiment or explore aspects of life that could enrich me. Simplified models of complex individuals encourage us to view one another as objects, types, or commodities measured by benchmarks we can't see and did not define.

Writing in the 1950s just as the personality testing business was taking off, the social critic Theodor Adorno argued that assigning different types to people facilitated their identifying with their own group at the expense of others. What later became known as the "minimal group paradigm" showed that categorization could be divisive, increasing conformity within one's own group, but also discrimination and hostility against other types.[14] Typing could polarize. Adorno's critique of the profiling business was informed by his sense that this was exactly what had occurred in Nazi Germany, "where the labeling of live human beings, independent of their specific qualities, resulted in decisions about their life and death." The very rigidity of types, Adorno argued, was itself indicative of fascism.[15]

He would probably be aghast today, at technologies that not only purport to tell us who we are but try to replace our personality and humanity with nudges, algorithms, profiles that at best interfere with developing self-knowledge and at worst attempt to condition it in the guise of perfectionism. Remembering that technology outsources human activity to a machine should be enough to steer us clear of apps whose ambitious developers hope will produce better humans than humans. Treating each other first as objects and then as groups, mediated by technological interfaces, just makes it cheaper, faster, easier to isolate and demonize one another. Relying on such systems means that we trade judgment for efficiency, reflection for obedience, inquiry for conformity, and independence for constraint. Only organizations or individuals that are implicitly authoritarian would arrogate to themselves the right to tell people who they are and what they might become.

But if forecasting fails individuals just because they *are* individual, it's reasonable to hope for more success by analyzing large human systems and identifying trends. We can't help but see patterns everywhere; it feels a logical assumption that extrapolating from them could reveal how success routinely unfolds. This was, in essence, what Vivienne Ming and the profilers were trying to do when they surveyed successful leaders in the past: draw a profile of achievement from a huge dataset. It's a seductive idea, particularly when coupled with the prospect of efficiency. If only we could glean how complex systems work, then we could invest heavily in productive people, places, and things—and spare effort on the rest. But that expectation of prediction proves elusive, too.

This is particularly frustrating when it comes to scientific discovery. Governments, businesses, and institutions around the world spend billions on scientific research. The work takes place within a vast ecosystem, with hundreds of interconnected fields, tens of thousands of researchers, and an overwhelming number of published results every year. It works accretively, which is to say that all researchers build on work done before and around them. Everyone wants a return on their investment of time, career, and money. So the question arises: How could science be organized to produce more and better results faster? The rhetoric that surrounds the "war on cancer" or "fight for the cure" implies that ruthless efficiency will solve complex problems: just double down on what works. The desire is sincere—everyone wants to cure cancer, MS, Parkinson's— but there's a reason why predicting outcomes in science is so often wrong. Science, too, is a complex system.

At certain moments in history, it has become obvious that particular lines of research have become feasible where previously they were not. One example is the Human Genome Project: a vast exercise that became practical when scientific knowledge, technological innovation, and computing power all coalesced at the end of the twentieth century. Like pieces of a jigsaw puzzle, it was only when these came together that the genome became describable. Just as the moment of the birth of the financial forecasting business depended on the simultaneous advent of trains, the telegraph, and statistics, periods of breakthrough require that knowledge, technology, resources, and human ingenuity align. Everyone would like more of those moments.

But other breakthroughs, like the discovery of penicillin or of cosmic microwave background radiation, exist at the opposite end of the spectrum: big, important discoveries that are flukes, neither predicted nor predictable. Everyone would love more of those, too—but they aren't planned; they emerge and are understood only retrospectively. There are also always "sleeping beauties,"[16] big powerful ideas—such as Mendel's concept of inheritance via the mechanism that we now call genes—that need other notable discoveries before the full import of their thinking is understood. Science has to advance on many other fronts before the sleeper subject can awake.

Across this spectrum—from the expected to the fluke—sits all the rest of science. It makes intuitive sense to imagine that if just some of this could be predicted, science would progress faster and more cheaply. But what principles could inform that process? Where might more investment predictably produce bigger, faster results?

Many propose that science needs to identify its superstars and just invest in them. But there is no profile of the breakthrough scientist. Great discoveries do come from scientists with a string of breakthroughs to their name, but they also come from newbies and overlooked veterans. There is no correlation between the impact of a discovery and its timing within a scientist's career.[17] What looks like a strong hypothesis—such as the Higgs boson—may take decades to validate. In the meantime, do you categorize Peter Higgs as a visionary or a flop? Mendel would never have been selected for his promise. He studied physics, not biology, missed much of his childhood education through illness, and regularly failed exams. The Nobel laureate Kary Mullis, the inventor of polymerase chain reaction (PCR), which accelerated decoding the genome, was a self-described surfer pothead whose best idea came during a nighttime drive to his beach shack.

If not superstars, could data mining predict where the new hot spots will emerge? Attempts to do so—analyzing publication counts, citations, recency, appeal—showed little more than the scientists themselves already knew; it's their job and passion to stay alert to developments in their field. Just as one risk of profiles (DNA or psychographic) lies in oversimplification, so the danger in making science efficient is the risk of inhibiting innovation, marginalizing underrepresented ideas, and discouraging new and multidisciplinary fields. However society might wish to make scientific progress efficient, the truth about complex systems is that trying to simplify them doesn't guarantee that they become more effective; it risks making them *less* effective. They function best when they are robust, throwing off a vast array of insights and understanding whose value may be realized over time. That means they can look wasteful, producing more than what is needed. But when you don't know what's needed, you're safer with more.

A useful analogy here is with air travel: Much in flying is predictable and efficient. You know passengers will check in, their bags will be loaded onto planes, they will want to eat and drink. Those aspects of flying are planned and managed with a beady eye on the efficient use of time, people, and money. However, once the plane is in the air, you cannot guarantee with absolute certainty exactly what will happen: whether geese will impact, or a part will fail. Too many factors are at work and beyond control to know for sure what will happen. And because the risk in the air is so much greater than on the ground, aircraft have been designed with more engines and operating systems than they usually need; if one fails, others won't. Robustness, not efficiency, is their protection against the unpredictable. In a complex system like science, the fundamental robustness of the ecosystem is variety, because it facilitates a rich range of insights and discoveries—like penicillin—whose value can emerge even when unplanned. The big danger in confusing a complex system (like science) for a complicated process (like loading bags on planes) is that, in striving for efficiency and predictability, the robustness of the system, its creativity and ability to withstand adversity, is killed off.

Science and counterterrorism might not look like they have much in common, but they do. Both are complex systems, where crucial events may be predictable or flukes. Both are full of routine events and total surprises. Understanding such environments and managing through them requires the capacity to distinguish between what can and cannot be predicted and tolerance for the ambiguity and uncertainties that lie in between. The chair of the Wellcome Trust, one of the largest funders of scientific research in the world, Eliza Manningham-Buller, has dealt with the complexity of both counter-terrorism and science. Her understanding of complex systems began when she worked in the British security services at MI5 between 1974 and 2007, the last five years of which she served as director general. Of the fifteen terrorist plots that Manningham-Buller faced during her time as DG, twelve were thwarted, including that of the shoe bomber, Richard Reid, and of the 21/7 bombers. Only the four suicide bombers of 7/7 succeeded fully, which means that MI5 had missed something or failed to act in time. Manningham-Buller knows that while perfect knowledge might be desirable, what matters more is the capacity to take action.

"It's a myth," says Manningham-Buller, "that you *ever* have all the information you need. When I was at MI5, we were always having to make tough provisional judgments based on pinpricks of light against a dark and shifting canvas. Whatever you do, when you make your decision, your knowledge is incomplete. At MI5 consequences could be lethal—but not acting could be lethal, too."

There is no perfect profile of a terrorist because who they are and how they behave keeps changing and adapting. While there are patterns in terrorism, they don't repeat reliably and there is no stable narrative. This is characteristic of complex systems. So one tragedy (like 7/7) might reveal information that is helpful next time but it also might not be relevant for years—or ever. Terrorism isn't defined by profiles or patterns; terrorists know that randomness protects them. For those trying to anticipate terrorist attacks, it can feel as though the sides have come off the billiard table and balls can drop off or arrive from anywhere. You don't know how many variables there are, or where they may come from, and you can't predict which, if any, will matter.

At MI5, Manningham-Buller required that people *not* tell her what she wanted to hear, but that they find the insights and courage to argue with her, to present alternative points of view in order to assess multiple possible realities. That takes time, of course, and can look inefficient. But in a context saturated with ambiguity, resisting the gravitational pull of certainty remains paramount. While Manningham-Buller always sought a robust sense of possible realities, her colleagues say that her tolerance for uncertainty was her strength.

"Make the call too soon, without enough evidence, people are released without charge. To do nothing is not an option. Too late and you're calling for hearses. So it has to be a mixture of judgment and how much you need to know to make a reasonable decision. It's a dangerous myth that if you plan enough, if you're efficient enough, you'll always get it right."

That's why the intelligence services attach probability ratings to their briefings: because they know that their forecasts, however scrupulous, are riddled with contingencies, accidents, luck, and change. Intelligence officers I know crave critical, independent readers who appreciate that it is impossible ever to provide what Manningham-Buller calls "100 percent prescience." But politicians hate the ambiguity in the numbers, seeking to give the public the palliative certainty that only fiction can provide. The probability ratings, just like the color-coded threat levels Manningham-Buller introduced, articulate ambiguity: that all information about the future is not equal, comprehensive, or conclusive. You get the "pin-pricks of light" but they could mean anything. You only ever get a bit of the picture and have to try to fill in the rest, all the while asking: What is it a picture of?

Staying open-minded to stray bits of information can feel inefficient, disorganized, or indecisive but it is the only way to ensure that decisions are as well informed as they can be. To think better requires more options, not fewer. When Manningham-Buller ran MI5, the number of intelligence operations increased five-fold. This might not have looked efficient; it aimed to be robust. You have to be alert, she says, to what doesn't fit your preconceptions. Never imagine that you know what will happen or even what you might need.

"About twenty or thirty years ago," Manningham-Buller told me, "the USA made a serious error believing that technology would get us all the information we needed. They thought the future didn't need human intel. It was a big serious error. It meant that after 9/11, they had no Arab speakers, no local network or knowhow. Of course, it's since been reversed."

Manningham-Buller and others in intelligence argue that depending too much on technology means that any information that isn't digital data too easily gets marginalized. The thought that you've captured all the data is what leads to error. No single, efficient process, profile, or narrative will prove robust enough for an environment characterized by change. Thinking so gets people killed. Human skills and talents are critical to a fuller picture. The temptation to try to simplify complex systems is how you get them wrong; just like profiling, just like any kind of model, what gets left out or what changes can turn out to be vital. This is why intelligence organizations frequently use multiple teams to examine and analyze the same data in real time: because doing so can tell more than one story. That variety might look inefficient but it imparts adaptability and responsiveness, essential qualities when you know you can't predict what the future holds.

The complex system from which we expect the greatest predictive power is genetics. Ever since we've been able to identify genes and begun to understand how they worked, DNA has been seen as destiny, capable of determining who we are—and who we will be. As the Human Genome Project got under way, public excitement positioned DNA as a kind of chemical horoscope: a code for every individual's future.

In reality, it has all turned out to be far more complex than even scientific researchers anticipated. If your DNA is any kind of profile, it is one full of potentials and probabilities but few certainties. There is no gay gene, nor a way to predict an individual's sexual behavior.[18] Genes do explain hair color, but even something as simple and heritable as this turns out to be complex, with only red and black hair predicted with 90 percent accuracy. More common colors are difficult; at least 124 genes determine what color hair your baby might be born with, and so far nobody knows what predicts some blond hair turning brown.[19] Nearly two million genetic variants determine height.[20] For each of us, just 4 percent of our life span is predicted by our parents' longevity. Heritable conditions such as sickle cell anemia, Down's, Edwards's, and Patau's syndromes, Huntingdon's disease, hemophilia, fragile X, and cystic fibrosis can be detected through DNA testing, but the DNA can't predict how the conditions will manifest, what quality of life the child might enjoy, or how long that life will be. Even here we are dealing with probabilities, not certainties.

This is not just because interpreting the tests for these diseases is difficult. It is also because what happens in your body, in your environment, and in your life influences the activity of your genes. This is clearly seen in studies of identical twins, born with exactly the same DNA. If one identical twin developed multiple sclerosis, then, if genes were destiny, the chance of the second twin also developing MS would be 100 percent. But it isn't—it is about 30 percent. Similarly, while the rate of breast cancer among women is roughly 10 percent, the risk for women who have an identical twin *with* breast cancer is 15 percent, not a hundred.[21] In his reflections on the human genome, Nobel laureate Sydney Brenner observed that identical twins develop different immune systems.[22] The experiences and environments of the two individuals, even with the same DNA, are different enough to produce life-defining differences. What happens along the way is life.

Since DNA testing has become easily available to the general public, more than 26 million consumers have chosen to see how much of their future might be detectable. Rupert tried the genetic testing kit 23andMe out of sheer curiosity; a lifelong technologist, he was open-minded about what he learned.

"I think what's interesting is what it doesn't tell you," Baines said, laughing. "There were a lot of caveats, likelihoods rather than absolutes. Likely doesn't have red hair. Likely dark hair, that kind of thing." The most useful thing Baines learned was that he was likely to have a strong response to the anticoagulant warfarin. That's useful if he ever needs to take the drug, which he hopes he won't.

Baines's test also revealed that he had a 20 percent higher chance of colon cancer than the population on average. Overall, the risk of colon cancer runs at about 4.5 percent; for Rupert this might mean his risk is closer to 5.5 percent.[23] He is unlikely to contract the disease but cannot be certain that he will not. Because his grandmother had glaucoma, he has his eyes tested every six months. Learning that he actually had a lower-than-average risk of contracting the disease was reassuring, but he hasn't changed his routine.

Rupert's greatest delight wasn't about the future but about the past. Learning that, on his father's side, his genes didn't come from Lancashire but from the Levant, maybe Lebanon, was a surprise. Knowing that his grandfather was a captain in the merchant navy and went to that part of the world with his wife set Rupert wondering what exactly happened there. A seaboard romance? A love triangle? It doesn't really matter now, he says, but it is fun to imagine. "Who it was, how or why," Rupert reflected, "we'll never know for certain. . . ." And he laughed again.

The revolution in our understanding of genetics has produced huge surprises but also widespread confusion, even among geneticists themselves. An informal audit of three DNA testing companies showed completely different results for the same DNA sample, largely because each firm uses different sets of reference data.[24]

Analyzing vast swaths of DNA now makes it possible to stratify people into trajectories for specific diseases, but the biobanks that provide the DNA have limited ethnic and geographic diversity and so may have predictive validity only for those regions. And even the boldest evangelists for genomically determined medicine concede that only 30 to 50 percent of the risk for many common diseases lies in our genes. Environmental factors determine the rest and some of these are still not well understood. Take, for example, some species of deer that drop off and regrow their antlers each year. When a notch is cut in one antler, you'd expect the new year's antlers to be pristine. But they aren't; they grow back with a notch in the same place. Where and how has that information been stored? No one knows. Epigenetics, the study of all the factors *beyond genes* that determine life, is revealing how much more complex inheritance is.[25] So when you get into the genetic determination of personality, prediction becomes highly problematic.

Some of the loudest claims come from Robert Plomin, best known for his twin studies. In his book *Blueprint: How DNA Makes Us Who We Are,* he makes what he himself describes as a "sales pitch" for the power of genetics to predict personality. It can, he writes, "tell your fortune from the moment of your birth, it is completely reliable and unbiased—and it costs only £100. . . . The fortune teller is DNA."[26]

As sales pitches go, that's impressive. The difficulty lies in the detail. What Plomin means is that no other *single* factor has as much influence as DNA. He is certain that genetics account for 50 percent of psychological differences—but what about the other 50 percent? Collectively the other half has equal influence—it's just that those influences are varied, diverse, random, and unpredictable. So while taken all together they are just as important as DNA, they're more difficult to study and to measure.

Plomin's is a loud voice in the genetics world, though he is not without his critics. A psychologist, he focuses on personality:

everything from the Big Five traits (neuroticism, extroversion, openness, conscientiousness, and agreeableness) to bipolar disorder and schizophrenia. But these characteristics aren't detectable by biological tests; they can only be determined through observation and assessment. Scientists have already raised concerns that statistics now risk overpowering biology, and they risk even more uncertainty when there's little established physical biology to study, only observed behavior.[27] Nevertheless, even while acknowledging that everything else constitutes the other half of the story, Plomin still insists that personality is defined by DNA. As a researcher, he's drawn to the factors he can measure, but this makes him as in love with his Big Idea—the genetic determination of personality—as the founding fathers of forecasting were in love with theirs.

Analyzing his own DNA, Plomin discovered that he had a high probability for schizophrenia. Because there is no evidence of schizophrenia in his life nor any history of schizophrenia in his family, the DNA analysis led him to wonder whether it explained his need for a highly structured, scheduled working life. This is a marvelous example of the Forer effect in action: told something is true, he starts to redefine himself in the light of the new knowledge.

Plomin frequently asserts that "prediction is the *sine qua non* of prevention . . . an early warning system."[28] But what might Plomin's parents have done with this knowledge? Would the pregnancy have proceeded? Perhaps his parents would have enrolled him in trials of prophylactic antipsychotic medication at the age of fifteen, but whether the drugs would have advanced or destroyed his academic promise is unknowable. Noting his predicted high level of educational attainment, his parents might have hesitated, worrying that acting on one prediction might undermine the capacity to fulfill another.

The discovery that DNA can predict school achievement thrilled Plomin. His own predicted academic achievement was so extravagant, he confessed, as to be "embarrassing."[29] But what is the value of this prediction? He argues that it would make parents and teachers of failing kids more understanding and forgiving, less likely to blame the student for their failure. But that risks stereotyping and giving up on the child, or provides the perfect excuse for rationing: Why bother investing in struggling students whose DNA says they'll never get that PhD? Or the reverse: The smart kid's going to do well anyway, so let's send the less well-endowed sibling to a really great school and provide extra tutoring?

We should never forget the other 50 percent of the equation. The genetic capacity for a PhD isn't negligible, but it is no guarantee of getting one. High levels of predicted educational attainment count for nothing, if the promising child in Syria or Venezuela hits school age just as the education system falls to pieces, or when parents can't afford the bus fare to less violent schools or older kids are made responsible for child care.[30] For Johanna, the absence of educational qualifications said nothing about her intellectual capacity but everything about other factors: her illness, an unfriendly school. Just because those environmental factors are impossible to predict doesn't mean they don't matter. Ever since Renner and Rosenzweig first pioneered research into neuroplasticity, we've been able to see physical evidence that the brain's capacity changes according to the richness (or poverty) of the environment in which it develops.[31] And what does educational attainment actually mean? It can't be seen under a microscope but is defined by bureaucracies that codify what it means to be educated. That changes over time; on its own, educational attainment predicts nothing more than further academic achievement. Good grades are helpful but don't, in themselves, predict success in life.

Confusingly, Plomin concedes that "genetics is not a puppeteer pulling our strings. Genetic influence means just that—influence, not hard-wired genetic determinism."[32] However random, complex, and hard to measure the other 50 percent of the equation may be, it makes a significant difference to what the future holds. Rich parents, a house full of books, being able to breathe clean air, to have breakfast, and to get to school, having neighbors who can help with homework or a friend who shares a passion for sport: any of these—or none—has a profound and real impact on life outcomes. A parent's decision to move their family to a different country provokes exposure to new experiences, which prompt different ideas and choices that in themselves lead to different choices, all unpredictable because there is nothing in the parents' or the child's DNA that predicts the move, the exposure, or the subsequent decisions. If Plomin at times seems confused and contradictory, it is because the evidence is confused and contradictory: the DNA matters but it isn't the only thing that matters. And what might change your life could be predictable—or not. Fifty-fifty.

The uncertainty and ambiguity implicit in DNA data is hard to explain, to understand, or to use for rational, safe decision making. I've watched well-trained genetic counselors struggle as they've guided educated, mature executives through the complex data that goes into polygenic scorings. Though they all sought to understand the consequences of the genetic information, the day ended with the audience dazed and confused by just how uncertain it all remains. Mark McCarthy, a geneticist at Oxford University, worries that "there aren't enough genetic counsellors on the planet" to manage the subtle interpretations of polygenic scores.

But, as always in the world of forecasting, there's money to be made from commercializing prophecy and imbuing it with moral urgency. Both Plomin and Anne Wojcicki of 23andMe believe it is a parent's duty to "arm themselves with their child's blueprint."[33] Duty to whom? Plomin's big idea and Wojcicki's big business trivialize the danger and mistake of emphasizing what's certain—the score—over and above what's uncertain—the other half that represents life. Stereotyping, rationing, discrimination, passivity, surrender: these are the very real risks produced when overstating the foresight afforded by DNA.

What should be done with this knowledge? More deliberative voices than Plomin's should be heard. Where Plomin gets excited by the prospect of "precision education" that would tailor schooling to genetic potential, he's loading the dice: amplifying with environmental contributions what the DNA shows as merely probable. He doesn't contemplate the decisions that might be made by the parents of a fetus demonstrating a high risk of schizophrenia. And like most clever people, he's markedly more interested in opportunities for the fortunate than danger for the unlucky.

But ever since Darwin described evolution, researchers into inheritance have been tempted by the prospect of the perfectibility of human beings, by amping up strengths and reducing weaknesses. Francis Galton (Darwin's cousin) posed the incendiary question: "Could not the undesirables be got rid of and the desirables multiplied?"[34] He coined the term "eugenics" and in 1869 wrote, "The time may hereafter arrive, in far distant years, when the population of the earth shall be kept as strictly within the bounds of number and suitability of race, as the sheep on a well-ordered moor or the plants in an orchard-house; in the meantime, let us do what we can to encourage the multiplication of the races best fitted to invent and conform to a high and generous civilization, and not, out of a mistaken instinct of giving support to the weak, prevent the incoming of strong and hearty individuals."[35]

The language of efficiency is unmistakable. Just like the engineers of Silicon Valley, life is idealized as simpler, better, if its complexity, anomalies, and flukes can be managed out. For decades, eugenics attracted a large and distinguished following from all parts of the political spectrum: Beatrice and Sidney Webb, John Maynard Keynes, and H. G. Wells believed that human "stock" should not be diluted by allowing "detrimental types" to have children. Bertrand Russell proposed that the state issue color-coded "pro-creation tickets" defining who was and was not allowed to bear children. Sterilization, segregation, incarceration were all proposed as means of eliminating those deemed to be "social rubbish." Writing to Prime Minister Asquith, Winston Churchill warned that "the multiplication of the feeble-minded is a very terrible danger to the race."[36] The mother of the Myers-Briggs Type Indicator couldn't have agreed more: "Multitudes of people are utterly worthless or worse than worthless, having no just claims whatsoever upon the civilization which they burden with the dead weight of their existence."[37]

Eugenics first moved from theory to practice in the United States. In 1923, the German geneticist Fritz Lenz observed that "Germany had nothing to match the eugenics research institutions in England and the United States."[38] In 1927, the Supreme Court upheld forceable sterilization when Justice Oliver Wendell Holmes argued in *Buck v. Bell*, "The principle that sustains compulsory vaccination is broad enough to cover cutting the Fallopian tubes. . . . Three generations of imbeciles are enough."[39] In parts of the United States, forced sterilization—of uneducated girls raped by older men, epileptics, those with low IQ, and those deemed too "feebleminded" to raise children—continued until 1977. Poor, uneducated, and black Americans were disproportionately affected.[40]

The advent of genetic testing in the 1970s brought eugenics back to life as newgenics: the use of abortion and prenatal screening to introduce some element of choice into having a baby. There were important differences; prenatal testing and selective abortions were performed with no state mandate and no centralized legal definition of fitness or unfitness. The advent of in vitro fertilization (IVF) introduced the idea of "procreative benevolence," which enabled parents to test which of their four embryos looked most promising and choose only those for implant. Many found (and still find) that reasonable.[41] Giving choice to individuals rather than to the state preserved variety and while some nations (such as Japan) preferred girls to boys, others (such as India and China) chose boys over girls. In 1980, a millionaire sunglass entrepreneur, Robert Graham, opened a Repository for Germinal Choice that called for elite sperm from men of the highest intellect (preferably Nobel laureates) to be inseminated into intelligent, healthy young women. His "genius bank" was widely ridiculed and, before it was disbanded, seems to have produced just fifteen children, none of any distinction.[42]

But as the mapping of the human genome progressed, the possibility of "improvements" moved from the level of the whole person to the level of the gene. This progress has taken two forms. The first, gene therapy, involves the manipulation of genes to treat major illnesses. These alterations last only one generation and are not inherited by future offspring. But the second form of genetic manipulation, known as "germ line gene therapy," does pass to future generations. Editing the genome of an egg or sperm through CRISPR (clustered regularly interspaced short palindromic repeats) offers the possibility of permanent genetic change. Some argue for efficiency: Why not, improve the quality of the future human genome through selection or editing? Others are deeply uncomfortable with the prospect and consequences of reducing genetic variety.

In 2015, recognizing that a fundamental turning point had been reached, genetic researchers called for a moratorium on the use of gene-editing and gene-altering technologies. CRISPR genomic editing had potential that neither old-style eugenics nor newgenics had ever had: to add or subtract information in the human genome. Francis Collins, who had helped to lead the Human Genome Project, was alarmed. "This reality means that germline manipulation would largely be justified by attempts to 'improve' ourselves. That means that someone is empowered to decide what 'improvement' is."[43] In 2018, a Chinese researcher (trained at Rice University and Stanford) horrified the scientific world when he created the world's first gene-edited babies, a pair of twin girls. As the Chinese government rushed to develop new gene-editing legislation, the researcher was jailed for three years and fined three million yuan for "disrupting medical order."[44]

Although James Clapper, when director of national intelligence, described genome editing as a weapon of mass destruction and proliferation, Jennifer Doudna, the co-discoverer of CRISPR, remains pretty sanguine. After the Chinese experiment, a second moratorium was proposed, which she did not sign. She's founded several CRISPR start-ups and joined the board of Johnson & Johnson, hoping to see the acceleration of her work. "The more efficiently you can do the editing, the more effectively you can deliver editors into cells, whether plant cells or the human brain or anything else, the better it will work," she said. "I've grown up in a capitalist society where you believe that as technologies become more capable, that it enables more companies to do interesting things. . . ."[45]

But this new science poses two fundamental questions that dog all those trying to determine the future through DNA. First: Who decides what is eliminated or amplified? Do we return to state-mandated definitions of improvement, as we saw in the Third Reich and in North Carolina? Or does the market decide, with greater choice ceded to the wealthy, making inequality not merely economic but also biological and heritable? Historically, both markets and authoritarian regimes have demonstrated an insatiable appetite for eliminating variety.

The idea of the perfected world, from which all difficulties and anomalies are removed, is a persistent one, attractive to individuals who already feel they have what it takes, and repellent to those who see in our diversity and interdependence the foundations of adaptive, creative, and sustainable societies. Watching the resurgence of eugenics, Victoria Brignell wrote a series of articles exploring why eugenics feels so disturbing. A professional researcher, she strongly identified with those who might be edited out. Left paralyzed from the neck down by a spinal tumor, she is looked after, day and night, by carers.

"Do we really want a society where, for example, everybody is equally good at maths—so we don't need each other's help? Where we don't need each other because we're all perfect in all the same ways? Society celebrates independence but without dependence, there *is* no society. Or any diversity. . . ."

She puzzled over the allure of perfection, finding it homogeneous and dull. Removing flaws might reduce uncertainty but didn't it also risk reducing variation in the population? Variation and mutation make evolution robust over time. Not knowing which qualities and traits the future will need, why increase risk by *reducing* the broad spectrum of human talents, insight, and capacity in our species? Concentrating on strengths today would constitute a big, dangerous bet, the consequences of which we can't even guess.

We can't see the future. Over the last hundred years, turning to models, data, history, profiling, and DNA has thwarted our craving for certainty. Models fail because they're reductive, subjective, ideological. Confronted by the inherent unpredictability of life, many individuals and organizations have shifted subtly from trying to forecast our future to trying to influence us, using salesmanship and propaganda. For some corporations, even that is too slow and ambiguous. Instead of coming to terms with ineradicable uncertainty, companies intervene to eliminate it. Rewards (air miles, discounts) and punishments (higher prices, being expelled) condition consumers to converge on some choices and turn away from others. Defeated by the ambiguity and complexity of human life, it has become more profitable to reduce free agency than to predict it. This is the thinking behind Amazon's anticipatory shopping patent.[46] Instead of customers making their own decisions, Amazon decides for them, sending what they want before they know they want it. It is, as one commentator noticed, one more step toward cutting out human agency altogether.[47]

In her book *The Age of Surveillance Capitalism,* Shoshana Zuboff quotes an unnamed chief data scientist who describes how he thinks about consumers. "We can capture their behaviors and identify good and bad [ones]. Then we develop 'treatments' or 'data pellets' that select good behaviors. We can test how actionable our cues are for them and how profitable certain behaviors are for us."[48] Instead of seeking better to understand ourselves, MIT's Alex Pentland celebrates the opportunity to deploy sensors and data to increase efficiency and to impose "a quantitative, predictive science of human organizations and human society." Proposing "social efficiency both as a design goal and a metric for the design of social network systems," he urges us to build "social network systems" as wondrous as the "rich legacy" of our financial system.[49]

This is a eugenics mind-set, applied to everything we do and everything we are. With CRISPR, would-be forecasters crossed the line into casting the future. This transition—from information to intervention—could not be more profound or challenging. In many ways, it acknowledges that the future cannot be foretold. Economic models aren't fully successful. Narratives prove misleading and history doesn't repeat itself reliably. Profiles of individuals or systems cannot overcome the ineradicable uncertainty of the complexity of life. For those determined to master the future, the only recourse is to force-fit a standardized model of a predictable reality onto a world that remains complex and rich but unpredictable in all its individuality. The appeal for large corporations is that doing so is hugely profitable. The temptation for us is the allure of a life that is convenient, predictable, and certain. No longer overwhelmed by choice, our decisions get edited for us, day after day, as surely as CRISPR edits human potential.

So we stand now at a crossroads. Can we live with the fact that neither professional forecasters nor historians or profiles or even DNA can untangle the systemic complexity, uncertainty, and ambiguity of our lives? All of our ancestors did so. Or is a more predictable life—calmer, easier, with less fear of error or surprise—too tantalizing to reject? The price of certainty is high: surrendering to a limited experience of life, designed by individuals and corporations who do not know us, whose interests are not ours. In this condition, convenience is passivity and choice obedience. In our hunger to know the future, is the alleviation of doubt and uncertainty sufficient reward for the loss of agency, of autonomy?

All of the advocates of eugenics or fully efficient social systems are eager to demonstrate their advantages: less suffering, less waste. They are reluctant to spell out the risks: not just conformity, injustice, and authoritarianism but the loss of meaningful social connection and diversity. In Pentland's utopia, where every bus arrives on time and medical appointments are magically scheduled just before you get sick, nobody needs anyone else. We don't need compassion, generosity, or trust because everyone is taken care of by a system. The meager reward is convenience. The big risk lies in the loss of diversity. With everyone equally dependent on the same system, this vision has no capacity for robustness. In this picture of predictable lives on a narrow spectrum, there are no flukes, no happy (or unhappy) accidents. Variety is not its defining characteristic, even though we know that that is what provides evolution with the capacity to adapt. As such, a world in which we are all reliant on an invisible system we don't understand seems the most dangerous response to uncertainty ever devised.

Every generation of human being has lived with uncertainty and unpredictability; that's how we developed our staggering human capacity for invention, discovery, improvisation, and creativity. Our ability to invent and explore came from necessity, not comfort. It's been in the interstices of uncertainty that we have found and used freedom. As Eliza Manningham-Buller found, trusting a single approach is dangerous but living with incomplete knowledge doesn't leave us useless or passive. Just because perfect success isn't possible doesn't mean we should all become Galton's sheep on Pentland's well-ordered moor. While we can never render complexity simple, we could embrace it as an adventure that calls us to investigate the infinite permutations of life that it contains. Surrendering agency, action, and adventure for convenience is a miserable bargain. In an uncharted world, who is content to be left hugging the shore when we could use our freedom to explore?

PART II

WHAT WOULD YOU DO
IF YOU WERE FREE?

CHAPTER FOUR

NO AVAILABLE DATASETS

A man can starve from a lack of self-realization as much as from a lack of bread.

—Richard Wright

Growing up on her father's small Devon farm, Rebecca Hosking didn't feel that she lacked for companions. Surrounded by wildlife who were both pets and company, she always felt most at home in nature. Studying photography gave her an excuse to get outside and wander. Now in her early forties, Hosking's weathered face shows she has spent most of her life outdoors; it's when she pulls the thick, curly blond hair away from her face that you notice she's beautiful. But chiefly the impression that sticks is one of tenacity, a rugged determination not to be daunted by stiff challenges. In 1999, after completing a degree in photography, her teachers had encouraged her to apply for a coveted BBC scholarship, working in the Natural History Unit. No woman had won it before, but Hosking did. Two years later, she was a producer, traveling the world shooting the documentaries that made the NHU so famous. Not all directors wanted to travel the world with a woman and many were skeptical that Hosking could cope with heavy film gear and tripods. She proved them wrong. But after six or seven years working on David Attenborough films, she was severely disillusioned by what she had seen in the wild.

"In all of these projects," Hosking recalled, "we'd go past hor-rific ecological devastation. Huge monoculture farms. Dead zones where you can't film. Climate change was seen as an annoyance, getting in the way of film shoots and messing up our schedules! A great subject staring us in the face—seen as an annoyance. I just got more and more cross."

Hosking knew she was in a privileged position: she had resources (her expertise, access to audiences); she had real passion for the environment and a crying need for something to be said about its spoliation. The BBC agreed to commission her film about Hawaii, but she had no intention of showcasing the glorious wildlife; the program was about the ruination of the ocean caused by plastic.

"I sold it as beautiful people saving animals," Hosking said. "But I didn't say what they were saving them *from*. The series producer knew. He kept telling me: you have to tell the series editor that every marine animal seen on screen would be shown choked in plastic, ingesting plastic. . . ."

Hosking's hypothesis was that if audiences could see the horrors she had witnessed, they would rise up and demand change. But when the film aired, nothing happened. Her hypothesis wasn't proved. What she learned was that people watch TV and carry on as usual.

She went home, severely jaded. Her achievements and her friend-ships now seemed superficial, pointless. Alone in her small flat in Modbury, Hosking wondered: Why hadn't people responded? Per-haps they didn't know where to start. What if she started small and just tried to persuade her village to give up plastic bags?

Friendly with the local deli owner, Hosking floated the idea: the first supporter. The art gallery owner thought it was a fantastic idea, too. The butcher agreed but asked what he was supposed to do about meat juices. If she could find a decent substitute, he'd go along with her. Six weeks later, all of the local independent shops supported her plan. She called a public meeting to confront the big retailers, challenging them to support the campaign, and they did, promising to give every household—1,500 people—a cloth bag. The night before the secret launch, each householder got their bag through the mailbox, with a note saying: "From Monday, we are not going to be using any plastic bags in the village." If her film couldn't change the world, Hosking hoped that she could at least change her little village.

She was wrong again. The world's media got wind of the story and arrived en masse on her doorstep. The *Guardian* picked up on it first, then other newspapers. Then, she said, it went stupid: CNN, Sky, Russia Today, NBC, Chinese TV crews, Canadian, French. Chinese officials presented Hosking with a bag that said: *Our Province follows Modbury!* They had banned bags overnight. Hosking asked them how many people lived in their province. Thirty-two million!

In 2007, the year of Hosking's experiment, Botswana, Ethiopia, Belgium, Rwanda, and China all either banned plastic bags, imposed a levy, or introduced laws requiring bags to be biodegradable. In China, bag usage fell by between 60 to 80 percent. In Ireland, it fell 90 percent. In the United States, bans were local, by state or city. In 2019, New York's governor, Andrew Cuomo, signed a law banning single-use plastic bags and, around the world, the trend has continued. In January 2020, the Chinese government went even further, banning all single-use plastic products, including bags, straws, and utensils. Why did Hosking's movie experiment fail when her second, small-scale one was so successful? Why did a 2017 film on plastic pollution in the ocean make an impact where hers had not? She will never know. But it is characteristic of complex systems that small actions can make a disproportionate impact. You just don't know, won't know, until you try. And try again.

As individuals, organizations, and corporations confront enormous problems—inequality, disease, injustice, technological disruption, environmental degradation, climate change—it's become fashionable to seek to define theories of change. What makes people and institutions abandon old bad habits and acquire new, better ones? Some argue that pressure eventually produces a tipping point, while others maintain it's all about the cogency or timing of the message. When large corporations and institutions require strategic change, investors and participants demand a theory of change that promises to contain or define their risk. But the test of a good theory is that it can predict—and what we know about complex systems is that, while aspects of them may repeat, they are inherently *un*predictable. So theories of change in highly dynamic systems might purport to offer certainty, where it often proves most illusory. The value of experiments is that they disrupt apathy, acknowledge ambiguity, and give people hope.

Hosking's experience reveals useful principles. Distraught by what she'd seen around the world, she didn't despair or whine or assume that somewhere someone else would take action. She refused to be passive; it was better to try something than to do nothing. When her first experiment failed, she didn't give up. Nor did she try to predict or game the outcome, so she made no promises; her experiment was genuinely open-ended.

What she brought to the problem were three assets: need, resources, and passion. She knew that there was a demonstrable need for a change in consumer behavior. She had resources: her knowledge, her media experience, and her relationship with the villagers who trusted her. In this she was smarter than many, who often assume that only professional colleagues are sources of power. And she had passion for the subject—essential if she was going to have the resilience and energy needed to keep going and to bring the project to life. If you think of those three assets—need, resources, passion—as a Venn diagram, she took action where they overlapped.

You could say that experiments are how we learn everything. We try to stand up, fall over, recalibrate, and next time find we can teeter for a second or two. Keep at it and mastery emerges. Misbehave and feedback provides fresh evidence that throwing food is a poor means of securing affection. An iterative process of approximation is how we learn. That life, work, love, politics are complex makes experiments more valuable, not less. They allow us to see the systems we inhabit. Since we can't see the whole of a complex system at once, trial and error is how we probe them to find out what works. The key quality of experiments is that we don't know what will happen. So they both spring from uncertainty and ambiguity and are a creative response to both.

The first half of *Hamlet* is a vivid, excruciating demonstration of this idea. A ghost tells Hamlet that his uncle murdered his father. But is the ghost reliable? Real? Is the information true? What if it isn't? What if it is? Ambiguity paralyzes Hamlet. What should he do? He does experiments. Putting on a play—*The Mousetrap*—is an experiment. When Claudius explodes with rage, evidence mounts that he is a murderer. But the evidence is still ambiguous; vengeance is justified only if he can find incontrovertible truth. When Hamlet opens a private letter from Claudius to Rosencrantz and Guildenstern, he is conducting another experiment, testing the good faith of all three men. Reading that the king has sent his two friends with a letter commissioning the king of England to kill him, Hamlet finds the certainty he needs. Now he can act.

The driving tension of the play derives from uncertainty: from Hamlet's agony in not knowing who he can trust, what version of reality he can believe, in his search for action that will honor his late father and himself. The play's genius lies in its capacity to show us that this is how we live our own lives—not because our fathers have been murdered but because we all agonize over choices we feel inadequate to make because we don't know enough yet. The future of individuals, organizations, and communities hangs on how we answer those questions. We need to know more, so we do what Hamlet does: we experiment.

Experiments are pragmatic ways to test out the future, but to have real impact requires that other people contribute. Hosking recruited the support of her village but she had been lucky that the world's media amplified the impact of her experiment; without them, she'd have had a victory, but a small one. However much we might adore the legends of heroic soloists overcoming daunting odds, the risk is that trying to do everything yourself limits what can be achieved. Experiments can make a bigger difference when they connect a variety of influences, players, and perspectives. That allows small, nimble players to make a disproportionate difference—but it also requires a backbone.

Wolfe's Neck Farm is a six-hundred-acre site on the southern coast of Maine. In this wild and rugged setting, the casual visitor might imagine that it is nothing more than another untouched beauty spot of the kind that has made Maine famous. But for nearly sixty years, it has pioneered new forms of agriculture. Today, under the more illuminating name of Wolfe's Neck Center for Agriculture and the Environment, this small, remote farm is hosting some of the most ambitious experiments in the world.

Everyone involved in agriculture is conscious that it accounts for about 14 percent of the world's carbon emissions—so attempts to address global warming must address the way farmers produce food. As Fiona Wilson, chair of Wolfe's Neck, explained, that means that farming has to change radically and fast. There are two pieces to the puzzle, she says. "Stop doing harm—and start thinking about how you could use soil to increase carbon storage, help stabilize the climate, and improve food security."

Wolfe's Neck couldn't take on such an ambitious goal alone. It works with Stonyfield, a commercial yogurt producer completely dependent on the dairy industry—which means that climate change poses an existential threat to its business. The company is working with Wolfe's Neck on a series of experiments to improve soil health and to educate farmers.

"If we can improve soil health, we improve yield and improve water retention," Stonyfield's director of organic and sustainable agriculture, Britt Lundgren, explained. "We might even be able to use soil to sequester carbon and pay farmers to do so." Experimenting together, they hope to make Wolfe's Neck the world's first carbon-zero dairy farm—and, by collecting and disseminating enough data along the way, to teach a global industry how to reinvent itself.

"The physical science is just the first issue," says Wilson. "The experiment is: Can you create behavioral change by getting large swaths of farmers to adopt what we learn? The goal is to create the world's first open-source ecosystem to address soil health and climate change. Can we do that at Wolfe's Neck, and make new agricultural knowledge available to everyone everywhere?"

Wilson is a gifted diplomat and communicator, low-key and unpretentious. Citing the work of Michael Porter, she argues that for individual experiments to make a collective impact on any ecosystem requires a backbone: a person or organization that keeps the work on track and ensures that, when experiments appear to fail, they don't stop.[1]

As the backbone of the Wolfe's Neck experiments, Wilson has to keep the farmers, the U.S. Department of Agriculture, Stonyfield, General Mills, the Foundation for Food and Agriculture Research, seven universities, and several technology companies communicating, honoring their commitments to each other, sharing what they find. If results disappoint, the group will need to design new approaches. All of the experiments demand clear metrics to demonstrate the experiments' validity and meaning. And the data must be compelling enough to make others wish to follow suit. After all, experiments in isolation may yield great results but have little impact if nobody believes, knows, or cares about them.[2] That, says Wilson, is why the difficulty of managing collaborative experiments is worth all the hard work: because they are how a small organization like Wolfe's Neck can make a big difference to the world. Working alone might be romantic but with a problem on such a huge scale, it would be like trying to stir the ocean with a spoon.

"You have to start where you are. This is bleeding-edge stuff, involving technology and human behavior," she says, sounding nervous. "Both those things are pretty unpredictable. We could never do this alone but we can't learn enough fast enough unless we can work together."

This isn't Wilson's day job. An academic, she works full time in public policy, social entrepreneurship, and sustainability at the University of New Hampshire. But she's willing to take on the work because she knows that, without a backbone, the experiments will lose focus and momentum. The world is full of small organizations founded by passionate people, but who make little impact because they won't collaborate and frequently run out of steam. They may address a real need, but lack resources and are unwilling to take on the unromantic grind required of backbone organizations. Wilson takes on that work because she's good at it, and because she knows that so big a challenge requires more than a single entity can provide.

She also knows that, when it comes to the climate crisis, waiting for an all-encompassing global strategy has wasted time. What technological advantage and hope we have today is due to scientists and engineers who didn't wait, but rather began experiments decades ago. Knowing that this will be the critical decade for change, Wilson and others seek to accelerate that progress, experimenting today instead of waiting for the perfect grand plan tomorrow.

But traditional management is addicted to grand plans. However much executives claim to want, and to support, innovation and so-called transformation, much of their enthusiasm runs tepid to cold. They want safety and certainty, not the creativity and risk that come with experimentation. The irony is lost on no one: the more they demand certainty, the more they constrain their chance to discover a safer future.

Nowhere has this constraint been more obvious than amid the bloodbath of retail, where companies seem to have taken to heart Hilaire Belloc's line: "always keep ahold of Nurse / For fear of finding something worse."[3] So afraid are they of failure that they plan shop closures and layoffs with meticulous efficiency—while failing to be inventive enough to keep those businesses alive. Market analysts may call this creative destruction but it's hard to find much that's creative about it. Experiments and innovation are almost nowhere to be seen.

Nowhere has this status quo trap been more obvious than in the automotive industry. Although General Motors helped to design the moon buggy—an electric vehicle that drove on the moon in 1971—the company expressed little enthusiasm for experiments in making terrestrial vehicles electric. Every now and then, the industry unveiled prototypes and PR statements, but real innovation progressed so reluctantly that, as the documentary *Who Killed the Electric Car?* maintains, executives schizophrenically both promoted and suppressed the initiative. Instead of pioneering new technologies to reduce emissions, we now know that many car companies preferred to find ways to cheat the tests. As it became clear that more money could be made from financing car purchases than by making the vehicles themselves, the last forty years were characterized by little in the way of experimentation or creativity. This left the field wide open when Silicon Valley spotted the value inherent in the world's largest manufacturing industry.

Yet inside behemoth industries always lurk a few individuals determined to buck conservative comfort with the status quo. At GM, Melody Lee is one such maverick. "I run towards ambiguity!" she said with a laugh. "It's how I express my optimism. It's always been my style. I joined GM when the company was in bankruptcy; people thought I was crazy. . . ."

At the time she was appointed Cadillac's director of brand and reputation strategy, the luxury carmaker was in free fall, selling just 270,000 vehicles a year, compared to 1.5 million Audis.[4] The conventional rebranding routine—new logo, multimillion-dollar meaningless tagline—would meet neither the business crisis nor Lee's ambition. Lee believed that the brand had failed because it had lost sight of its pioneering heritage.

"This was the *first* luxury brand in the world—before Rolls-Royce, in 1902! And it invented everything—like the electrical starter. In an age where people dressed up to go driving, people still had to crank the engine—but not a Cadillac! That was the brand's legacy and it became, I guess you'd call it my cause, to restore that spirit to greatness."

The challenge of experimenting with old products in an old company is that the gravitational pull to the norm is so strong. Lee knew that doing the same old things with what she called the "old boy's club" would get her nowhere. Frequently the youngest, and often the only woman, in the room, she embraced risk, arguing for the bold and expensive relocation of the entire team to New York City.

"*Nobody* in New York was driving Cadillacs. I wanted to get us out into the world, where we needed to succeed. It was an unbelievably contentious decision—leave Detroit, are you crazy?—and the battle to get that approved—just approved—that took two years!"

If brands are all about experience, Lee and her team reasoned, why not sell the Cadillac experience? Test drives were lame—but what if you could book a Cadillac where and whenever you wanted it? Thus was born what Lee calls "the Netflix of cars": a subscription model whereby, for a monthly fee, you can have a Cadillac delivered to you whenever you wanted. Following the trend of twenty-first-century business models, the car could become a service, not a product. At the time, the idea was without precedent, so the first pilot offered just fifty spots—but 15,000 people signed up. Expanded to Dallas and Los Angeles, the pilot tested a variety of pricing scenarios and different service models. Lee wanted to test and learn from the market as fast as possible before competitors copied the experiment. When Volvo and BMW did so, Lee said that her consolation was that this was the first time that the Germans had followed GM's example since the 1960s.

"The experiment isn't the business," Lee cautioned. "It's designed to test acceptance, to reveal all the problems. To that extent, the experiment worked—it showed that we could work differently, that we could still be pioneers." Lee had demonstrated that GM could think and experiment with the future. It didn't have to be held hostage by planning.

Experiments might not *be* the business, but being good at them is one way to stay in business—even when they fail. For years, 3M has surprised competitors and the market by the company's ability to innovate at remarkable speed. How do they move so fast? The answer is that they don't always. They experiment and many of their experiments fail, at first. But they aren't abandoned, they're remembered.

In the 1980s, a service engineer at 3M with a passion for flying thought that the company might be able to increase planes' fuel efficiency with an abrasive that reduced wind resistance. But years of experiments showed that, while Trizact worked, customers didn't like it because it was too different; it didn't look or behave like the abrasives they were used to. In 1996, however, the burgeoning silicon wafer industry had fewer entrenched processes and demanded extremely high levels of performance of a kind Trizact could deliver. Suddenly 3M had exactly what this bigger, richer market needed. An overnight success story had taken more than a decade.

Experiments at 3M never really end. The refusal to condemn or retire experiments as failures keeps their ideas alive; doing that, the company says, links the past and the present with the future. It looks messy; why not get rid of those dead ideas? In 2000, when James McNerney became CEO, he replaced 3M's process with Six

Sigma, a rigorous data-driven quality improvement process designed to eliminate defects. In essence, McNerney was trying to maximize successful experiments and stop failures. But that required, of course, that he be able to predict what future markets would need. The company quickly began to lose its innovative edge—and the next CEO, George Buckley, took a different tack. "Innovation," he said, "is by its very nature a disorderly process. You can't put a Six Sigma process into that area and say, 'Well, I'm getting behind on invention, so I'm going to schedule myself for three good ideas on Wednesday and two on Friday.' That's not how creativity works." 3M's century of innovation depends on experiments, failure, and memory to maximize serendipity that can't be planned.[5]

Where companies used to operate in three stages—forecast, plan, execute—in theory now they can't do this long-term, because forecasting is so difficult. But companies still grind through the three stages, not because their executives believe that these are accurate—Melody Lee says they're always wrong—but because institutional habits are hard to shift, you have to start somewhere, and even an old broken system offers security, however false. Have decades of strategic planning left companies paralyzed, unable to explore without a map, incontrovertible data, rock-solid guarantees? Are firms now like travelers who dare not stray outdoors without a GPS, afraid of what they might find—or not find?

"Lots of people have only ever known control, so they think change has to come wholesale from the top. Life is a lot easier when you think the system locks you in," is how Oliver Burrows describes the push to experiment versus the pull of the status quo. "So I've been quite deliberate, provoking people to challenge the constraints they work under, to ask if they're real or meaningful—or just an excuse for keeping life simple."

Burrows is scarcely your traditional picture of a revolutionary; he is the chief data officer at the Bank of England. His department of 150 people already processes more than a billion pieces of data a year. But he knew that the workload would increase. A tougher regulatory environment now demands more data, analyzed with increasing granularity. Resources wouldn't increase in proportion to workload and just making people work harder wasn't a sustainable strategy. So how could the system cope with the demands he expected to be made on it?

"At my level, we all have quite a lot of freedom to decide how we achieve our objectives," Burrows reflected. "But it is a social norm *not* to use it. There's more constraint in the head than is real."

Burrows chose to use his freedom. Excited by the idea that experiments could loosen up the hierarchical culture of his organization, he hoped they would reveal smarter ways to work better. After all, if nothing changed, tension and stress would just escalate. What he didn't do was sit at his desk and try to map out a new organization. Instead, he called for volunteers and for ideas; that was an experiment in itself, showing how much more appetite there was for innovation than he'd anticipated. People were inspired by the prospect of inventing change, rather than having it thrust upon them. Together, they mapped out twelve experiments, some of which worked and some of which, Burrows shrugged, didn't.

"I made the decision to open up our senior management meetings to anyone who wanted to sit in; at first, lots turned up but over time they drifted off. Turns out: it wasn't all that exciting! We made the annual appraisal process a lot more participatory; that worked well. Some very technical coding projects were suggested that nobody in the management team would ever have thought of, or been brave enough to do. They tried them and they worked! I'm really proud of that."

But the big win, Burrows found, was that he started sourcing lots of strategy ideas from the bottom up. In the past, people had thought strategy was the preserve of management types—which meant: not them. Burrows found an unexpected source of new ideas, becoming an early pioneer of what is now called "open strategy":

sharing the task of forward thinking with a larger part, or all, of the organization. The bigger experiment for Burrows had been to test how much freedom and power he had, within the bank and in his own mind. What had stopped him in the past? Fear: the sense that he needed certainty before he could start. His experiments had revealed sources of insight and capacity—in himself and in others—that he'd never seen before. Experiments release human imagination because they give people hope.

Caught between uncertainty and ambiguity, it's easy to fall into the trap of imagining that the only way to solve hard problems is to start with a clean slate. When I was at the BBC, I recall executives arguing that the best way to confront change would be to build a parallel corporation and, when it was ready, turn it on and turn the old one off. It is what the Irish might call a "you can't get there from here" problem that usually becomes the alibi of inertia. Experiments are one way to shift that inertia.

Working as a home care nurse in the Netherlands, Jos de Blok was miserable. He didn't lack for passion or expertise but he hated the industrialization that had overwhelmed the work. Every patient had a contract, every contract had a code that specified the exact level of service that nurses were told to provide: Personal Care, Personal Care Extra, Personal Care Special. De Blok had originally trained as an economist, but quit when he found the work too dry and inhumane. Now in nursing, he saw the same trend. The bureaucracy meant that people—patients—were being treated "like apples on a farm: just picked and packed off." The introduction of so-called modern management methods—Key Performance Indicators, targets, productization, metrics, and efficiencies—had made the work elaborate, expensive, and meaningless.

He distinguished between two parts of the nursing system. The first, issuing a contract to get the nurse to the patient, was simple and didn't need an ornate bureaucracy. The second part, helping the patient recover, was inherently complex, because no two patients are identical and the work cannot be predicted or prescribed. That part, de Blok thought, should be left to human judgment. Would that make the system any better? The only way to find out was to experiment.

De Blok invited the Dutch health care minister to listen to twelve nurses talking about their experiences in industrialized medicine. Tears ran down the minister's face as she heard how the bureaucracy forced nurses to treat their patients like objects. She supported de Blok in his proposal to experiment with a team of twelve nurses whose only instruction was: do what's right for the patient.

When the accounting firm EY audited the experiment, they showed that, using de Blok's approach, patients got better in half the time, because nurses were free to use their judgment on the spot. And when the experiment was expanded, costs were shown to be 30 percent cheaper. A single simple experiment had proved a revelation and kick-started a revolution.

When asked what about the experiment had surprised him, de Blok's answer was succinct. "I never imagined it could be so easy to make such a huge difference so fast," he said, laughing. His discovery couldn't have been found sitting at a desk or a computer screen. Since then, de Blok named the company Buurtzorg (which simply means Neighborhood Care), and with 10,000 nurses it now provides two-thirds of all home care nursing in the Netherlands. The success spills over into the rest of the health system: emergency admissions are reduced by a third and admissions tend to be shorter. EY estimated that two billion euro would be saved if the whole of the Netherlands adopted the system and that, if scaled to an American population, savings would be $49 billion.

The success of his experiment proved de Blok's hypothesis: that separating the ineradicably complex (patient care) from the merely complicated (assigning nurses to patients) radically reduced costs and enhanced motivation and meaning in the work. Though both aspects of the work are necessary, they don't have to be run the same way. Separating the two can be a good way to identify opportunities for experimentation.

I spent a day visiting patients with Ani, a Buurtzorg nurse. With one patient, she spent just a few minutes because family members were there and the patient was doing fine. With another, she spent nearly an hour; the patient had recently lost a close friend and was distressed. Ani is part of a team that looks after forty or fifty patients. All their notes, treatments, and schedules are shared via tablets, so that, covering for each other during holidays or illness, they can retrieve any information they need. The team also decides where or whether to have a team office, to hold meetings, and what expenses to allow. They share a team credit card so everyone can see what team funds are available and can decide how to use them. Often, they are spent on the team's own experiments. No two teams are identical.

When making decisions for their team, Buurtzorg nurses aren't aiming for perfection. They don't seek consensus, because that may be impossible; there often is no perfect solution. But if no one has a principled objection to a proposal, it will be tried. That way, if it turns out not to work, the topic can be revisited without recrimination. Trial and error is how Buurtzorg and its nurses learn. Absent fear of failure, better ideas and more experiments emerge.

More recently, de Blok experimented with the insurance companies that pay for the nursing, trying to create a contract simpler than the current hundred-page monstrosity. They got it down to six. Now he is working with neighborhood schools where there are closer parallels with nursing and where the relationship between students and teachers is ripe for an overhaul.

De Blok hadn't tried to second-guess the outcome of his experiment. He didn't predicate future decisions, strategy, or structure on information he didn't have yet. Instead, he focused on pain and aimed at the best possible outcome, concentrating on what mattered to the people who mattered most: the nurses and their patients. Similarly, when Brian Chesky founded Airbnb, he had only the loosest idea of what his company could or would become. He did what most businesspeople do: he talked to customers. But he didn't ask them about existing products or make them fill out dreary surveys. Instead, he interrogated them about their fantasies. What would a six-star experience be for a customer? To be greeted with a bottle of wine and nice toiletries in a great place to stay. A seven-star experience? A host who knew you liked surfing and had booked lessons, or knew you liked Vietnamese food so had reserved a table in the best restaurant in town. Like de Blok, Chesky sought to understand what the best might look like. That way, he said, you get away from marginal improvements of something fundamentally inadequate.

Although small experiments can yield disproportionate results, their scale isn't always designed to minimize risk. One of the biggest experiments in the United States today is designed to tackle the world's most expensive health care system. Less well known than its exorbitant cost is the level of dissatisfaction among American physicians: after ten years of practice, 50 percent of doctors now say that they would get out of medicine if they could.[6] One who has persisted is David Ring. An orthopedic surgeon at Massachusetts General Hospital, David was a model of a modern medical man: tall, dark, handsome, powerful, and a Harvard professor. But his work kept throwing up questions he found harder and harder to answer. Why were patients persuaded to accept ineffectual and expensive medical procedures? Why were medical mistakes the third-largest cause of death in the United States—and why, when doctors made them, were they urged to deny and defend their actions? Why was it so hard to have a decent, straightforward conversation with patients? An outspoken critic of the role that money plays in medicine, he found the fact that hospitals could do well by serving people so badly to be unacceptable.

Ring wasn't alone in asking these questions. Experiments? The whole system felt like a failed experiment, bloated, corrupt, too big, too old, and too complex to change. But in 2009, just a year after the worst financial crisis since the Great Depression, the University of Texas decided to found a medical school.[7] In a city that is economically the most segregated in America, Dell Medical School's big experiment is to make it the healthiest. Leaving Harvard was a big step for Ring, but the spirit of ambitious experiments proved irresistible.

The new dean, Clay Johnston, had come from California for one reason only: to reinvent American health care. Unlike Silicon Valley salesmen, he didn't pitch the vision that the only way to do that was by eliminating doctors and replacing them with machines. He hoped, he said, that "starting from scratch, we can design a medical school that empowers doctors to work collaboratively *and* embrace new technologies *and* perform cutting-edge research. All of that *together* is how you serve patients better." From its opening in 2017, the school had a contract to serve the uninsured. It will have to prove, ultimately, that its services are so good that other health insurers will want to join in. That's a huge experiment in itself. But for now Johnston's goal is to prove that he and his team can deliver better health care at a better price by focusing only on what matters: patient outcomes. That goal might seem self-evident but achieving it requires challenging every orthodoxy, every tradition, every assumption.

Austin isn't an easy place to start. Most of the uninsured live a long way from the health center, so seeing a doctor can require expensive travel and time off work. When Ring arrived at the new medical school, a waiting list of two thousand patients greeted him, all needing to see a hand surgeon. The wait for a neurologist, dermatologist, or orthopedist was even longer. The hospital contract allowed for video consultations and Ring hoped these would help him reduce the list more quickly. But he was wary. He already hated how often consultations felt like transactions and worried that the technology would exacerbate that problem. But he was willing to experiment.

"Most consultations give the doctor all the power: *my* time, *my* place, *my* office, *my* fifteen minutes—and then you're out. This time, the whole idea was: to help you, I'll come at *your* convenience, just text me! We can talk in your home, on your laptop. It's about you. You can spend time setting up the camera, we can build some rapport. It's like a house call and it feels more like a relationship. It's surprising, because the average person might think this was cold. But it isn't, because it levels the hierarchy."

On one occasion, he phoned a patient whom he knew he couldn't diagnose or treat over the phone. But he reasoned that he could get a conversation started and maybe be helpful. At least she wouldn't feel abandoned. When he called, she gave him an earful: "You make people wait, how dare you?"

" 'You're right,' I said, and let her vent," Ring remembered. "Then I asked her to describe what was happening with her hand. I explained what the options for treatment could be. She needed to feel that something could and would be done. She had started off just being *so mad* at me—but by the end of the call, she was apologizing and promising to come in. And she said: 'The first thing I'm going to do when I come, I'm going to hug you.' "

Two weeks later, the patient came into Ring's office and hugged him. Then they sat down to discuss her choices. It had helped her to have had time to discuss her decision with her family. She had concluded she would be happy with a simple procedure that Ring did there and then. When she left, she turned to Ring and said: "Well done!"

Ring had hoped that calling the patient directly would disrupt the hierarchy implicit in the doctor-patient relationship, and it did, in ways he hadn't expected. He hadn't anticipated being screamed at, or that absorbing the patient's ire would prove valuable in building their relationship. But his bigger discovery was that for the patient to have time between the call and the appointment—time to do her own research, to reflect on her choices with her family—led to a better decision that the patient felt was her own.

The insight that power leads to poor and expensive decisions has had a huge impact not just on the way doctors work at Dell Medical School but on the entire design of its hospital. One of Clay Johnston's many experiments has been to create a companion Design Institute for Health, charged with co-creating simpler, better systems and a better environment for patients and doctors alike. Most hospitals have waiting rooms but, to Stacey Chen and Katherine Jones at the institute, these felt like factories, pushing bodies along a conveyor belt where each encounter was a billable event. Sitting in a holding pen full of sick people was demeaning, depressing, and frightening and set up the relationship between doctor and patient for failure. Why not reverse the power equation and give ownership of the exam rooms to the patients?

The idea of handing over control disturbed a few physicians, but it confounded all the architects. They argued that every hospital had waiting rooms. But Dell was set up explicitly *not* to be like all hospitals. The architects offered to simulate patient flow using analytics software to show how useful waiting rooms could be. But Chen and his colleagues rejected the offer, because there was no alternative to use for comparison. They had to do the experiment themselves because, as Chen said, "the future has no available datasets—there was no evidence one way or the other about *no* waiting rooms . . . !"

The fight lasted for two and a half years, with architects deeply uncomfortable doing something new and the Dell team determined that experiments were what they had come for. Chen worked through the logic: poor decisions derive from anxiety; anxiety comes from a lack of control. If you reduce anxiety by giving control to patients, they will make better decisions. If, rather than intimidating authorities, doctors could be seen as experienced guides, then the relationship between doctor, patient, and caregivers could change outcomes. Changing the patient experience is part of the treatment. Creating individual "care rooms" controlled by patients, in which they could sit with friends and family, could reduce stress, enhance doctor/patient relationships, and produce better choices, leading to better results.

Along the way, new issues arose—What if the patient got lost? What happened if they arrived hours ahead of time?—but were resolved. Chen and Jones even managed to replace intimidating examination tables with sofas and chairs that can convert to tables if needed but otherwise don't put the patient in so exposed a position. When the clinics opened in 2017, patients went directly to their care rooms, where doctors, nurses, social workers, the whole integrated care team came to them, where they waited in calm social surroundings. The geography of the experience put the patient in control.

David Ring now spends most of his time on his feet. Knocking on the door, he entered a care room to meet a Hispanic woman who was sitting with her son and a friend. Ring sat down level with her, eye to eye, not behind a desk, speaking Spanish. Holding her hand gently, he asked about numbness and tingling. The cyst was quite noticeable and she wanted it removed. Ring asked her if she knew what it was. She didn't, so he explained that it was joint fluid, that most people get them, they're entirely benign and go away eventually. Ring is alert to the possibility that the problem might not be orthopedic; if she had had pain, he would not want to operate because it wouldn't help, because the real problem would have to be elsewhere. But no, it wasn't painful.

"Tell me what you're thinking," he said.

"I want it out," she replied.

"Okay," he said, "we will remove it in a month." He wanted to give her time to think about it because on reflection, 80 percent of people cancel the unnecessary surgery. In a more traditional setting, Ring would make more money from the surgery. Here he doesn't.

His only interest is in the patient making what feels to her to be the right decision.

In the central area between the care rooms, nurses, nurse practitioners, psychologists, and social workers hover, moving from room to room, conferring with their colleagues about patients. Ring talks to one about the difficulty of working through translators; how much subtext gets lost, how patients sometimes simplify what they're saying. Communication is a central subject at Dell.

"We've been working with psychologists on the best questions to ask," Ring explained. "I used to come into the room, introduce myself, 'How can I help you?' But the immediate response is always: 'Oh my aching. . . .' It's too quick. There's no time for rapport. We thought: What if we started with a positive question: Who are you at your best? What things do you love to do? What makes you laugh? You learn so much more about the patient and their life that way." Better questions means Ring learns, faster, about the lives his patients inhabit and which may influence their choices and recovery.

"When doctors ask: 'Is there anything else you want to talk about,' the answer is always no. But if you ask: 'Is there *something else* you want to talk about today,' if there is, you'll find out."

How does he know? At Dell, talking is also part of the experiment. Erin Donovan is an academic who works with Ring and his colleagues at understanding and improving communication with patients. She knows that medicine is saturated with uncertainty and anxiety and teaches her doctors and students to understand concepts such as tolerance of ambiguity.

"Natural science students do not have high tolerance for ambiguity and don't understand why some people do," Donovan said. So she teaches a seminar on uncertainty management. Some students experience uncertainty as full of hope and opportunities, others as danger and risk. Her students learn why a patient won't ask a scary question or might not call back for test results. More positive interactions help patients to remain hopeful and open.

Doctors are often unfairly pilloried for being poor communicators, Donovan said. But when you measure and price every minute of each interaction, hoping to increase efficiency, communication takes the first hit. In many American pharmacies, a red light flashes if prescriptions aren't filled fast enough, so of course pharmacists make mistakes. The same is true for conversations: the more doctors consider the financial cost of every minute, the more mistakes they make. At Dell, doctors, communicators, and designers are experimenting together, exploring and devising what they now call "interpersonal medicine." This approach accepts that improved human relationships between doctors, patients, and caregivers is associated with a 19 percent gain in patient adherence to therapies and improved outcomes. It recognizes that a patient is a person, not just a body; there is more to medicine than data and statistics, and the next big leap in medicine depends on making health care interactions more human.[8]

Dell is full of experiments under way and planned. The old hacksaws that surgeons still use have now been replaced by a cold laser tool designed at the hospital. Dean Johnston hopes consultations can be documented using voice recognition software. Self-care websites are being prototyped. New systems catch opioid overuse early. They engage informal caregivers in every conversation. They educate family doctors about when MRIs help and when they don't. There are experiments into community impacts on health. The goal is to experiment, learn, and build out only what works. One consequence of this principle is that, just like de Blok's Buurtzorg, experiments start low tech—paper prototypes, whiteboards—to ensure that the human element remains front and center and that snazzy technology doesn't get in the way.[9]

There are so many experiments going on at Dell, it can be hard to see how the day jobs get done. But the day job *is all* experimentation, each consultation an experiment in doing one thing better. There is no org chart yet. Johnston wants to get Dell's culture right first before imposing a structure. So far, Johnston's organization sketch looks more like a web, designed for people to move in and out of collaborative experiments with ease, unhampered by departments, hierarchies, silos, and functions. That way, he hopes, new projects can start quickly, people come together easily, and, if the project proves unproductive, everyone can move on to the next challenge. It's a complex skein of questions, experiments, learning, and improvement in real time on real patients leading real lives.

The overarching hypothesis at Dell is this: if you change the power relationship in medicine by putting the patient in charge—not the doctor, not the infrastructure, not the technology salesmen or the insurance companies—you get better, more affordable, and more sustainable outcomes. It's a big bet, expressed and explored through hundreds of experiments because there's no other way to find out. Johnston, Ring, Chen, and all their colleagues have a lot going for them: with U.S. health care seen as an extravagant mess, they have the mandate that comes from a failed system. They have the enormous privilege of starting with a clean slate with the active support of the community they serve. Already they can demonstrate that Dell produces better care, at a lower price, with a better experience. Because the funding comes directly from citizens' property taxes, there is a tight coupling between patients and the hospital. They succeed together or not at all.

It can be tempting to argue that you can't change the future without that neat blank slate. It's a seductive idea and often a dangerous one. In software development, there's always a moment in bug fixing when the number of errors seems so overwhelming that the cry goes up: Wouldn't it be better to throw this code out and start again? The implicit belief, of course, is that *this time* we will write it flawlessly, this time we will get it right. It never works that way; the fresh version just has different bugs, different problems. Perfection is an illusion.

Similarly, many have been tempted recently to look at democratic institutions around the world and condemn them as impossible to change or to reform. Time to throw them out and start again. Those making such arguments make the same error as the rookie software coder, their idealized future blissfully empty of error, violence, and recrimination. Their sense of crisis isn't misplaced but a crisis isn't the moment to give up on experimentation. It's the time to start.

Ireland in 2008 didn't look like a promising seedbed for anything new. Even in the context of the global economic crisis, failure in Ireland was extreme, as all of its institutions had failed at once. Bank failures brought the economy close to collapse and when the most unpopular government in the country's history signed a punitive bailout agreement, democracy seemed moribund, too. Those who had caused the banking crisis were left largely unscathed while the rest of the bewildered populace were left to pay for their reckless-ness. The Catholic Church, which underpinned all of civil society in its running of churches, schools, and hospitals, was revealed as an abject moral failure, guilty of perpetrating and covering up the abuse of children, the illegal sale and burial of babies, and the exploitation of young women. With the failure of the banks, the government, and the church, the survival of a democratic society suddenly seemed fragile.

That concatenation of crises lured David Farrell home. He'd been teaching politics at the University of Manchester and knew how badly Ireland's institutions needed renewal. He and his colleagues believed that the rich, recent history of democratic experiments could be helpful. In 1994, the American political scientist James Fishkin had conducted his first experiment in what he came to call deliberative polling. He brought together a representative sample of the British population, provided them with fair, impartial briefing documents on current topics, such as crime, and asked participants to discuss and debate them. His experiment tested how a random national sample would interact, how seriously people would read and consider their materials, how civil (or otherwise) the discussions would be, and, crucially, how far anyone would change their minds.

"And it worked beautifully," Fishkin says. "The sample was representative. The discussions were civil. They had knowledge gain and there were coherent and identifiable changes of opinion that were statistically significant. So the big thing I learned is that, while my colleagues in political science mostly think that the public is stupid and easily manipulable, it's not stupid." Since then Fishkin has conducted more than one hundred such polls around the world, all showing that such public discussions can be an effective way to enlist citizens in political issues of consequence: budget priorities, voting reform, and constitutional amendments. These experiments encouraged Farrell and his colleagues to launch one of their own.

But in arguing that Ireland needed a form of deliberative democracy, David Farrell and his colleagues anticipated opposition—and they got it. Ireland already had a parliament; people are too daft; why trust ordinary, uninformed citizens? But they kept pushing and in 2011, the Labor Party and Fine Gael formed a coalition government that included a promise to hold a convention of citizens—one-third politicians, two-thirds ordinary citizens—to explore amendments to the constitution. The new government made no promises regarding the outcome, save a commitment to respond formally and debate any recommendations in the Oireachtas, the Irish parliament. It was an experiment in democracy that went largely unnoticed except by cynical journalists who were convinced it was just a fig leaf: a pretense at action.

The outcome surprised everyone. Of the many sane, coherent recommendations emanating from the convention, one proposed a referendum on the legalization of same-sex marriage. On May 22, 2015, the referendum was held and approved by a clear majority: 62 to 38 percent. Although those who had participated in the convention believed it should be continued as a valuable and important addition to democracy, Taoiseach (Prime Minister) Enda Kenny disagreed, declaring it the kind of exercise applicable only to the lifetime of a single parliament.

But by 2016, another coalition government—Fine Gael and independents—again found citizen deliberation a useful way to sidestep intractable social issues on which the electorate demanded action. No politician and no political party wanted to take a public stand on the subject of abortion: the topic was simply too toxic. Once again, the idea of consulting ordinary people was derided and Enda Kenny pilloried by all sides for "kicking the can down the road," using the device of a Citizens' Assembly to sidestep action.

On the day she returned from maternity leave, the civil servant Sharon Finegan was assigned the task of managing the assembly. Her colleagues warned her not to touch it. The issue and the process were too risky.

"I was warned," she said. "You'll be personally attacked. It could damage your career. I took a different view—I thought it would be incredibly interesting. And if it was to be done, I thought it should be done well and I thought I could do that. I thought it would be an enormous challenge."

A lot was in play during this experiment. Nobody knew whether the assembly's deliberations would be useful or if their conclusions would be accepted as legitimate by politicians or the electorate. Not everyone was convinced that such thorny issues could be understood by ordinary people. Would the assembly strengthen democracy or merely reveal how impotent and irrelevant it had become? At a time when politics seemed increasingly driven by ego, vanity, and corporate interests, and when the binary nature of elections grossly oversimplified every issue, commentators and citizens speculated about what good a bunch of barmen, parents, electricians, nurses, and truck drivers could do.

Finegan had a huge job. The assembly required ninety-nine ordinary citizens who were an accurate demographic reflection of the country. They would be asked to sacrifice twelve weekends over a period of eighteen months, when they would come together just outside of Dublin to listen to a series of presentations by lawyers, academics, doctors, and advisors on four topics: abortion, the aging population, term limits, and climate change.

This time, no politicians would take part; it was to be an assembly of ordinary citizens only. The earlier experiment had suggested that professionals might dominate discussions—and the politicians were eager to keep their distance. At the request of the chair, Supreme Court justice Mary Laffoy, an expert advisory group assessed and prepared every expert presenting to the citizens. At the end of each meeting, members were surveyed to see if they had gotten all the information they needed. If they wanted more or different input, Finegan's team of four sourced it. Those procedural changes to the experiment paled in comparison to the big change: overwhelming public scrutiny.

"From the very beginning, the chair was obsessed with transparency," Finegan recalled. "We had to do everything with utter transparency and clarity, otherwise, we'd always have to justify everything we did." So every presentation, every paper was put online, in English, Irish, and in sign language. Every session was filmed. The whole country could watch and contribute by submitting their own views and arguments. But the full burden of the work fell on the one hundred citizens, recruited door-to-door, to reflect the demographic of the Irish population. Few had heard of the assembly or knew exactly what would be required of them.

The assembly opened at Dublin Castle with a welcome from Enda Kenny: "We chose to go about our business this way so that as a nation and as a society we could move from a position of contention, even of contempt, and find in valuable consensus some common coordinates in a matter so privately and publicly tender." But unlike many grand opening ceremonies where heads of state preside, Kenny didn't just say his fifteen minutes and leave. He stayed and listened as Justice Laffoy set the tone for the next eighteen months with an introduction that was pragmatic, straightforward, wry, and punctual. The next day the members were treated to a master class on ethics: what they are, the role of disagreement, the meaning of decisions, and their impact on others unknown and unseen. Members left impressed, serious, intent.

Few assembly members appreciated what they had let themselves in for: eighteen months of some of the most intense work and homework they'd ever done. Briefing documents. Presentations. Discussions. Debates. Hundreds of hours of work—even before they met for weekends in Malahide. Like many of his fellow members, ventilation technician John Long worked long days Monday to Friday, then came home to fifteen lengthy briefing documents to be read before the weekend. He didn't want to be sitting at a discussion table unprepared, so he took his new work seriously.

"You'd be sitting round the table and someone would say something and: gee, I'd never thought of that! They came at it from a direction I'd never have thought of—whether I agreed or not! You come along this big arc—the *way* and the *reasons* you'd never think of yourself. . . . Some of the sessions were head-melting, there was so much legal, medical information. But the process—the roundtable discussions, the questions and answers. Q-and-A. At the end, you understood."

Barman Peter Patrick said he had no idea how important the work was until the end. But nothing about the process intimidated him. "I am a relatively quiet person in the group," Peter Patrick said. "But the facilitators ensured everyone's voices were heard. It could get slightly heated but you could always ask questions and overall there was real respect for every point of view. Some had strongly held views but still there was total respect. . . ." Patrick appreciated Sharon Finegan's secretariat. They ruthlessly excised jargon from papers and presentations and made it easy for any member to ask questions. Another member, Deirdre Donaghy, felt that the insistence on straightforward language made it comfortable for people to challenge each other in debate that was reasonable and respectful, without grandstanding or point scoring.

More than thirteen thousand members of the public made submissions regarding abortion, more than a thousand on climate change. The process rejected lobbying organizations and pressure groups but welcomed those with firsthand experience or nonaligned expertise. For the hardworking secretariat and for the ninety-nine members, the experience was unforgettable, a source of intense work, new friendships, and huge learning. Understanding how far behind Ireland was on climate change forced theater technician Oisin Heraghty to reexamine how he lived his life. Given facts about the country's aging population made him explore choices and consequences he'd never considered before. Being given reliable information made him more thoughtful; that, he said, was what the assembly did for him.

Although they had the other topics to consider, the nation as a whole remained transfixed by the way in which deliberation of the eighth amendment (on abortion) played out. The assembly's radical transparency didn't extinguish the firestorms that typically accompany any discussion of the subject, but it did counter it with nonpartisan speakers, documents, and a wide range of perspectives. The spillover of information and argument—much of the assembly's work was replicated by coverage and debate on RTE, the national broadcaster—connected the public at large with the assembly's work, enriching what became a national conversation.

On April 23, 2017, the Assembly voted 64 percent in favor of a referendum proposing the liberalization of abortion up to twelve weeks. According to Finegan, the perceived wisdom in political circles was that this was so far from public opinion as to be useless. Media headlines concurred, asking how on earth this extreme view could be watered down to make it palatable to the population. Had he been asked the night before the vote, Farrell said, he'd have guessed that the referendum would be lost. But it wasn't. On May 25, 2018, in an almost perfect mirror image of the assembly, the electorate of Ireland voted by 66 percent in favor of legalization.

Not everyone, of course, was happy with the outcome of the

referendum. But everyone accepted its legitimacy. For David Farrell, the result had been a cathartic moment in Irish history, a time
when citizens saw that they could learn, work, and live together even
amid disagreement. Assemblies weren't, he insisted, a substitute for
parliaments but an important and valid addition.

"Right now," he said, "we have an ongoing crises across the
world: climate change and a populist challenge to democracy. This
is the perfect time for us to adapt these devices to take charge of
the debates on immigration, multiculturalism, and let the mainstream political class engage in debate with their citizens. I think
this device is perfect for those big ideas to be tackled, explored so
that the people feel involved in their own future."

Judge Laffoy produced a thoughtful report with recommendations for improving the process. The time commitment had been
extreme; one item at a time would be less exhausting, with a mini-
mum of two weeks deliberation for each. Members should serve for
a maximum of six months and Parliament should consider paying
them a modest stipend. The experiment wasn't over; there was still
opportunity for improvement and discovery.[10] In February 2020, a
new assembly began to explore issues of gender equality.

Sharon Finegan had plenty of ideas, too, about how to improve
the process but, for the time being, was happy to be going home
to have another baby. Her greatest praise went to the members,
their hard work, their dedication, their sense of agency: of being in
charge. On the day that the assembly had been launched in Dublin
Castle, she had listened as Michael Manning, the chancellor of the
National University of Ireland, warned the newly minted members
that their deliberations would test them to the full, but he believed
that they already had what they most needed.

"You come here," Manning said, "as free citizens, bringing with
you your own life experience, your own sense of duty, your own
values and insights. . . . The great quality you bring to this process
is your freedom to be yourselves."

"It actually works," Peter Patrick reflected. "I just came back from Berlin—and I went down to where the former SS headquarters was. Looking at it, I thought how quickly a country can change. Democracy can just disappear because something that isn't democracy takes over. You can just get rid of people, livelihoods. So you have to keep working on democracy, because countries can change very quickly. It made me realize how very fragile we are."

Once we accept how unpredictable life is, experiments are where to start working toward future goals—like carbon-free agriculture, patient-centric health care, or a more responsive democracy—that we don't know how to reach today.[11] An antidote to helplessness or passivity, they set us on paths that reveal new knowledge and choices. They can be done alone but need resources to get started and passion to keep them going. Simply attempting to experiment can identify give in the system, and illuminate where untapped talent and energy lie. So they are a means of exploration, but they reveal more under certain conditions.

Distinguishing between the complicated and complex parts of a problem is helpful, because each requires different, but compatible, approaches. Repetitive processes will yield to efficiency, but unpredictable ones need to prioritize human judgment. Led by volunteers, not recruits, means they are in the hands of people who care and who aren't daunted by ambiguity and complexity. Knowing who else to draw in is crucial to their liveliness and legitimacy. Bringing in others enhances impact—though big experiments founder without someone to keep them on track. A crucial antidote to slow, unwieldy master plans, they impart a sense of urgency and agency to even the most disillusioned individuals and staid institutions.

Experiments are not pilots, with their intricately preconceived definitions of success and failure, and freighted with power struggles. They're designed to be open to whatever is found, good or bad. That doesn't mean they're just messing around. Proving their effectiveness—as de Blok did with auditors, as Wilson aims to do with metrics—is crucial but has to come after, not before, the experiment is designed. Otherwise they risk being too constrained, achieving too little or overlooking unexpected results. Conceptually they have to be loose, but in their execution they must be tight, meticulous about detail, so that their conclusions are convincing. Above all, experiments are ambitious. They don't tinker with incremental improvements to mediocrity but, stemming from deep hopes and fears about factors that matter, aim for the best imaginable outcome. They start from, and impart, a primal optimism that the future can be better than the past.

CHAPTER FIVE

GO FAST, GO FAR

If you want to go fast, go alone.
If you want to go far, go together.

—African proverb

One morning in 2010, Alberto Fernandez woke up to discover that his world had changed. Nine men were hanging from a bridge over the highway that led to Monterrey, Mexico, where he lived. In later days, executed bodies were found around the city. People he knew were hijacked and killed. The homicide rate increased by 650 percent in one year, kidnapping by 293 percent, and violent robbery by 392 percent.[1] He had to buy a bulletproof car. His sister, married to the president of the country's largest newspaper, had to leave the country. The biggest problem, Fernandez reflected, was apathy; it was so much easier to blame others than to take action.

Fernandez is one of the most successful businessmen in Mexico. A serial entrepreneur, he has started, run, and sold telecommunication businesses, a construction company, restaurants, a beverage business. He could see that the sudden eruption of violence signified attempts by drug cartels to infiltrate one of the country's wealthiest, most modern and industrialized cities. Everything Fernandez prized, his family, his home, and community, his companies and his employees, was under threat.

His instinct was to do something, to act where passion, need, and resources intersected. After thinking about the violence, and the apathetic response to it, Fernandez concluded that a fundamental failure to believe in the rule of law was what allowed violence to flourish. In a country where 80 percent of people said that they would break the law for personal benefit and young guys believed it wasn't worth being honest, he felt the population had become silent accomplices. Tackling those attitudes was where Fernandez decided to intervene.

He started by founding an organization to promote the rule of law. After consultants delivered a fancy, complicated marketing strategy, he turned to his cleaning lady, explained the concept, and found that her way of describing it got to the heart of the matter: *Hagamoslo bien,* which, roughly translated, means *Let's do it right.*

Fernandez's prominence in the community allowed him to reach out to anyone and everyone who mattered. All of the churches backed him. Both universities. Community leaders. Museums. Businesses. Schools. A world racquetball champ and both rival football teams: popular heroes whom everyone would listen to. The coalition started to research and experiment. Online courses reached fourteen thousand people. Activist workshops. Negotiation workshops. Workshops for parents. Street experiences. Courses for *Evolucionarios* in corporations, the fire department, and the police. Family rallies. Student-led programs to eradicate cheating at university. A huge campaign against texting while driving. Major employers, such as OXXO (the Mexican equivalent of Walmart), started to redevelop public spaces in ways that would encourage transparency and safety. Educationalists worked at integrating ideas of trust and trustworthiness into the curriculum.

Tall, trim, slightly balding, Fernandez looks every inch the corporate citizen. But if there is a stereotype of a business leader or entrepreneur, he won't fit it. As we were driving around Monterrey, his conversation wandered. A love for the poetry of Pablo Neruda. Banksy and the power of graffiti. The architecture of Tadao Ando and the technical demands of building with reinforced concrete. A passion for Shakespeare. The importance of carpooling. The genius of Issey Miyake. But the leitmotif was always the same: how to provoke change. As Fernandez put it: it's not a question of changing the landlord but how to stop being a dog.

By 2018, Fernandez's passion for the rule of law was unabated, refueled by success. The number of people who'd said that they would break the law if they could had fallen to 28 percent. But a mind as energetic and complex as Fernandez's wouldn't be satisfied by survey data. Violence had receded from Monterrey but remained a looming threat across Mexico. In 2014, forty-three teachers and students in the state of Guerrero disappeared, later found murdered, the police unable or unwilling to help. Each year corruption costs the country between 2 and 10 percent of its GDP.[2] There had to be more he could do. So when colleagues approached him about scenario planning for the future of Mexico, he didn't quite know what that would entail but he was definitely up for it.

Scenario planning had been pioneered after World War II by the Rand Corporation and the American military. As a process, it grew out of an understanding of complexity and the recognition that it was impossible ever to identify all the forces at work that defined the future. This made traditional planning dangerous: it would always contain too many assumptions to be reliable and risked offering certainty where none existed. The best one could do was to identify a plausible variety of futures and interrogate them for implications and consequences. Scenarios are different from experiments because they are conceptual and operate on a far larger scale. Where experiments reveal immediate internal features of a complex system, scenarios explore where the internal organization meets the external environment, where uncertainties lurk beyond anyone's control. Scenarios identify and test how and where the future and the present meet.

The military still deploys a variant on scenario planning today. It has to, because it functions across multiple time zones: the immediate present, the near future, and the distant future, decades out. As chief of the General Staff in the British Army, General Sir Nick Carter confronted two competing demands: his organization had to be ready to respond at a moment's notice, but he also had to plan today for the fighting force Britain will need twenty-five years from now.

"You have to distinguish between determined strategies and emergent strategies," Carter explained. "Because the future is inherently unpredictable, a determined strategy won't be successful. We think that the future emerges and therefore we can only really take one step at a time, building alliances and hedging opponents' behavior along the way. But you need scenarios to get a general idea of what parts of town you're aiming at and to check your steps are in the direction of your ends."

Reconciling the tension between the internal, immediate demands of the army and the external realities of the world in which it operates, scenario plans separate predetermined certainties (the army has these capabilities and resources) from uncertainties (where the army might be called to intervene). The goal is both to protect what's critical now and to identify early what might bestow advantage in the future. Scenarios bridge inside and out, immediate and future.

"My replacement is being recruited now," Carter explained as we sat in his office, surrounded by photographs of his predecessors. "A platoon commander who joins at the age of twenty-four is commanding a battalion fifteen years later. But we don't know what they will be asked to do in fifteen years so we have to train now for a deeply adaptive mind-set. It is exactly the opposite of the gig economy."

Carter can't know what challenges the army will face fifteen or twenty years from now. What he does know is that whoever leads the army then won't be able to rustle up the skills he needs the minute he or she discovers he needs them. The lead time to develop that talent is too long. So he works from a variety of models of the future that help define a range of possibilities for which his men and women will be trained. He's learned that, while it's easy to talk about adaptive leadership, it's hard to produce.

"In my second tour in Afghanistan," Carter told me, "it was interesting seeing how twenty-five battle group commanders behaved. Of the twenty-five, only two or three were generally tactically adaptive. Building an army where that is the norm cannot be done overnight."

Carter received a lot of flak for ads that specifically aimed at attracting as diverse a range of recruits as possible. Traditionalists scoffed at questions like "Can I be gay in the army?" and "What if I get emotional in the army?" But Carter insisted that he was trying to craft a fighting force that looked like the nation it would defend—a force for the future, not the past. Every five years, he develops multiple scenarios, war-gaming them and drawing conclusions about the capacity the future army will need. He knows how easy it is to get this wrong. Over the last fifteen years, he said, Western armies have concentrated on stabilization and counterinsurgency. But other areas—cyber security, underwater warfare, drones—got overlooked. He's using multiple scenarios to try to ensure that future strategies don't leave such gaping exposure.

Scenario planning began in the military, but it was at Shell Oil Company that it became most developed. In the early 1970s, all the oil companies ran a sophisticated, bureaucratic form of centralized planning (called the "Unified Planning Machine" at Shell) that assumed business would continue into the future without significant change. But however big the Planning Machine was, it focused almost exclusively on financial information. Pierre Wack, an idiosyncratic French oil executive, regarded the forecasts that emerged from these systems as wholly inadequate, a dangerous substitute for real thinking because it was too easy to mistake financial models for reality. Instead, he argued that external volatility (what he called "the rapids") would increase as countries began to nationalize their natural resources and the power of OPEC grew. To Wack that meant that the companies themselves could lose control over price. How could they plan for this?

In what became one of the most famous scenario planning exercises in history, Wack and his team designed a number of stories describing a changed world. One challenged the conventional wisdom that finite natural resources would always command rising prices. Instead, it asked the planners to consider what useful responses might be feasible if the oil price *fell*. This proposition appeared absurd, barely worthy of notice. But in 1973, when oil prices did fall and everyone else scrambled to understand what was happening, Shell was ready. The corporation had already decreased stockpiles, restructured to cut costs, and decentralized, anticipating that the price shock would affect nations in different ways. The exercise enabled Shell to move from the weakest to one of the strongest of the "Seven Sisters" of the global oil industry.[3]

The scenario planning Wack developed at Shell, and that the company still conducts today, follows certain rules. Multiple scenarios must be produced (usually two to four) based on the same rigorously researched and reliable datasets. Like the evidence presented to the Citizens' Assembly, data cannot be ideological, nor can it be vague, opinionated fantasy but derived from verifiable facts that are consistent and plausible. That means that they can be explained. Each has to be considered as seriously and fully as any other; Shell's team has always rejected assigning probabilities to the scenarios. Soft data (cultural differences in different markets, for example) is as important as hard data. Financial planning is not allowed to dominate. Scenarios should focus less on predicting outcomes and more on illuminating the forces at work across the organization and the environments in which it operates. They must be relevant and challenging, pragmatic not ideological. And that means that they won't be tidy; like life, they are bound to be messy, patchy, full of paradox and contradictions. Using scenarios, Wack argued, "is as different from relying on forecasts as judo is from boxing."[4] If you understand outside forces, you might be able to make them work to your advantage.

Shell attributes to this planning process its capacity—not always, but often—to be ahead of the curve. It helped them adapt to a second oil crisis in 1979, to the collapse of oil markets in 1986, and to the fall of the Soviet Union in 1989. They claim that it brought the company early to address the rise of China as an industrial force, in putting sustainable development on the corporate agenda and seeing natural gas as an intrinsic part of that. They do not claim that the technique has given them control or the ability to predict accurately. Rather its strengths lie in highlighting options and alternatives, in revealing possibilities otherwise obscure, and in building within the organization the imaginative and creative capability that derives from asking "what if?" and "so what?"

In 2013, Shell published what it called its New Lens scenarios. These define three paradoxes at work in the world today: a Prosperity Paradox (economic development raises millions out of poverty but increases strain on resources and the environment, and increasing prosperity doesn't always increase well-being), a Connectivity Paradox (the digital world sparks creativity but also makes it harder to protect or derive livelihoods from creative products), and a Leadership Paradox (the greater the need for collective long-term solutions, the less the appetite for individual sacrifice). It then argues that industries and nations typically find themselves in one of two places: either with room to maneuver, which makes them resilient, or trapped by institutional rigidity, which causes them to delay or prevaricate. India, China, and Brazil proved to be relatively resilient, for example, to the 2008 financial crisis because they had financial, political, natural, and social resources that provided immediate options for quick response. By contrast, many European countries proved less resilient as they drifted, procrastinated, and got stuck for years. These concepts, coupled with the three paradoxes, give rise to questions from which the scenarios emerge: Which paradoxes are most acute where, and for whom? Which industries, nations, and groups have room to maneuver—and which are trapped? How will capital, collaboration, and creativity develop? How will power and influence be distributed?

From these lenses and questions, two scenarios emerged: Mountains and Oceans. In Mountains, power remains concentrated in elites; entrenched power hampers globalization and economic development, making political reform difficult. Individualism remains a prevalent mind-set, with a belief that people get what they deserve. The Internet becomes balkanized, with elite access for the few. Oil loses ground, shale gas becomes a global success; clean coal and nuclear energy expand while renewables struggle to compete. Mass migration drives defense spending. Mountains portrayed a world of volatile peaks and valleys.

Oceans, by contrast, describes a world of greater cohesion, where power is more broadly shared. That makes reform slower but more effective in unleashing economic productivity and ambition for reform. Social justice emphasises solidarity over individualism: people believe that *systems* get what they deserve. The Internet remains open, so political and business innovation are widespread. Rising prices make more expensive forms of energy viable. Prosperity is more widely distributed and pervasive but resource stresses become acute. As climate change renders some parts of the world uninhabitable, populations migrate in search of food. Solar energy overtakes liquid fuels and coal, but weak policies strangle the growth of natural gas. The combination of biomass, carbon storage, and solar power reduces greenhouse gases—but late.[5] Oceans portrayed a world of swirling, dynamic growth.

Neither of these scenarios is ideological or simple. Shell is an energy company, so its scenarios examine the world through the lens of its concerns—consumption, transport, CO_2 emissions, water, weather, migration, food, political institutions—while ignoring social trends they don't expect to affect them, such as genetic engineering or gender blending. But there is much about the underlying stability of institutions and the rule of law, both of which global companies need to thrive. The scenarios challenge organizations to consider: In this story, what can we do now and what should we prepare for? Do we have any capacity to influence the story and, if so, where and how? Just as General Sir Nick Carter has used scenarios to address today the need for adaptive leadership in the future, scenarios can reveal the requirement or opportunity to address today what the future will need tomorrow.

A diaspora of executives who worked in the Shell Scenario Unit has disseminated this way of working across industries and institutions around the world. The process has evolved according to context and its most stalwart advocates readily acknowledge its challenges. The scenarios themselves aim to be morally neutral but one Shell scenario planner "found them too promiscuous in their willingness to envisage almost anything, even the most disagreeable events."[6] At Shell, there was some reluctance to publish the 2013 scenarios, because they posit that the world would fail to limit the increase in global average temperature to 1.5°C, as called for in the Paris Accord. Do scenarios run the risk of habituating people to prospects that are ethically repugnant? Might they provoke despair rather than creative thinking?

Today, some permutations of scenario planning have become technocratic, dependent on artificial intelligence and far less amenable to the soft data that, for all that it is hard to quantify, makes a measurable impact. Pierre Wack regarded computer modeling as the enemy of thought. Once quantified, he believed, models become too rigid, their makers so wedded to them as to become blind to disconfirming data.[7] Numbers acquire more authority than they justify. One scenario planner, Angela Wilkinson, compared computer models in scenario planning to "a heavy axe in the hand of a fireman—even if it hinders his escape from a fire, a fireman is reluctant to drop his axe. The axe is a help most of the time, but a dangerous burden in extreme events." Some researchers regard big data as a twenty-first-century Maginot Line, purporting to offer more security than it can provide.[8] If you entrust scenario planning to data scientists, there is a real risk that strategy and data bifurcate so severely that the plastic, creative exercise of integrating them fails. And while it is clear that scenario planning demands a diverse range of people who are open-minded, with deep intellectual curiosity, expertise, and a capacity to think freely, those people can be hard to find.

As global head of intellectual property, Michael Kock used to run scenario planning exercises within the global agrichemicals business Syngenta. He is evangelical about the process. On one occasion, he explained it to a group of senior British executives who were keen to understand how it worked. He outlined a scenario of abundance that he had developed at Syngenta. The falling cost of photovoltaic cells, coupled with improved energy storage, has made energy cheap and plentiful. Clean water is abundant and forests are regenerating. Food can be grown easily wherever it is needed with agritech providing cheap, renewable sources of nutrition. Robotics ensures everyone has ample time and big data systems underpin efficient, cheap safe transportation systems. Pervasive connectivity makes all data available everywhere and virtual reality gives you any experience you want, anywhere, anytime. There are downsides: With more data, decision making gets harder because there's more bad data and it's harder to distinguish noise from signal. Anything can be copied, so fakes abound. More fundamentally, our economic systems derive value from scarcity, but in this scenario, there isn't any.

The gathering broke into small groups to discuss it. What would this world feel like? What would you stop doing and start doing?

What would make you unhappy? Many enjoyed what was, for them, a playful process: free, creative, eye-opening. The scenario upended many assumptions about modern economics and allowed them to explore questions they'd never considered before. What happens when laws of supply and demand *don't* influence price or consumption? In an age of abundance, scarcity itself would become scarce; perhaps underproduction could be a new goal.

But one group was paralyzed. Kock's scenario was too much for them. They could not imagine a world in which so many age-old, tested rules no longer functioned. Arguments about probabilities got nowhere. So much change was just too frightening to imagine. Kock said he had seen the phenomenon before. The most amenable to scenarios, he'd found, were young people who play a lot of computer games. Those are all forms of simulation where play is how to find out what happens next. Avid game players don't just get used to trying out different strategies; doing so is their idea of fun. It could even be the way to win. So they bring to the exercise a wholly different mind-set, one that is open, fluid, and optimistic that change isn't just possible but positive. The same is sometimes true in business school simulations, where teams less obsessed by winning find delight in trying out radical decisions that impart no real cost. This is, of course, how they learn. But corporate executives, Kock concluded, "need certainty like an addiction and they are so afraid of being wrong that they have lost the capacity to think freely." A year later, Kock left Syngenta disappointed "that they just couldn't let go of where they are today. So they are in a death spiral."

Thinking imaginatively is harder than many people expect. We are all born with the cognitive capacity to reconfigure the knowledge we have, but how boldly we are prepared to do so becomes a matter of habit. Sterility and paralysis might be blamed on corporate cultures but I've encountered it when running scenario exercises for individuals who find it cognitively or emotionally impossible to leave their past behind. They can't imagine changing industries or jobs, learning a new skill, or enjoying more freedom. They don't love where they are, but fear of change and addiction to certainty traps them, making present misery more comfortable than future hope.

At Shell, one scenario planner said that team members needed to feel free enough "to push within an inch of being fired." But the planners hadn't started with the luxury of such an open, free-speaking culture. For decades, the company had been a byword for formality and hierarchy. But being required to argue, on the basis of context, data, and imagination, has become a hallmark of the way Shell works. At its most effective, this kind of thinking requires that everyone involved has to be able to ask anything, to make space for conflict and have the emotional and intellectual capacity to endure disagreement. Hierarchy and seniority lose some of their power. Where Kock had found that the conservative, obedient culture of Syngenta couldn't accommodate this, Shell discovered that the process itself had shifted the company's culture, making it more responsive and adaptable.[9] One of the great insights from scenario planning has been that the act of doing it can change the systems it strives to describe.

In 2015, the government of Slovenia confronted the paradox of prosperity that Shell had defined two years earlier: quality of life had improved steadily since World War II, with high levels of educational attainment and personal security, but Slovenians felt that their quality of life was worse than in the past. Despite being a relatively equal society, its citizens didn't feel they enjoyed equal opportunities when it came to schooling, jobs, and housing. An aging population absorbed a high proportion of resources and, while Slovenia was at the forefront of Europe's digital revolution, there was a widespread sense that the direction of technology was beyond their control. Perhaps most profound of all, citizens did not trust one another, having more trust in European Union institutions than in their own. And that habit of distrust translated to weak democratic participation, with voter turnout among the lowest in Europe.

But the government of Slovenia had promised to develop a new vision and strategy for their country. Most had expected that, as usual, this would be a secretive gathering of elites holed up in a swanky hotel, drafting policies that would be dumped on the electorate. But instead, adopting the tools of scenario planning, the government tried to bridge the gap between daily party politics and wider, long-term social concerns. Fifty participants from government, regional communities, civil society, and the business world, a balance of gender and age groups, used scenarios to galvanize discussions around the kind of society Slovenes wanted to create for themselves in the future.

One of the guides through the process was a veteran of scenario planning: Betty Sue Flowers. A professor of English at the University of Texas, her literary finesse had drawn her into scenario planning with Shell in the 1970s. She is an excellent listener and a gifted editor—all qualities heavily in demand when trying to capture the complexity of a collective vision.

Working on the Slovenia project, she noticed immediately that the problem of trust threatened to stall the entire exercise. Participants weren't open or willing to argue and debate together. If this obstacle weren't removed, she realized, the project would go nowhere.

"The problem dated back to the Second World War. Some families had backed the Germans because they were anticommunist and other families had backed the Russians because they were antifascist. That was all still in the room," Flowers recalled. Scenario planning always surfaces conflict and there is always a moment when everything seems to fall apart. But getting the conflict out in the open, constructively, is critical; it's how and when people start to acknowledge and consider alternative perspectives. "That's how the facts, and then the trust, emerge."

Breaking through the barriers of distrust felt painful and slow. Flowers and her colleagues were trying to describe a world that the participants would feel able to inhabit—but they worked only from what they had been told. When the facilitators unveiled the systems map they had drawn to reflect everything they had heard, the group erupted. "When they saw their own thinking in front of them, they really hated it," Flowers said. She had known such moments before, but none quite so intense and personal. "They looked in the mirror and said: 'We don't want to be that!'"

Flowers and her colleagues kept their nerve. Not liking what they saw in the mirror motivated the group to come up with an identity they could like better, and the project sprang into life. A new vision began to emerge that wasn't just a wish list, or a bunch of campaign promises, but a map showing how trust, well-being, and social innovation could build on each other. The group began to share a dawning recognition that economic growth alone wasn't good enough. A more meaningful measure of prosperity was social well-being. From this epiphany, the first draft of a Vision for Slovenia emerged.

The group didn't stop there. Through workshops and surveys, they spread the vision across the country, arguing that "while the future cannot be predicted, societies can still make choices that shape their future. As such this is an antidote to the habit of distrust. . . ."[10] Published on February 9, 2017, the vision provoked an explosion of cynicism. How could a few pieces of paper change the whole country? But one sentence captured the public imagination: "In 2050, Slovenians are a happy people." Everywhere those words incited debate and discussion. What did they mean? What *should* they mean? What would make people happy—with their country, with each other, with themselves? Who was responsible for making it happen? Why wait until 2050? A national conversation drew in everyone and catalyzed debates that drove the agenda of the next election. The new government's development strategy turned that agenda into action, identifying where, how, and by whom action would be taken to move the country toward this goal of a better life for all. But the critical change, Flowers said, was when the scenario of a happy Slovenia became more than a story: the government put a budget against it.[11] "Sticking inside you is how the scenarios become real outside you," Flowers explained.

Every scenario planning exercise is different. At Shell, it's a well-oiled process, part of business as usual. In Slovenia, no one predicted that the vision would be so swiftly translated into policy. It wasn't just that scenario planning had elicited vivid, bold conversations where once stalemates had prevailed. The conversations had changed the way the country could think about itself.

That what started as a military framework and had morphed into a corporate tool could have such progressive, emotional, and cultural power has been a discovery. Nowhere was this more profound than in South Africa in 1991, when Adam Kahane, a scenario planner working in Shell's London office, ran an exercise in South Africa. With Nelson Mandela out of prison and the African National Congress legalized, political transition was gaining momentum. But what direction would it take? What kind of transformation would it be? What would the future of the country look like? No one imagined it would be easy or susceptible to central control. Perhaps scenario planning would be a safe way to illuminate possibilities.[12]

Kahane recalls a popular joke at the time that defined two options: the practical option, in which everyone went down on their knees and prayed for angelic intervention, and the miraculous option, in which people learned to walk and work together. Asked what kind of team the project would need, Kahane specifically requested "awkward sods" and got twenty-two current and potential leaders from across South Africa: black and white, left and right, business, unions, academics, activists, and politicians. Kahane asked them not to bring predictions or advice but to explore only possibilities, what *could* happen.

Four scenarios emerged and, true to form, they were given descriptive titles: Ostrich, Lame Duck, Icarus, and the Flight of the Flamingoes. The connections between the scenarios illuminated the key decisions the new government would face: whether to negotiate a settlement, how fast the transition needed to be, and how sustainable its policies should be. Each scenario was written up at length, illustrated, and distributed in all the national newspapers, reaching politicians, businesspeople, and NGOs around the country.

Did it make a difference? Kahane says that the discussions, between participants and then across the entire country, shifted what people thought was possible and what they believed was necessary. Complex and richly imagined, the scenarios discouraged binary thinking and forced people to face the real and immediate choices facing their new country.

Kahane and his firm, Reos Partners, have worked on more than thirty national or regional strategic scenario projects, tackling issues such as education, health care, climate change, and energy supply in Brazil, Canada, the United States, and Australia. Each exercise addressed problems that spanned multiple, complex organizations subject to external shocks beyond their control. They were all ambiguous, riddled with internal contradictions. And so, as the epidemic of violence in Mexico raged, Kahane's process and experience looked like they might offer a way out of a seemingly intractable crisis.

"We had tried to do something like this before, in 2006, but our timing was wrong," Rossana Fuentes-Berain recalled. By training, Berain is a journalist. She has the alertness of a bird, quickly turning to catch everything happening around her. Together with a business consultant, Julio Madrazo, she approached Kahane to see if his process could help Mexico. Without some methodology, they felt, the current crisis would just continue. One of the first people Madrazo approached to join them was Alberto Fernandez.

The working group (*grupo de travajo*) was spellbindingly diverse: an archbishop, police chiefs, members of the military and of organized crime groups, indigenous farmers, union leaders, politicians, household workers, bankers, doctors, academics, judges, civil and women's rights leaders, economists, state and national senators. The aim was not that the group be representative but that collectively members could see how different people experienced Mexico's problems from separate perspectives.

On November 27, 2015, fifty people gathered in Cuernavaca: close enough to Mexico City to be easy to reach, far enough away to avoid distraction. Emotions in the room ran high. Fear: at the coffee break, one participant thought he might have to leave because his family had received a death threat that he believed emanated from a group represented in the room. Curiosity: I never in my wildest dreams imagined being in a room with these people, never mind having a meal with them, talking about our families! Hope: this is different, perhaps something different will come of it. Relief: my job is to oppose you in the media or the senate and I thought this would be a disaster but here we are talking to each other.

Every participant got to know the entire group. Paired walks brought together those otherwise too wary to talk. A gay person and an archbishop. A policeman and a criminal. But the hard work started with discussions of the present. Some believed that it was mediocre but manageable; others thought the country was heading for civil war. Coming to terms with complex reality was painful as they all came to see that there wasn't just one Mexico.

If you build a model of the world that excludes the people, ideas, and forces you don't like or understand, of course your vision appears perfect to you. But nobody else inhabits that world or recognizes it as true. Scenarios aim to capture ways of seeing the future that are recognizable to everyone. So they can't pay attention only to economics or only to politics; they can't exclude social cohesion or natural resources. Incorporating all of this tricky, unprogrammable soft data, of the kind so important to Pierre Wack, makes the work richer—but harder.

"Making something binary seems simple but it is a way *not* to have a conversation," the facilitator Elizabeth Pinnington explained.

"It's a form of bullying. Sure, you can say, 'this person shouldn't be here, we have to annihilate drug traffickers' but that resolves nothing; it exacerbates the problem."

By the end of the first weekend, the participants were tired. Almost everyone was glad they'd come and most experienced both disappointment and relief. The problems were harder than they'd thought—but they were developing a means of communicating. At the second meeting, in February 2016, detailed work producing the scenarios began. They were titled *Mexico Posibles*. "We started," Pinnington said, "with the idea of possibilities: nobody is expert on what hasn't happened yet, so we aren't writing plans." Once people got clear about the scenarios, Pinnington explained, there was always a very strong desire to improve them. She and a team of editors worked hard, sometimes through the night, to incorporate all the ideas, caveats, and refinements that participants insisted on.

"The night of the initial edit," Pinnington recalled, "we started with fifteen scenarios and got it down to six drafts. When they saw the drafts, people were everywhere from interested to panicked: this isn't right, this isn't sharable! They were learning how to participate. Our editors would propose questions for the next draft: here are some options, what do you think is the most realistic? We did eight rounds of that. It's slow but it gives people the opportunity to say what they're thinking and to come to terms with what other people are thinking."

By now, everyone knew each other quite well; a desire not to let each other down kept them going. But so, too, did Kahane's well-honed methodology. Everyone could speak, but no one for more than one minute. When the bell rang, they had to stop. An archbishop got the same amount of time as an indigenous woman; the laborer was as readily heard as a senator. It can be shocking, Kahane told me, when a household worker and a senator are treated equally, but it makes the process feel democratic and fair. Everyone is more willing to listen and the work doesn't get bogged down.

But as the scenarios were crafted, the world outside was changing—and the organizing group felt some innovation was required. "After Brexit and Trump," Julio Madrazo recalled, "some of the scenarios were irrelevant because reality had already moved beyond them." A fresh, second generation of participants joined the initial group. Where the first generation was composed largely of senior leaders working on a national level, the second was younger and had a more regional focus, working at city and state level. On February 24, 2018, the two generations came together for the final session in Puebla, an ancient colorful city in the center of Mexico. At the meeting in a former convent, now a hotel, the atmosphere was one of a family reunion: warmth, excitement, anticipation.

The scenarios had been whittled down to three: *A Hostile Mexico, A Paralyzed Mexico,* and *A Responsible Mexico.* But now the second generation wanted to introduce a new one, *A Failed Mexico,* that described a Mexico fractured by guerrillas, gangs, and paramilitaries. Huge, orderly debate ensued. Might organized crime and far-right or far-left extremists make common cause? Was inertia really the country's greatest enemy or did greater threats lurk outside the country? Nothing in this discussion felt theoretical; personal experiences in the group made each detail real. The fourth scenario was accepted and joined the rest for more editing, re-editing, and polishing.

On March 21, 2018, Mexico Posibles presented their four scenarios, on paper and as short videos, at the Palacio de Minería in Mexico City. José Woldenberg, the first president of the country's Federal Electoral Institute, opened the event, saying, "The future is built from today. . . . There is no law of history that condemns us to be better or worse in 2030. These options are possible and their nuances and folds are infinite."

A history of the project preceded a brief explanation of the process, explaining that a scenario is "a history of what can happen." Many participants strove to describe how the process had changed them. An indigenous woman, Tukarima Carrillo, told of her amazement at being listened to and taken seriously. "Today I do not feel alone," she said. "You solve social problems with social processes." Others spoke of their initial skepticism, losing their prejudices, the need for reconciliation. Many spoke about victims of violence, about migrants trying to make a future for their families. Everyone referenced a powerful network of trust. And Alberto Fernandez spoke of his own initial ignorance.

"Businessmen do not know what the big problems in Mexico are," he said. "The vision of the problems that I had of this country was wrong. I learned that it is no use trying to implement solutions if you do not know with total depth and certainty the problems we have in this country. . . . Only when we learn to break and create bonds, only when we pay attention to the differences between us, but realize that the same blood runs in the veins of all Mexicans, only when Mexico works the way that Mexico Posibles worked—to feel what others feel—can you start to understand what is happening in other parts of the country. And when we can work like that, no one can stop us finding the solutions to our beloved mother country."

The speech was a startling confession, of how little Fernandez felt he had understood of the country he loved. Shocked by the limitation of his very curious mind, he emerged from the experience with a hugely enhanced sense of the complexity of the problems Mexico faced, but also with a deeper appreciation of the human talent that it contained. The weekends rife with conflict, with irreconcilable perspectives, had given Fernandez new pictures of where he and the country might go. It was, he said, a life-changing experience.

Months later, participants recalled one particular session when they'd gathered after dinner with a glass of wine, in an old, round room, sitting in concentric circles, talking as night fell. Each was asked to tell a personal story. No arguments, no opinions or theories: only unvarnished personal experience for one minute. More than anything else, it was these raw testimonies that changed people.

"These stories were so powerful and new to me," Fernandez remembered. "I was sitting next to Rosina and she told a story about when she was twelve and living in Oaxaca and her father told her she had to get married. She said no, she wanted to study. Her dad said no, so she stopped eating. Her father said: if you are so strong, you can leave. So she left. She took the first bus in her life and went to the next village. Years later, she came back to run as mayor! They didn't elect her, because she was a woman so she said, okay, I will change the laws. And now, four hundred indigenous women are being elected in Mexican communities! That created such a feeling of admiration for the group and broke all the walls of differences."

Other participants understood for the first time why some had chosen organized crime as a direction, but they also appreciated how it felt to be a military commander totally outnumbered by criminals. A policeman struck up a tight relationship with a terrorist who'd thrown three bombs. He could see now, he said, that they each wanted a better Mexico. What emerged from the exercise were deeply adaptive minds.

The general election that followed in 2018 was one of the most violent in Mexico's history; more than a hundred political figures were killed. The result was dramatic: all the established political parties were trounced by a left-wing populist, Andrés Manuel López Obrador, who won the first outright majority since 1988. "At first, I was scared of the new government but it was probably what we deserved," Fernandez reflected. "But then we met with them and we realized: we are nonpartisan, we are not self-interested, we don't have any party alignment, and we are everybody in Mexico. And so we went to the government and said: How can we help? Where do you want us to work?

"It was really good. They told us one area where they needed our help was primary and secondary education. So we have another project! We are going to bring people from the best universities, from rural schools and all this diversity across the whole system, so we can work together. Not just so the children have better Spanish and math but to transform the lives of kids and their communities. We are not a political party—so we can be very open and work with everyone."

Scenario planning originated with the recognition that much in the world is too complex to be predictable and that the future is too malleable to be revealed by hard data alone. Absolutely accurate forecasting is feasible, but only where everything is known and predetermined—and nowhere is that true. General Sir Nick Carter dismisses such forecasting, not on ideological grounds but on pragmatic ones: if he imagines the world is fully determined, he "won't be successful." Instead, scenarios illuminate the contingencies, contradictions, and trade-offs of the real world, where no one interest or single perspective is in control. That's why they produce conflict but also epiphanies.

Scenario planning exercises demand that we acknowledge that we all inhabit complex systems, only parts of which we can see or influence. They force individuals and organizations out of their narcissism to confront how much of their success depends on others. This can illuminate opportunities for experiments or trade-offs; it also engenders humility. Bringing together the powerful and the powerless forces both to accept that while each has hopes and visions for the future, neither fully knows how to achieve them. They also reveal that win/win is usually a lie and that progress demands adaptation and sacrifice. That's when they become uncomfortable again.

Scenario planning changes the people who do it. Seeing ideas, people, trends, and the immense nonlinearity of life is chastening. It's difficult, accepting the complexity of the world and the ambiguity of personal experience. It's even harder to learn how to participate. But one way to address social processes is *with* a social process, one that enhances alertness, sensitivity, and imagination. Most participants treasure the experience—eventually. They come to see how opposites can be reconciled and that positive change emerges only when they are. No longer alone or intimidated by the fear of conflict, making the future starts to feel viable, practical, and real.

But perhaps the most potent way in which scenario planning changes people is by shifting their sense of time. In Cuernavaca and in Puebla, the future—2030—seemed close and personal. It was no longer an abstract idea, not someone else's problem. It stared everyone in the face and it didn't feel a decade away; it felt like tomorrow. The Mexico Posibles scenarios end: "The future is not . . . written. We have no time to waste."

CHAPTER SIX

THINK LIKE AN ARTIST

The only true voyage would be, not to visit strange lands, but
to possess other eyes.

—Proust, *The Captive*

A London theater, packed. Onstage, characters explore a past that
is murky, uncertain, infused with corruption. They struggle with
a present that is impoverished and dangerous, where no one can
imagine a future not mired in lies and fantasy. The central image of
the play—a wild duck that has been wounded but rescued—lives
in the attic, alive but trapped. Each character is full of contradictions; every sentence bristles with ambiguity. And yet the play grabs
attention. When the trap in the plot is sprung, the audience gasps,
seeing for the first time how tortuous these relationships have always
been. When the play is over, they erupt in cheers.

After the performance, many stay behind for a discussion with
the cast. The questions are electric: How uncomfortable is it to play
these roles; how different is each performance; is it about Trump or
Brexit; how do you decide which version of the truth to act? Most
in the audience have come new to the work; few know anything
of its history or author. At the end of the evening, walking from

the theater to the subway, a group of friends continue their fierce debate as one sighs: "I need to go to sleep but my brain is whizzing."

How is it that Ibsen's play *The Wild Duck*, written in Italy 135 years ago by a fussy, middle-aged Norwegian man, holds this cosmopolitan audience rapt? On publication, readers condemned it as nauseating, bizarre, archaic, and empty, its characters as total idiots, morally dead, morose and tired; today it is considered a masterpiece, one of the many Ibsen plays produced every week around the world that denote him the creator of modern theater.[1] Artists are frequently ahead—that's what "avant-garde" means—but what makes that possible? How does art stay relevant in times and circumstances well beyond any future its makers could have imagined? What is it about the way that artists live and work that puts them in touch with ideas and themes that last so long?

What endures is, to some degree, random or accidental. We don't know whether ancient Greece had greater playwrights than Aeschylus, Sophocles, Aristophanes, and Euripides, only that they are the ones whose work has been found. You need only look at the wildly hyped but now-forgotten authors touted in the backs of old books to see how ephemeral art can be. But all generations go back to art, discovering or rediscovering sources of meaning and insight that their makers could never have planned. There's no evidence that artists contemplate "future proofing"—artists don't see the future as something to manipulate or guard against—yet we look to them for insight, perspective, ways to understand our own times that they themselves did not know. And, in work made decades, centuries, millennia ago, we find what we're looking for. Unforeseen, unforeseeable: What do artists do that makes their work endure?

If artists have the capacity to make work that defies time, it is because instead of trying to force-fit a predetermined idea of the future, they have learned to live productively with ambiguity, to see it as a rich source of discovery and exploration. Instead of trying to reduce complexity, they mine it, undaunted by contradictions and paradoxes. Working in the interstices of uncertainty is how they forge their identity, making future works and worlds that they can't see before they get there—and which they may only dimly understand on arrival. They are propelled by a strong sense of agency, knowing that their work won't exist if they don't make it. As such, they are the opposite of the hapless executives too terrified by future scenarios to think for themselves. In this, artists have much to teach us about how we ourselves could address the future with imagination and independence. In addition to thinking about what to do, the artist's method suggests that we should think about how to be.

In the pursuit of industrial innovation, it's become fashionable to try to define recipes or algorithms for creative success or to derive from neuroscience the cerebral patterns that generate imaginative work. This implies that we (or machines) can all be Bob Dylan, Picasso, or Beethoven. That is both statistically implausible and crass, as one of the deep rewards of art lies in it *not* being formulaic.[2] Generalizations about art always fail at some point because there are no rules that always work and no rules that are never broken. It is personal, human, and unique. Nevertheless, artists do have routines, ways of sensing and of making sense. Where experiments and scenarios offer ways of working into the unknown, artists illustrate ways of being that more tactical approaches to life miss. We may not all be artists but we can learn from their habits.

Paying Attention

Ibsen was a prodigious noticer: remembering guests who had shared his hotel years before, noting their reading habits, wondering whether a young man's light appetite might indicate disease, worrying about another guest's. Nothing seems too small for his attention, not clothes, food, weather, or syntax: he notes that the way people speak changes as the day wears on, that men and women end sentences differently. His acute social awareness scans the horizon for silent flares of anger or injury. He's an inveterate earwigger, overhearing and reporting other people's conversations. In the two decades he lived in Germany and Italy, his visitors always commented on how up-to-date he seemed. A tremendous gossip, he received Norwegian newspapers wherever he lived so that he could follow the ups and downs of friends and enemies. To write, Ibsen said, was to see.

In this, Ibsen is like most artists: febrile, alert, receptive, a mind like a street sweeper. The historian James Shapiro says this is true of Shakespeare: how acute his observation, how aware of the vast importance of trifles. Many artists are super-sensors, their humility manifest in their alertness to the small and unimportant. Colm Tóibín writes of Proust that he is always "noticing, registering, sifting evidence and studying what lay on the surface, seeing what people wished to reveal of themselves when they appeared in the social world. . . . He was intrigued by what was visible in a single moment in a room, at a gathering, how many generalizations he could make from a single glimpse or glance or change in the social air. He was concerned with manners as a painter might be interested in shade or contrast, as a composer might be interested in melody. . . ." Paying attention for artists is a habit of mind.

The visual artist Katie Paterson says that she is always tuning into something—but without obvious intent. "Nature always. Telescopes. Observatories. Zen temples. Water. Iceland. Japan." Paterson laughed, recognizing that the list could go on. Much of what Paterson tunes into is sensual; physical texture, smell, light, sound are, for her, as full of meaning as data and news. *Hollow*, a sculpture completed in 2016, brings together more than ten thousand tree species, from the oldest tree in the world to the youngest; standing inside of it is to experience the feel and smell of time. Paterson's work starts with detail. "It needs," she says, "to be accurate to be imagined." That means not being too busy to pay attention

to surroundings, not walking down the street staring at a phone. Similarly, when he isn't in the midst of production, the filmmaker Mike Leigh needs to give his mind free range.

"Every time we finish a film, the gang always says: Where's the next one? They want to do it! But it's so important to have time to do nothing. I don't mean nothing, of course; that's just what it looks like. I read all the time. I look at pictures. I like being alone, you need time alone just to sense: What's going on, where are we right now? Nothing happening *is* something happening."

Similarly, the science fiction writer William Gibson immerses himself in the present. He doesn't start by thinking about new technologies and how they might play out and his process, he says, has nothing to do with prediction.[3] Margaret Atwood describes something similar behind the genesis of *The Handmaid's Tale*: a steady collecting of clippings, each real, all gradually coalescing into a picture of rigidly enforced misogyny that wasn't a figment of the future but obvious to her around the world, once she started to notice.

These descriptions are strangely reminiscent of Eleanor Maguire talking about the minds of her London cabdrivers: individuals stocking their minds and memories with rich, random observations, the raw ingredients for later compositions. There is little didactic about this process; it seems to be constant, diffused, and undirected: scanning, noting, collecting. Heads up, eyes, ears, minds open. This includes reading that, at its deepest level, is experienced as life itself. Virginia Woolf describes reading as "absorbing at every pore" and her mind is saturated with it; it is, she writes, an addiction—but not an opiate. Almost the opposite, in fact. For musicians, natural sounds seem to provide the same effect; Olivier Messiaen in particular was the great collector of birdsong, but natural and found sound has been a basis for music for as long as it has been written.

This mind-wandering is free of an agenda, with no promise of reward, but, consciously or unconsciously, artists are incapable of not doing it. It is what shaped Samuel Beckett, who described

himself and his father as "fanatical trampers. . . . We were never going anywhere, just on our way." It's what preoccupied Dickens as he prowled city streets at night, what Ibsen did in his long daily walks, what Virginia Woolf sought when she set out across London: absorbing the minute details that others might ignore or overlook but which artists collect. Where there is intention, it is inchoate: there is, as yet, no plan. Instead, this way of being is drawn to the unfamiliar, anomalous, ambiguous. This is not a quest for confirmation or certainty. A form of imaginative immersion, its purpose is undefined—and much in this collection of raw material will never be used. So it looks inefficient, even wasteful, collecting observations for no immediate purpose, which simply trigger questions or provoke a train of thought. At the age of ninety-three the theater director Peter Brook recalled an experience that has stayed with him since he was a young man, traveling in Afghanistan.

"I saw a man sitting in front of a prison," he said. "He was just sitting and looking at the prison. He offered to share some of his food with me but I didn't have the courage to take it so I said 'no.' Now it seems a shame, not sharing. At the time I didn't know why he said that or who he was. I just had endless questions. . . ."[4]

The experience stayed with Brook, latent for more than fifty years, available until needed. If needed. For anyone craving certainty or wedded to plans, this way of life is excruciating. There are no measurable goals, no reassuring benchmarks of progress. This way of life is not for the Pavlovian dog but for the independent cat: attentive and meandering.[5] Experienced artists learn over time to trust that something of value will eventually emerge; their apprenticeship entails not just the acquisition of skills but of patience. It requires what the poet Patrick Kavanagh called "sensitive courage and sensitive humility": the humility to pay attention to the marginal and the nerve to explore beyond predictable pattern recognition, interrogating what isn't obvious, important, or inviting. To find anything original requires respecting the elusive. Where this occurs

doesn't matter—as much richness might be found in a gas station as a grand museum.

Kavanagh also drew a telling distinction between two opposites: the provincial and the parochial artist. The provincial, he argued, "has no mind of his own; he does not trust what his eyes see until he has heard what the metropolis—towards which his eyes are turned—has to say on any subject." So the provincial craves patterns, cares about fashion, and longs to be on point. His mind is so full of preconceptions, editing, and ranking that it is almost closed. He longs for predictions, signposts, and pathways, not daring to explore alone. For Kavanagh, the provincial's is not the mind of an artist, because it is crammed with prescribed agendas, seeing only what others have already seen.

But the parochial mind digs deep and keeps digging, confident that the parish is universal. It is here that timelessness might be found. Elena Ferrante's portrait of female friendship over a lifetime is a classic piece of parochial perspective, tracing in the dirty, poor streets of Naples the tensions of friendship and rivalry that transcend time and place. Richard Linklater's film *Boyhood*, twelve years in the making, knits together moments of growth and failure familiar to all families. James Baldwin's novels and plays speak as directly today to the excluded, overlooked, and undervalued as they did to African Americans caught in the rage and heartbreak of the civil rights movement.

Simmering

The great documentary filmmaker Frederick Wiseman believes in daydreaming, which he described as paying "as much attention to peripheral thoughts at the edge of my mind as to any formally logical approaches to the material."[6] Because explanation is not their game, ambiguity is productive for artists—though it takes courage and stamina to endure it. For Sebastian Barry, a novel takes a year of waiting "and waiting is very frightening and humiliating."[7] Unlike expedient work, imagination doesn't move directly from observation to action but from noticing to gestation. What do particular images, stories, observations mean? What are they saying? Mulling over the accumulated impressions and sensations internalizes memories, turns them into source material, available for interpretation. A French contemporary described Ibsen as having two eyes—one reserved for observation, the other for reflection—and both his letters and play drafts reveal him toggling between the petty and the meaningful, the detail and the story. His daughter-in-law recalled how, when she brought him town gossip, "one always had to tell him a story twice. First he listened, the second time he always asked very searchingly for details."[8]

Of all these accumulated sensations, which ones matter? Artists must decide what to work on. The choice of subject comes with no guarantees but must override all other options. After his encounter near the prison in Afghanistan, Peter Brook spent half a century doing other work; his productions of Shakespeare and Beckett, the revolutionary devising of *The Mahabharata* established his reputation as the most admired theater maker in the world. The memory of the prisoner didn't leave him, he said, it just wouldn't come to the boil. Artists use any number of words to describe the process between collection and making: gestation, filtering, percolating, simmering, mulling, distilling, digesting, waiting. No one I've ever talked to or worked with can explain how or why clarity emerges; they simply trust that it will. In practical terms, this means that artists wait for meaning to emerge.

"Be patient towards all that is unresolved in your heart," Rilke wrote, advising a young poet, "and to try to love *the questions themselves* like locked rooms, like books written in a foreign tongue. . . . *Live* the questions for now. Perhaps then you will gradually, without noticing it, live your way into the answer. . . . [T]his is what you must work on however you can and not waste too much time and too much energy on clarifying your attitude to other people."[9]

There's an echo here of the CERN scientists who glean over time where physics might be going next. But where they collect and review data, artists use themselves and their lives as the colliders, the place where collisions occur, where signals can be traced and interpreted. What propels the work are questions that reverberate incessantly: What do these images, words, signals mean to me? Why won't this idea leave me alone? With no specific end in mind, the answers are undetermined and unpredictable. For most artists, the decision of what to work on remains unconscious and personal.

"I know the premise will come," Mike Leigh told me. "It'll come from my own preoccupations . . . eventually! I'm old enough to remember before 1967, the Abortion Act, when people had unwanted pregnancies (though I was never responsible for one myself). I just remember that. And for about forty years, I had this notion of making a film about it. And eventually I did, in *Vera Drake,* but not till 2004. But why then, not earlier, not later? I don't know. I don't really care." He laughed.

"It is always an interesting question, which to work on," Katie Paterson said. "I have a massive editing process going on, with all these ideas going on all these years. In a lot of my works now there is a practical element involved—I have to consider what is physically possible. But otherwise, it's just quite instinctive."

Although his works hang in the Rijksmuseum, the Museum of Modern Art, and the Tate, the artist Norman Ackroyd, widely recognized as one of Britain's foremost landscape artists, doesn't consider the ultimate destination of a work when he starts on it. His subjects emerged as he found himself drawn to the northernmost coast of Scotland. Patterns in an artist's work might be discernable looking back, but in the moment few claim any kind of foresight.

"I've never had any grand plan," Ackroyd explained. "I just wanted to see those outliers—this little group of islands sitting off the edge of Europe that sits on the end of Asia and then you've got three thousand miles of ocean before you come to America. So it really is the edge of everything. I want to try to squeeze the essence out of it."

Observations, details, themes, experience coalesce into a starting point that uses, but is not, the artist's life. For the novelist and playwright Sebastian Barry, a few facts may be enough to triangulate a beginning: *The Secret Scripture* started with an aunt who had been a piano player in an uncle's band and who was sectioned. His son's coming out and an uncle in the American Civil War initiated *Days Without End*. These are starting points, where the work begins to define itself inside and outside the artist. But at any moment the story could change.

"It's not like a diary, it's more like a system of thought," Tracey Emin explains. "How I work and how I think about life and how I think about things. I might be thinking: Is sex to do with love? Is this a connection or is it not, is it completely separate? Is it lustful? Is it void of love? Is pure love nothing to do with sex? . . . I have to trust myself."

Such questions may reverberate for years, with no guarantee that anything meaningful will emerge. Only the concatenation of other life experiences prompting further questions drove Peter Brook finally to create *The Prisoner*, his play in which a man is condemned to sit staring at a prison. This gestation defies planning and forecasting because its sole function is to sift through observation and experiences in search of new meaning. Waiting for that to emerge isn't for the fainthearted. Looking and feeling unproductive, this time demands self-reliance and optimism, the courage to wait. That makes the working life of an artist unpredictable and precarious. But the capacity to tolerate uncertainty equips artists (and might equip us) better to function in a world that is unpredictable and precarious, too, because to be artists also requires finding the impetus to keep moving. The way to understand all those observations is to make something of them. For the work to take on a life of its own, the ideas and experiences that gave rise to it have to move from the artist's mind to the canvas, the etching plate, the score, the workshop, or the page.

Starting

Artists begin without being asked. That is the acid test of agency: not just having ideas, but acting on them. Where experimenters may carefully calculate need, passion, and resources, artists supply all three themselves. The need and passion are internally generated. The resources are ideas and time, but time is not infinite. So choosing one subject means abandoning the rest, with no guarantee that the choice is right. The only way to find out is to start. Almost every artist describes their way of working as a curious combination of invention, which is conscious, and discovery, which is not.

This process of unfolding can be seen when the printmaker Norman Ackroyd produces the first state of a new aquatint; what is, for many artists, deeply internalized work becomes visible, captured on film during a day in his Bermondsey studio in *What Do Artists Do All Day?*[10] For all that this is "a big production day" and despite decades of experience, for Ackroyd the process remains uncertain and unpredictable; he doesn't quite know yet what will emerge.

Ackroyd's etching of Muckle Flugga, a small rocky Scottish island north of Uist, aims at something abstract. The great things of art, he says, "are the human figure and the landscape it lives in. I am just trying to get a resonance of humanity." But he can't quite see what he is making. Because etching requires engraving with acid on copper in reverse, the plate shows a mirror image of what will become the final image. Years of experience and technical expertise mean he's not working in the dark—but neither can he be entirely sure what the image will look like.

"There's a huge desire to make the marks; that is the heart. I let the eye look at it and the hand do what the eye and heart wants and I just respond to it, because I feel I want to do it, so it's very instinctive."

As he handles the copper plate, it's impossible for the untrained eye to discern a defined image. To give the picture tone, Ackroyd grinds pine resin to a fine powder that falls onto the copper plate, randomly like snow. He then heats the plate so that the resin melts into it. At any moment, the image could still change. He takes breaks, careful not to overwork the image. Etching with acid is, he says, a high-wire act because he can't go back. In common with many artists, Ackroyd doesn't quite know when the work is finished. Every step along the way is a choice: Does the piece still earn attention, would he do better to move on, what else could he be working on?

By the time he puts the plate into the press, Ackroyd has a feel for the piece but he still can't be confident of the result. Every stroke, every drop of acid, each fleck of resin is a decision but what all those choices add up to remains to be seen. When the print emerges, it is a strong image, simple and pure. Ackroyd is acute in his appraisal. "It just needs a little more nip," he says. "A thinner blanket on the back. That's a good start, a few little things need adjusting. As a first state, that'll do."

It has taken days to make this first state of the print and months more to think about it. But Ackroyd's routine—doing, thinking, reflecting, doing some more, assessing—is much like a musician composing, an author or poet writing: moving in and out of focus, trying to get a feel for something that doesn't exist yet. Sebastian Barry once described how he spent nine months writing a long, dark opening for his novel *Days Without End* only to wake up one morning and throw out all but a page and a half, at which point he didn't know whether he had a book. Only finding the first sentence—"The method of laying out a corpse in Missouri sure took the proverbial cake"—did he begin to discover what would be a new style.[11] Afterward, he could not remember writing the sentence and, to this day, faces the fear that the next word won't come.

Getting started doesn't necessarily determine the ending; much still remains open and contingent, a matter of both invention and discovery. That means the work can continue to evolve and adapt over time—but it also means that at no point is the work without worry. So it takes stamina. Tracey Emin talks about being intimidated by canvases, her need sometimes to draw as a form of warm-up to overcome her trepidation. Some of Emin's paintings sit for years, waiting to be finished or developed—or changed completely.

"*Hurt Heart* was a great painting, with two small figures holding each other and it was really, really sweet. And I thought: I can't live with that. And then I painted over it. And I was going to write 'Heart' over the top, but I spelt it wrong and put the *U* and then I just wrote 'Hurt' and I crossed it out and then I put 'Heart.' I didn't expect to be making that painting. . . ."[12]

"With every single project," Katie Paterson told me, "there is always a point where I think: What's going on? It is never going to work. It's usually a bad sign if I *don't* have that moment." Lack of certainty is uncomfortable but it doesn't paralyze her. "If it seems possible here on earth, I will go for it, keep going for it. I've never been daunted by ideas not being possible. So far, I've never had to totally give up. . . ."

Paterson's latest project, *Future Library*, is defined by uncertainty over time. In 2014, in the Nordmarka forest outside Oslo, she planted a thousand trees that will produce paper to print a book in 2114. Once a year, for a hundred years, authors will submit manuscripts commissioned for the book. These can be stories, poems, a novel, a sentence, that no one but the author can read until, nearly one hundred years from now, the complete book is published. The first author was Margaret Atwood, in 2015 David Mitchell, in 2016 the Icelandic poet Sjón, in 2017 the Turkish novelist Elif Shafak, in 2018 the South Korean novelist Han Kang.[13] The idea came to Paterson, she said, when she found herself drawing tree rings that she associated with chapters in a book. She felt certain that this was one of her many ideas that would never come to fruition—but she was wrong.

"The project is very much about ideas and imagination," she said, "but they're physically expressed: in the room where the manuscripts wait, in the manuscripts themselves, in the trees which will make the paper. When I started, I didn't even know if writers would be up for it. It is so meaningful for me because it just keeps evolving, as a continuation of our lives into others people's lives. . . ."

Paterson doesn't allow herself to read any of the manuscripts; the only people who know their contents are their authors. Just as in Ackroyd's printmaking, there is much in this work that remains deliberately unknown, to be discovered, not predetermined. Paterson can't be sure the work will be kept going for the full hundred years, that its sponsors won't abandon it, that authors will continue to be entranced by the invitation. She cannot know who the people are who will read the final book or what they will make of it. But it is the unknowability of the whole project that makes people love it. Such work cannot derive from second-guessing, by trying to nail down the future. It can only be imaginative, provisional, and fragmentary, on the part of Paterson, her authors, and all those who flock, once a year, to watch a new, mysterious manuscript being handed over.

A good project, Paterson said, is one that keeps evolving; the more you explore, the more you find, so you have to keep alert to what you might not expect. The reason that artists so prize openness and are attracted by ambiguity is that not solving problems ahead of time keeps the work alive, capable of adaptation and variation—and it makes the work itself live. For Mike Leigh, the starting point for *Vera Drake* was the forty-year-old memory of the Abortion Act. That made him consider the kinds of people who performed illegal abortions, which led to the creation of the character Vera Drake by the actor Imelda Staunton. But filming starts without a script.

"We never rehearse the details, just the premise," Leigh explained. "We improvise on location." Leigh's shooting script is thin, a list of scenes that identify only the practical details that the crew needs. No one knows how each scene ends. When Vera Drake is arrested, the actors playing her family members did not expect this would happen and they didn't know what she was being arrested for. This is Kavanagh's "sensitive humility" at work: daring not to assume knowledge but letting implications play out. "We discovered what happened next by being there, and watching what happened," Leigh explained. "You arrive and the end presents itself. All sorts of forces, practical and spiritual and thematic and psychological and emotional, objective and subjective bear on events but how—well, you have to be there to find out." Not rehearsing a scripted scene, Leigh believes, gains in raw truthfulness what it might lose in perfectability.

Working this way isn't easy. Not knowing for long periods of time what will happen to their character, how important (or not) they will be to the final film, is precarious for actors already pursuing an insecure career. What's rewarding, for them and for us, is that what happens feels so real because it grows out of detailed knowledge of the characters they have created. It's through the detail, Leigh says, that you hit bedrock. "The stuff that's real and that is always there, if you keep looking. That is the stuff that lasts."

Of course, not all filmmakers or directors work this way. But most hope for something unforeseen and often unexpected in the moment, in rehearsal or when shooting, that brings the work to life. Instead of denying ambiguity, artists illuminate and explore it. When they are successful, the work creates a context in which we can experience some of the complexity and ambiguity of our own lives. When Ibsen wrote, he used what his biographer Michael Meyer calls "double-density dialogue": a language at once ordinary but oozing ambivalence and subtext that got under the skin of his audience. At the time, this language was entirely new: the idea that what characters said might not be true was revolutionary. It infuriated his critics, who insisted life wasn't like that, but his plays endured because it is. Ibsen understood that there is no freedom—not for him, not for us—without uncertainty. So he created stories and a language that threw his audience off-balance, unsure how far they were responding to Ibsen's play and how far to the discoveries they were making about their own lives. Investing his characters with our own beliefs and fears, private associations and public parallels, he made us a living part of the action.

Explain less, mean more. That way the makers and recipients of art become what Toni Morrison called "co-conspirators."[14] Being true to a single moment is how to stay true to all moments. Even the most solitary of artists, therefore, work with others: their readers, viewers, listeners. Most accept that they can't control the response provoked by their work; that's where humility comes in—again. Much is a matter of trial and error and, because trial and error is how children learn, and because it often looks like play, this way of working and being is also frequently misinterpreted as infantile. No rules (unless self-generated), no hard targets, no concrete goals: it doesn't look like work as it's commonly understood. But artists are among the toughest, and most tough-minded, people I've ever worked with. Katie Paterson says she tried *not* to become an artist, because she knew how hard the work and the life would be. There is a paradox here: that free, imaginative work requires tough mastery of discipline and detail.

"Once we got going," Peter Brook explained, "*The Prisoner* took a year and a half to develop. We started simply by just enjoying every sort of idea. Try. Try. . . . At the end of the day, you think, we've really got somewhere now. Then the next morning, you go through it and think: what a lot of shit. If you go home thinking it's in the bag, you're in trouble."

Failing

On completing *Days Without End,* Sebastian Barry concluded that the book would sell so poorly that he would need to write another one fast. In fact, it made him the first author ever to win the Costa

Book Award twice. Artists are often poor judges of their own work, if only because success in art depends not on the work alone, but on how it lives and breathes in the world. In our data-obsessed age, pseudo-scientific attempts have been made to measure the success of art, largely according to how often works are read, viewed, performed, or sold. This is nonsense, of course. Judged by this heuristic, for two hundred years *King Lear* would have been judged an abject failure, because it was regarded as too dark and difficult to perform—until today, when it seems the most modern of Shakespeare's work. For nearly a hundred years, little serious attention was paid to the nineteenth-century poet John Clare; his working-class origins and prolonged periods of mental illness accorded poorly with Victorian ideals of poetry. Yet in the middle of the twentieth century, his voice, his story, even his lack of punctuation suddenly appeared modern. The times had risen to meet Clare. His work, as W. H. Auden wrote, had been "modified in the guts of the living" just as today, a whole new generation of readers and artists are rediscovering James Baldwin, an artist who, by the 1980s, felt himself to be overlooked, underrated. This gave him no pleasure but neither did he accept it as the final judgment. He knew that the times rise, and fall, to meet or leave artists.[15]

Appreciating the complexity of the environment in which they work means that artists know that they can't control the reception to their work, that they can neither predict nor force the future. For many, the disappointment of a finished work merely points the way to the next one. Only after finishing his first film, *It's Impossible to Learn to Plow by Reading Books,* did Richard Linklater say he knew how to make his next movie. The playwright Peter Barnes told me that when two huge plays, *The Bewitched* and *Laughter!,* were greeted with damning rejection, he realized that he wanted to start again, reconstructing his craft afresh. He started with monologues, then dialogues, then trios: a conscious act of renaissance. Like many, he recognized that the best he could hope for was better, not best, never perfect. "A perfect poem is impossible," Robert Graves wrote. "Once it had been written, the world would end."

Better is the chance to change. The future isn't something to be nailed down, defined, and programmed. The only way to influence it is to keep noticing. While an efficient mind-set prizes predictability and continuity, an artist's passion for exploration develops the capacity for change. For years now, we've been encouraged to develop "the brand you," to adopt, as businesses or individuals, an unwavering, fixed positioning that everyone can recognize and rely on. But for artists, brands are toxic, suppressing the lively evolution that keeps them growing. Just a few weeks into rehearsal, Peter Brook says, a director isn't the same person; the work reveals and develops them. That is what the work is for.

Artists often change before they have to. Fans and followers frequently deplore these moments of evolution, when musicians adopt or abjure new technology, when painters change media, when writers shift style or genre. Ibsen was forever frustrating his champions by his furious refusal to be tied down by their definition of him. Picasso's shifts in style baffled critics. Fans of Schoenberg's gorgeous classicism were dismayed and disgusted by his adoption of the twelve-tone scale. Even James Joyce's staunchest supporters balked before diving into *Finnegans Wake.* Many Miles Davis fans never forgave his electric years. It took decades before Bob Dylan's fans got used to the idea that change was the point, that the developing self was Dylan's subject.

"Ninety percent of me has changed," Tracey Emin says. "I want to see new things. There's no point looking over your shoulder to see who's coming up behind you; you should just enjoy the run, be with it, and do it in your own way."

Minds digging deep can't predict or promise where they need to go next. They pursue no agenda, except perhaps the need to be free. "If you stand outside any position," Patrick Kavanagh wrote, "you aren't at its mercy." That is the benefit of doubt. It is why authoritarian regimes fear artists and why their citizens look to artists to be truth tellers: because they don't simplify but clarify. Search Shakespeare as closely as you like, you will find no ideology, no program. Artists with staying power know that art isn't about finding answers, defining solutions; it's about better questions. Beckett, often asked to explain what had happened in his plays, said he didn't know. No Ibsen play ever really ends; it leaves the theater in the heads of the audience. Writing of Joyce and Chekhov, Virginia Woolf observed that their work leaves questions "to sound on and on after the story is ended," flooding us "with a view of infinite possibilities." Drawing conclusions, Chekhov wrote, is up to the jury, not the artist. Art lasts not because it nails down human experience, but because it refuses to do so.

What the patterns of an artist's progress show is the human capacity to find meaning and to make lasting work not by planning it but by remaining open to the possibilities they see inside and around themselves. This argues against forcing predetermined expectations and goals onto our experience of life and for an alert way of being, open to noticing and responding to the future as it emerges. We think ourselves efficient when we squeeze our lives into schedules, itineraries, and plans, asking of apps that they tell us what to do, where to go next. But what we lose is the freedom to notice for ourselves, to filter and reflect for ourselves, to craft our unique sense of who we are and what we wish to make of our lives. The way that artists live and work is, in many ways, opposite to the linear, cause-and-effect, rational assumptions and efficient goals that underpin much of modern life and institutions. Instead, artists respond to the complex system that is life with the complex system that is the human mind.

The capacity to wander, pay attention, make sense, act, and change ahead of the curve is today the holy grail of most organizations and nations. When the investor Warren Buffett and the economist Ian Goldin describe themselves as artists, they imply that following prescribed rules can't give individuals, companies, or countries the alertness they need to evolve and adapt. Andy Haldane, chief economist at the Bank of England, depends on long city walks for sense-making, trying to perceive how the world feels as he's contemplating interest rate changes.[16] In an age of uncertainty and change, being able to sense what to do in advance of reliable prediction can make businesses or nonprofits smarter, more inventive, and more relevant. The intuition for change and the capacity to pursue it energetically is what markets applauded in Steve Jobs, a man who wasn't an artist but thought like one. That is what many organizational strategists yearn to emulate. The billions of dollars spent on corporate transformation programs start with the dream of turning hierarchical, bureaucratic, data-driven organizations into visionary sense-making machines. If only everyone could think and act like an artist. . . .

It's a tall order and frequently frustrated. Few leaders are prepared to give their workforce the kind of freedom that artists seize for themselves. The prevailing efficiency ethos and an addiction to planning and measurement are too embedded, and the risk too great, to do what Jos de Blok did with Dutch home care nurses: let people think for themselves. Each time I talk to chief executives or boards or senior leadership teams about less management and more freedom, they understand the opportunity but cling to the ancient reassurance of scientific management. Standardizing and measuring work is what they are good at, and most are more comfortable reading surveys about employee engagement than talking to people about what it feels like to work in their company. They're up to their necks in a status quo trap, believing that a well-measured if scary present is less risky than an ambiguous future.

But not everybody's quite so stuck. Investors look to start-ups to find in them the rewards that thinking like an artist bestows: a greater sense of zeitgeist, a willingness to probe, the freedom to change and to experiment. When they are less enslaved by competition and overheated markets, the entrepreneurial ecosystem could be seen as a vast network of sense-makers, all aspiring to the creativity that forges a future instead of incrementally improving the past. Huge corporations appreciate that sensing what's possible is an urgent strategic demand that requires freedom to explore. Some build slack into their planning and budgeting, hoping to enable discovery by loosening the pull of efficiency. Many work hard at developing more open cultures of high trust and safety, hoping that less rigid systems will support more flexible minds. Corporate hackathons such as Microsoft's One Week, when the entire company comes together to "dream big" and work together on thousands of different, speculative projects, provide time once in the year to think off-piste. A week isn't much, and it could be more. The fact that it is an event signals how profoundly this way of thinking is not business as usual for most organizations. Companies famous for their ethos of self-management—W. L. Gore, Arup, Morning Star, Patagonia—have found that letting people choose what to work on energizes the imagination and intelligence of each employee, not just the few at the top. They flourish in large part because, where people grow and change, organizations do, too. Company cultures are deeply implicated in their capacity to be creative but, as you'd expect when dealing with the complex system that is the mind, it takes more than a single structure or a few workshops to release and enhance human imagination. A deep tension prevails between the need for freedom—required to generate the creativity that keeps a company relevant—and the desire to maintain control.

When it comes to the future, it matters more to invigorate the search than to try to determine the outcome. Many artists, and people who think like artists, are inimical to formal organizations and the feeling is frequently mutual, with managers fearing or scorning whatever, or whoever, can't be easily predicted or managed. Allowing people at work to think like artists takes more than colorful

walls, toys, murals, and open spaces. To have insights that are relevant to life requires having a life, one rich in experiences and the
time to internalize them. That requires trust: that the difficulty, the
not-knowing, the periods of confusion and frustration, will amount
to something worth the effort and the risk. For organizations to
cultivate people who can think like artists requires that they trust a
process that is inherently inchoate, unpredictable, and risky.

That's why several Silicon Valley companies intentionally recruit
employees who show a high tolerance for risk—because they know
that those uninhibited by risk are more likely to be daring and to
spur innovation. But these employers are routinely disappointed
when the new hires' appetite for adventure seems to evaporate the
minute they hang a corporate lanyard around their necks. Why?
Because everything about the environment, from the badge to the
bonus, KPIs, assignments, and deadlines, speaks to the corporate
need to stop minds from wandering, to streamline periods of reflection, to predict outcomes before projects begin. Like the former
CEO of 3M, many companies try to make the unpredictable process
of invention predictable, the complexity of imagination simple. But
both require mind wandering, time, space, agency. When employees'
time, their online actions, keyboard strokes, and even their movements around the office are being tracked and recorded, it's hard to
convince employees they're free.

Independent thought can be enhanced by corporate cultures
but it isn't born there. For many, thinking like an artist is the only
way they know how to be. For others, it is a deliberate choice:
to make the effort to notice where they are, what's around them,
what's missing, to make the time to reflect on what it could mean.
That means wandering streets without a map, visiting buildings not
listed on TripAdvisor, having unnecessary conversations with people
whose profile isn't known. The automation paradox doesn't apply
only to autonomous vehicles or GPS; it pertains to how we choose
to experience life. We could be more adventurous, thinking without

bannisters. To be where we are sounds simple and it feels like an easy habit of mind to instill. But creating and retaining memories, and developing the capacity to mull over them—the foundational activities of imaginative work—are diminished when we let technology take the strain. Taking photographs results in poorer memory of what we've seen. Online research gives us information faster but it doesn't last as long. The more we multitask, switching as frequently as every nineteen seconds between diverse sources of information and entertainment, the less capacity we develop to pay and hold attention.[17] As scans reveal the physical changes this activity imposes on our brains, the downside of neuroplasticity becomes visible: all the gestational work of artists slips from our grasp.

What we lose is not just the opportunity for intimate experience, but the chance to create from it our own sense of the world, our place in it, and the future we could create. The more time we spend visiting places that others have described for us, the more we follow the paths laid by others, reading what we're told, seeing what the algorithm recommended, listening to what crowd-sources have heard, and eating what's already been photographed, tasted, marked, and measured, the less capacity we have to see what we didn't expect, to hear what we weren't told about, or to ask questions that haven't already been answered. We lose our unique perspective and contribution and in this, everyone is impoverished: our selves and anyone who looks to us in vain for fresh insight or understanding. Artists try to make the most of their minds. In the quest for predictability, we risk making the least of ours.

Artists think for themselves. In doing so, they claim the right to influence the future of their own lives, of their work, and of anyone who witnesses it. These aren't the stale, frightened minds of executives who can't imagine even participating in a different scenario but the highly adaptive minds that seize, in uncertainty and ambiguity, the freedom required for adaptation, variation, and change. That's what they can teach us, too.

CHAPTER SEVEN

CATHEDRALS

Standing in the middle of a golden cube, three stories high, it's easy for the three of us to feel small. Walls pleated like ice cube trays await 800 metric tons of liquid argon, whose brutal cold (-303°F) will make the walls shrink on impact. Outside the cube hang two huge steel frames, each covered with four thousand invisibly fine cables designed to capture signals from neutrinos, subatomic particles similar to electrons but with no electrical charge, whose mass may be zero.

We are standing inside protoDUNE, a neutrino detector that represents the next generation of machines at CERN, the Center for European Nuclear Research. DUNE stands for Deep Underground Neutrino Experiment, and when the prototype phase is finished, the full project will consist of two detectors like this one—but each twice as high, twice as wide, and seven times as long as the model. A tunnel running eight hundred miles from the Fermilab in Chicago to the Sanford Underground Research Facility in South Dakota will connect them. In particle physics, the smaller the particle you're trying to catch, the larger the machine needed to catch it—and neutrinos are very, very small. DUNE is just one of the twenty-five projects under way at CERN today. Each involves scientists and engineers all over the world tackling potentially insoluble questions. What they will find, whether they will discover anything, how long it will take, how much it will cost, and how much value will be produced: all of this is uncertain; it can't be planned, predicted, or forecast.

CERN is a cathedral project. The phrase is Stephen Hawking's and he used it to describe "humanity's attempt to bridge heaven and Earth."[1] Like the great medieval cathedrals of Europe, they are destined to last longer than a human lifetime, to adapt to changing tastes and technologies, to endure long into the future as symbols of faith and human imagination. They are distinct from megaprojects such as dams, bridges, spacecraft, and power plants because they have no end date. Cathedral projects contain experiments but are also their opposite, because they start with a clear vision of what they hope to achieve. So the longevity and scale of their ambition makes them intrinsically ambiguous, uncertain, and full of risk. Who could write a thousand-year plan? What new technologies might render any plan too long, too short, too expensive—or irrelevant? What kinds of people and skills are needed? Cathedral projects challenge to the utmost our capacity to imagine and adapt to a future we can't see or predict. And their success illuminates just how far we can expand our capacity to deal creatively with what is uncertain, complex, ambiguous, invisible. Not knowing the future can unleash a freedom to invent and to improvise. But they also demonstrate just how far robustness depends on legitimacy: the public understanding and support that allows them to endure.

Cathedral projects don't start with a business case; their primary aim isn't to be drivers of economic growth or to solve practical problems. At the end of World War II, when most nuclear physicists in the United States and the Soviet Union found themselves locked into developing nuclear weapons, CERN was founded on the guiding principle that the search for human knowledge was valuable in its own right and to all people. Its creation was deeply informed by the experience of the war and a determination that working

together could be one way to stop the world falling apart again. Many great pioneering researchers had remained in Europe—Niels Bohr, Erwin Schrödinger, Raoul Dautry, Edoardo Amaldi—but they lacked facilities and resources. So in 1953, twelve founding nations came together to create a new European Organization for Nuclear Research, with each country providing both funding and scientists. Its mandate was specifically pacific and collaborative, its guiding ambition the pursuit of particle physics knowledge on a global scale. Beyond that, everything was born in ambiguity. How it would operate, with whom, on what timelines, to what end, at what pace: all of this had to emerge.

Conceptually ambitious, the beginning of the project was modest and messy. Giuseppe and Maria Fidecaro started their work in a muddy barracks near Geneva Airport, a site full of people, as Giuseppe says, "sometimes lubricating, sometimes friction." Now ninety-one, with a shock of white hair and stooped with age, he looks like Mr. Burns in *The Simpsons*—except that the gleam in his eyes isn't malice or greed, it's just abiding excitement about physics. From the day they started at CERN, change was their norm. Maria had expected to work on a new accelerator—but when new technologies made it possible to generate ten times more energy, her original design was thrown out. Maria shrugged off the change of plan with nonchalance. It's all very well to plan, she said, as long as you accept that the future will not be what you expected and you stay open to happy accidents. The uncertainty of this work, she said, was nothing compared to the war she'd just survived.

Straddling the Swiss–French border, the CERN campus is littered with huge pieces of discarded accelerators; you'd need a very open mind to view them as sculpture. They are testament to a core capacity at CERN not to get too wedded to specific designs, plans, or theories. The mind-set at CERN is both tight and loose: rigorously committed to doing physics that matters at a level of acknowledged excellence, but loose in its responsiveness to new ideas and technologies. Scientists must demonstrate the kind of adaptive leadership General Sir Nick Carter prizes so highly. Plans aren't sacrosanct but accuracy is. This paradoxical combination of superhuman scientific detail with human improvisation requires a mind-set that is open to change, to disconfirmation and correction, but which can function in a discipline that demands absolute precision. Such punctilious flexibility is a CERN hallmark, as critical to the institution's management as to its science.

As director general between 1994 and 1998, Chris Llewellyn Smith led one of the most ambitious phases of CERN's existence: the funding of the Large Hadron Collider. In 1983, the W and Z bosons had been discovered at CERN: a discovery for which Carlo Rubbia and his colleague Simon van der Meer were awarded the Nobel Prize. This proved the existence of bosons (a particle, named after scientists Bose and Einstein) and spurred the hunt for the Higgs boson, as first proposed by Peter Higgs in 1964. But the collider that had found W and Z wasn't up to the next task and a new collider—bigger, of course, and far more complex—was expected to cost $3 billion, more than had ever been spent on a single machine at CERN. In leading what he expected to be a huge battle, Llewellyn Smith dispensed with the large bureaucracy he had inherited and instead created a small team to help him master the intricacy of raising such vast funds. Being an outstanding physicist wouldn't be enough; now he needed to adapt, too, becoming a politician and a diplomat.

"This was the greatest financial risk CERN had ever undertaken," Llewellyn Smith recalled. "The British were very anti. The Germans were struggling under the cost of reunification. There was no public support. We were prohibited from taking out loans." To reduce the budget, Llewellyn Smith agreed that the new collider could be built in two stages and, because they were so costly, to leave out every third magnet. Nobody knew if this was technically feasible; they simply believed they could figure it out along the way. He also won agreement that any new funds wouldn't reduce member contributions but instead would be used to accelerate the project.

Llewellyn Smith was forever being asked to predict the financial return on the project. But nobody could guarantee the value of work that had never been done before. If the experiments were too tightly constrained by financial promises, then there would be no discoveries and the work would be worth nothing. On a voyage of exploration, how can you price what you'll find before you even set sail?

In the United States, when the discovery of the W and Z bosons had been announced, a *New York Times* editorial had summed up national ignominy with the headline: "Europe W, US not even Zero." Mammoth cost overruns and poor management caused the Americans' own supercollider project, the SSC, to be canceled and it became obvious that, for U.S. scientists to stay in the forefront of particle physics, they would have to join CERN. For Llewellyn Smith, that was a piece of unforeseen luck. The hard part would be persuading the United States and Japan—wartime foes and scientific competitors—to work together at CERN. He convinced the Germans to relax their opposition to loans and persuaded other member states to adopt a more realistic approach to the $9 billion budget. But his primary, unwavering argument focused on the value of pure research. Transistors had come about, not from searching for them but from the study of wave mechanics and the quantum theory of solids. Computers weren't invented by people wanting to build computers, but by physicists who needed to count nuclear particles. Induction coils in motorcars weren't made by people wanting to facilitate motor transport—but by Faraday centuries earlier.

Margaret Thatcher's assertion that "[t]he value of Faraday's work today must be higher than the capitalization of all the shares on the Stock Exchange" might be true—Faraday's discovery of electricity did inaugurate the modern world, a contribution too vast to quantify. But it didn't fully explain the foundational belief at CERN: that great, valuable discoveries derive not from planning but from adhering to a total commitment to the pursuit of new knowledge. Cleaving to that guiding ambition, refusing to constrain the work with guarantees, made the gigantic cost of what became the Large Hadron Collider a tough sell for Llewellyn Smith. Billions of dollars—and *no* forecast return?

That CERN has generated valuable spinoffs, however, is unarguable. Today, smaller accelerators of the kind pioneered at CERN are used in the semiconductor industry, for sterilization of food, for sewage, in hospitals, for nondestructive testing of materials, and in cancer therapies. The superconducting cables developed for particle accelerators are now fundamental components in MRI and PET scanners and are also used in control systems, cryogenics, high vacuum systems, and electrical engineering. Solar energy collectors use thin film technology. But the most famous CERN spinoff of all is the World Wide Web.

Because CERN grew into an international organization committed to the open sharing of its data, from the earliest days it had attracted pioneering computer scientists who built the information systems to do this work. As the amount of data expanded, so did the complex requirements of the network designed to support it. By the 1980s, CERN had email and scientists were able to send files—though they needed a PhD in computing to understand how to do so. By 1989, CERN was the largest Internet node in Europe. Tim Berners-Lee identified the need for a standard language and protocols, but his early ideas attracted little interest. Along with his Belgian collaborator, Robert Cailliau, he needed a catchy title to capture the scale of the project's potential. He'd wanted to call it "Mine of Information" but in French the acronym "MOI" sounded rather self-centered. "The Information Mine" (TIM) was no better. While "world wide web" sounded bigger, the little abbreviation—www—more accurately reflected the fact that CERN, at the time, possessed just two primitive servers. Eventually, on his third attempt, a supervisor's comment—"vague but interesting"—gave Berners-Lee the backing he sought. Many insiders questioned the investment—was it really core to the mission of CERN? Not a single commercial company expressed any interest. By the time he was done, CERN had invested twenty-eight man-years in the project and, in accordance with all its work, released it free to the world.

None of these spinoffs had ever been part of any plan or forecast. They have emerged from the way that work at CERN is done. Huge projects, like the LHC, are undertaken without certainty that they will find what they're looking for—or find anything at all. They require technology that hasn't been invented yet, materials stretched beyond their known limits, and collaborations with institutions and commercial corporations that may not have been identified. What gives the twenty-two national members and the directors general of CERN confidence is the way people work there.

The colliders and the experiments are designed by young scientists, because that's where the newest expertise lies. Parts of the enormous machines are built in eighty or ninety institutions all over the world, each taking responsibility for their part of the project. It has to work that way, Llewellyn Smith argues, because it's too complex to centralize. Shared belief in the guiding ambition—new knowledge for peaceful purposes—compels the creation of complex networks of trust and expertise, inside and beyond CERN itself, all enlisting on the same voyage of discovery. It's a simple but forceful way to address complexity.

For young scientists working on the CERN campus, the work can be confusing at first. They don't strictly have bosses but join a group that interests them and then that group decides where to start. Many but not all groups combine hardware and software people whose expertise is phased. At one stage, welding may be the central issue, then the focus may move on to electronics. Once a piece of equipment is built, physicists take over. The ebb and flow—between theory and experiment, between science and engineering—has to be loose to facilitate the emergence of the best idea that will move a project forward. Bearing in mind that everything done at CERN will never have been done before, there can't be any rules about how to do it: Where would they come from?

Engineers demand detail and specificity; physicists have to ensure that the theoretical aspiration of the experiment isn't compromised. Both must succeed but neither can take precedence. Shared ambition drives avid collaboration: not to fall short, not to let each other down, to bring your best with a passion to do together something that could never be done alone. Everyone has expertise but everyone also needs help for the project to yield results.

So much of the talk at CERN is so abstract—invisible particles, complex theories, unproven hypotheses, amorphous organizational structures—that it is a surprise to see, at the entrance to the Large Hadron Collider, a wall of giant wrenches. The test of pure theory turns out to be mightily mechanical and, until DUNE is up and running, the LHC is the biggest single piece of machinery in the world. Inside it, proton beams (and sometimes heavy ion beams) are aimed at each other to produce collisions. These can't be seen but pass through detectors that send signals to one thousand computers at the rate of millions of gigabytes per second. The LHC control rooms receiving the data operate 24/7 and everyone, from professors to students, has to do time here. (When one famous British scientist made it clear that he regarded such work as beneath him, he was sent home.) The LHC was built for the community, by the community, and must be maintained by everyone whose work it supports and develops. That will remain true for as long as the machine runs, which (for now) is estimated to be until at least 2030. Since every collider ever built at CERN has outlasted its plan, even the LHC shutdown date is uncertain.

Marzio Nessi, the technical coordinator of the LHC, oversaw its construction from the first drawings to its first operations. In his hard hat and overalls, he looks and sounds like any site foreman. Italian by birth, he showed off the site with an eloquent mixture of pride and humility.

"I thought it was impossible!" he said. "So many problems: how to develop electronics in such a hostile environment, how to handle the radioactivity produced by so much energy and so many secondary particles, how to build something so big. But there is an incredible network of knowledge here at CERN and you have to believe that somewhere there is the right idea. When you manage a project like this, you are managing the network of two hundred institutions, forty nations, thousands of scientists. Nobody has done something like this so you can't have a hierarchy, you can't have prima donnas. You have to respect everyone and ask for help, share the problems, and believe that between all those minds, the answer will come."

Nessi's professional pride isn't in the LHC's physical grandeur but in the spirit with which it was achieved. His eyes light up as he recalls years of tension and debate. Pointing out where, in the giant complex, teams from China, Pakistan, and Israel worked side by side he recalls how, at first, Pakistani scientists were reluctant to work alongside Israelis—but after a few months nobody cared where anyone came from. All that mattered was the quality of the thinking and the credibility of ideas. Professional respect develops tolerance; people are judged by their work, that's all.

More than ten thousand people contributed to the design and construction of the LHC but most weren't on the Geneva campus. Thousands of commercial companies helped CERN answer its questions and most say that their collaborations have forced the companies to be more ambitious: working to higher technical specifications than they thought possible, generating new products they might not have considered or thought themselves capable of making, thinking beyond planning, acquiring expertise and luster through their association. The scientists on-site and the thousands off-site are testimony to the human capacity to rise to challenges previously thought beyond reach. The difficulty of the work isn't an obstacle: it is the draw.

"We hope the companies take with them our way of working," Nessi said. "The understanding that you can't have prima donnas, you need team players who aren't trying to prove, they're trying to understand. People who are open and share and like searching for surprises. That aren't always worrying about the outcome, aren't always thinking about themselves. People have to share knowledge or the cathedral can never be built."

Pulling in all the expertise and thinking he could find, Nessi made no distinction between age or background, public or private sector, nationality or status. Ideas respect neither hierarchy nor bureaucracy; his job was to hand great problems to people with the energy, courage, and commitment to figure them out. In the creation of something so new, everyone was a novice.

Not everybody feels comfortable with the radical democracy and freedom that such experiments demand. But those who do best accept that nobody knows all the answers. And this, he argued, is the only way to address complexity: not by trying to simplify it or pretending the work is easy, but by presenting problems of mammoth difficulty as opportunities to experiment with one's own intellectual, imaginative capacity to grow with and through each other. Nessi's fundamental task was to make this way of working normal.

Much of the work takes place in the vast lunchroom: big, long tables, huge windows. Everyone is there: the Fidecaros, Nessi, Llewellyn Smith when he was DG, and Fabiola Gianotti, who is director general now. You can't tell the difference between the world's leading theoreticians, visiting laureates, artists in residence, and the newest arrivals. All day long, the space is full of clusters of scientists gathered in informal seminars and working groups. In this easy atmosphere, it can be hard to remember how much is at stake. It isn't just that the cost of CERN is comparable to the entire budget for Oxford University or that the LHC was the costliest project ever undertaken at CERN.

For years, CERN's theoreticians and mathematicians explored and designed experiments to prove string theory. They failed. Llewellyn Smith isn't sure that those who worked on it wasted their lives—they made some contribution to mathematics—but there's little to show for it. In one office, a skeleton (ostensibly a dead physicist) hangs with a sign around its neck: *SUSY: You'll be in my class when we discover the first SUSY particle.* It's supposed to be a joke. SUSY stands for SUperSYmmetry, a theory that might explain some peculiarities of the Standard Model. Researchers tell me it's a nice theory; it should be true. But eighty years of work have failed to find any evidence that it is and the scientists working at CERN could be dead before anyone knows for sure. There was some hope that finding the Higgs boson would rule SUSY in or out; it did neither. The scientists who devoted their lives to this work can't go back now and start on something different.

But the longevity of the work is central to the motivation of those who take part in it. The work has meaning, because it's audacious and because it connects this generation with all the generations of scientists on whom their research builds. Everyone I met working on the protoDUNE was eager to tell me that the idea to use liquid argon had come from the Nobel Prize winner Carlo Rubbia, who discovered the W and Z bosons in 1983. Their work sits on his shoulders. However small, however short-lived their work, these young researchers have had the opportunity to be part of something that goes back generations. That continuity outweighs uncertainty, infusing the work with a sense of grandeur and importance that touches everybody. Scientists working there today hope to be the shoulders on which future young scientists can stand tomorrow. The future casts a very long shadow over CERN.

"The cathedral is the people," Marzio Nessi insisted, then corrected himself. "Not even the people but the way the people work together. Being able to work in this way, to share what you know, what you learn, on the way to knowing more and understanding more: this is what is CERN. Bigger than the colliders, bigger even than the questions and the knowledge: the ability to find out knowledge together, no matter how big or small or difficult: that we can do this all together, that is truly what is CERN."

Unwittingly, Llewellyn Smith and Nessi and their thousands of collaborators have evolved a way of working that is the inverse of most corporate organizations. Since the nineteenth century, those have typically started small. Success causes them to scale up and, along the way, the division of labor requires increasing specialization. As organizations grow, hierarchies and bureaucracy develop—bigger companies, smaller jobs—and measurement and rules drive standardization and efficiency. As the work becomes atomized, it loses meaning and motivation is supplied by targets and rewards to keep the work on track. Such institutions have succeeded when uncertainty has been largely absent. But as they grow and complexity increases, their own hierarchies and bureaucracies overwhelm them. Eventually the only way to function is by adopting shorter and shorter time frames: quarterly returns or just-in-time production processes limit uncertainty. But the shorter the time frame, the smaller the ambition, the more ephemeral the human rewards. Obsessive managerialism, with its measurable, predicted targets, narrows perspective and shrinks meaning.

CERN is exactly the opposite: It didn't start small and get big. It was born in huge ambition with just one guiding principle that has remained constant: the pursuit of particle physics knowledge on a global scale for a peaceful purpose. This is its lodestar, shining light on what new might be discovered now, which in turn defines what the work could be and how it is to be done. With everyone's eyes on uncovering new knowledge, coherence is achieved but flexibility and adaptability aren't lost. Just as important: motivation isn't dissipated when everyone identifies so closely with the work. It's an elegant way to address complexity, because it can contain change while compelling commitment and imagination over long periods of time without becoming rigid or sclerotic. This is another of CERN's unplanned discoveries.

CERN demonstrates that uncertainty, complexity, our inability to predict need not constrain aspiration. We aren't condemned to short-term, atomized work just because we can't see far into the future, but can become more expansive and imaginative when looking further ahead. CERN has succeeded not because it denies the uncertainty in which it functions—but because it embraces it as a motivator. The very scale of the place drives its scientists to explore and test new ways of working that they could not predict. Where more traditional management structures depend on clear forecasts, measurable goals, promised rewards to incentivize their workforce, the work at CERN suggests that ambition is intrinsically more motivating. If all the uncertainty were eliminated, so, too, would be excitement and meaning.

CERN isn't unique. All cathedral projects start with a galvanizing guiding principle that releases and energizes the capacity to adapt and evolve and allows the future to emerge. The Human Genome Project shares many of CERN's characteristics: an open, international collaboration at ease with uncertainty. Begun at the Sanger Centre in Hinxton, Cambridgeshire, in 1990, at a time when the emergence of new technologies suddenly made gene sequencing feasible at scale, its initial phase was riddled with controversy and backstabbing. What had started with global cooperation rapidly turned into a fistfight between academic scientists who wished to make all of their findings public, and Craig Venter, who claimed that his venture-backed company, Celera, could do the work better, faster, and cheaper—but who wanted to make gigantic profits by privatizing the data and selling access to it. The public fight made Venter look big and bold, but commercializing the genome was an old-fashioned, petty ambition compared to the vast potential of releasing it to the world. Sanger's first director, John Sulston, another scientist/diplomat, inaugurated and led the public project with American colleagues. He had already won a Nobel Prize for his work in genetics but his colleagues later thought he deserved the Peace Prize for the way in which he fought for and won open access to the data. But when the first sequencing of the human genome was published to great fanfare in 2003, the work wasn't over. Many predictions about genomes had turned out to be wrong and new features of genes had emerged that nobody had anticipated. It turned out that we didn't need one human genome; now we needed thousands of them to understand and interpret all of the associations within genetics.

The next phase of the work has been institutionalized as the Wellcome Sanger Institute, still in Hinxton but now a sprawling bucolic campus that is, like CERN, a magnet for scientists from all over the world. Those who wish to work as superstar soloists aren't welcome; the work favors team players who appreciate that the only currency that matters is a good idea. And these scientists, too, approach discovery with enthusiasm.

"We don't know what we're going to find," Julia Wilson, associate director of the institute, told me. "We aren't trying to prove something one way or another; we don't start with a hypothesis. We're tackling big unanswerable questions with infrastructure and the political, financial, intellectual freedom to address them. So the scientists that we bring into Sanger have to have big ideas; the only limit is their imagination."

The Sanger's guiding ambition is the improvement of human health. Like CERN, the work is conceived in five-year cycles. The work is divided among thematic programs—cancer, aging, cellular genetics, human genetics, parasites, and microbes—and researchers are expected to contribute across these. Yet, just like Clay Johnston's Dell medical center, the organizational structure is designed to accommodate change. In 2018, work started on creating a map of the genes in DNA sequences of every cell type in the human body. The hope is, ultimately, to be able to zoom into a kidney cell to understand its genetic design and what it does. A huge undertaking, it was nowhere in the 2015 plan. But because the idea came along and was feasible, because the technology is available, because it can contribute to human health, and because it follows the Sanger's guiding ambition of uncovering new genetic knowledge, free to the world, the project was approved. The data is tight, the structure is loose. At the Sanger, there are no targets, no Key Performance Indicators, and no benchmarks. The only standard that matters, Wilson said, is excellence. How could you measure what you don't yet understand?

But work so open-ended, without guaranteed, predictable outcomes, requires public support. For that reason, the Sanger invests significant resources into the public understanding of their work. It is considered essential that citizens appreciate what genes, genomes, and genetics are, what they can and can't do, what scientists should and should not do with them. The emergence of gene editing, controversies around genetics, and the synthetic creation of new organisms have made that mission more urgent than ever and Wilson was distinctly uneasy when I raised the issue with her. But were the public to lose trust in the science or the scientists, the future organization could lose the freedom it enjoys to determine its own path. But everyone I spoke to recognized that the Sanger, and the scientific community at large, is falling behind on these issues.

After her career in intelligence at MI5, Eliza Manningham-Buller now chairs the Wellcome Trust, which provides the bulk of the Sanger's funding. Better than most, she understands the fundamental requirement for public trust and understanding—and the speed at which that can be lost.

"On ethics, we are behind the curve. If you are creating organoids, synapses in petri dishes, the science will be moving so fast that we won't have adequate ethical work being done to support it. We are still fixated on issues of consent: Who has consented to our using their DNA? We haven't got that right yet—but meanwhile, other, bigger issues are emerging and will keep emerging." This isn't just an issue of who owns what data, how it's used, or how to reassure the public that their contribution will be anonymous. Poor public understanding of genetics threatens to make people reluctant to contribute their DNA, suspicious of the therapies that emerge, and resistant to new discoveries.

Legitimacy—the public trust that the work is valuable and relevant—secures the longevity of cathedral projects. Guiding ambition produces coherence internally but that's inadequate if it isn't shared externally by a wider, broader audience. Only as long as the public believes in them can they preserve the freedom to pursue difficult work that takes time and is hard to predict and articulate. That legitimacy isn't guaranteed. A failure to explain, or to manifest public accountability, is their biggest threat. In 1978, the birth of Louise Brown, the first so-called test-tube baby, prompted such a challenge to the scientific community: Was science moving too fast? Were the new techniques of artificial insemination and in vitro fertilization morally justified or socially acceptable? Fearful that public ignorance and misunderstanding would prevent the development and availability of these new technologies, the British government convened the Warnock Commission in 1982, giving it two years to produce guidelines that might enable the new science to develop public support and understanding.

By training, Mary Warnock was a philosopher: a helpful background, she told me, not just because "philosophers really have no subject of their own." Unlike scientists or lawyers, they have no vested interest in anything except thinking. Her commission, made up of doctors, lawyers, health care executives, and social workers, was essential, she believed, if scientists weren't to run away with the new technologies, having never forged any public support. A leader in the field of fertilization, the British government didn't want to lose economic advantage, but that alone wouldn't be enough to secure social acceptance. Banning their innovations couldn't be the answer, either; everyone on the commission agreed that the "sheer awfulness of infertility" meant that some accommodation had to be made. The most divisive issue was the destruction of human embryos that research and in vitro fertilization necessitated: Could this ever be sanctioned?

"We wanted to look into the future," Mary Warnock told me, "but not in a sci-fi way, in a pragmatic way. We had excellent briefings so that everyone was in full possession of the same information. And we were able to craft an answerable question: not when does life start (which is philosophically unanswerable) but at what point do we attach *value* to human life?"

At the age of ninety-four, Warnock recalled how deep divisions ran; one member organized secret meetings behind her back. But all agreed to reach a conclusion based on "argument rather than sentiment." At the end of two years, Warnock submitted her report, endorsed by the full commission. There were two dissenting opinions—a virtue, she wrote in the foreword, because it showed how broad the discussion had been. The report explicitly rejected any kind of cost/benefit analysis, arguing that the moral nature of the subject demanded asking whether such technologies were ever right. No calculation of aggregate economic gain could answer such a question. Its conclusion recommended a rule banning research on any fetus more than fourteen days old. The rule became law and remains to this day. The Warnock Commission was celebrated for creating a consensus that most could accept and everyone could understand.

Cathedral projects rest on a foundation of such public appreciation and support. Without it, they are exposed to vicissitudes in taste, social mores, and political volatility. For the Sanger, that need lends an urgency to securing better understanding of genomics. With it, their work could continue for generations to come. But throughout history, scientists have been shocked by the unintended uses to which their work has been put. The journalist Clive Thompson calls these "holy crap moments," citing the moment when the atom bomb was dropped and twentieth-century physicists recognized that they were moral actors in the event. Such moments of moral reckoning, if not addressed, jeopardize the survival of genetic research. Cathedral projects endure when people believe in them as public goods—but only as long as people do. Nowhere was this more extravagantly tested than in the long, tortuous history of the Sagrada Família in Barcelona.

The idea for the church was rooted in sacrifice and suffering. As the modern city of Barcelona expanded, the Spiritual Association of the Devotees of Saint Joseph acquired the land for a huge cathedral, funded only by alms and private donations given to atone for personal and societal sins. In 1883, within a year of laying the foundation stone, the original architect, Francisco de Paula del Villar, resigned, ceding the work to the thirty-one-year-old Antoni Gaudí. The young architect had never attempted anything on the scale of a cathedral and he was expected merely to oversee the completion of Villar's neo-Gothic design. But Gaudí was too original, too zealous, and too devout to create a religious building according to generic traditional principles. Over time, he reconceived the church in an extravagant and idiosyncratic direction: a vast ornate statement of fervent religious devotion. His vision required extreme innovation in craftsmanship, engineering, and artistry. It would also demand money on a scale that no one could foresee when he started and no one fully appreciated at the time of his death, forty-three years later, when just a quarter of the building was complete.

Gaudí's vision for one of the last cathedrals built in Europe overflowed with radical architectural and iconographic invention. Leaving behind detailed drawings and plaster models, Gaudí hoped that his assistants would complete his vision, but his plan didn't take politics into account. Even before Gaudí's death in 1926, churches had become targets for violence and revenge but for much of this time, local love for the Sagrada Família left it unscathed. That support fractured in the Civil War. In 1936 the Iberian Anarchist Federation (FAI) attacked the church, burned down Gaudí's office, smashed plaster models and sculptures, and destroyed notebooks full of calculations. Correspondence and writing that detailed Gaudí's intentions were trashed. Twelve people associated with the Sagrada Família were killed and two years later Domènec Sugrañes, Gaudí's assistant who had loyally continued the work, also died. By 1939, the crypt had been turned into toilets.

Peace, of a kind, came with Franco's rule, but his hatred of Catalonian republicanism ensured no state funds or support for the Sagrada Família. In the 1940s, when starvation was used as a weapon against dissidence, a vast expensive, unfinished building garnered little support and work on the cathedral slowed to an almost invisible pace. Black-and-white photographs from the period show tiny old women on the street, selling cakes and raffle tickets as they try to raise meager funds for the extravagant fragments of a church that dwarfs them. Supported by nothing but the will of Barcelona's citizens, the building had become the city's icon of persistence, devotion, and endurance.

That the Sagrada Família was under construction at a time not just of political volatility but also of artistic turmoil rendered Gaudí's project even more precarious. Not everyone liked—or likes—the exuberant complexity of his color, glass, stone, and steel, the exotic mash-up of abstract and figurative styles. Whatever Gaudí's mixture of Gothic and art nouveau was called, by the time of his death it had fallen out of favor. *Neucentisme*, a specifically Catalan form of modernism, rejected Gaudí's ornate figurative style. Picasso detested Gaudí's work while George Orwell described the Sagrada Família as "one of the most hideous buildings in the world." Gerald Brenan, a great writer on Spanish culture, observed, "Not even in the European architecture of the period can one discover anything quite so vulgar and pretentious."[2] Postwar buildings like Mies van der Rohe's Seagram Building, the Matisse chapel in Vence, France, and Basil

Spence's Coventry Cathedral articulated a confident, technological future, not the remnants of an unfinished nineteenth-century church designed before cars and electric light.

Only Gaudí's disciples and supporters kept the work alive. By the 1950s, fund-raising and sculptural work started to gain some momentum. An archive and small museum brought together what remained of notes and plans. By the 1960s, the site began to attract curious visitors. But in 1965, such persistence also drew more ire from young intellectuals and architects, including Joan Miró, Alvar Aalto, and Le Corbusier. If the cathedral was Gaudí's great work of art, how could it be completed by other artists whose interpretation of his intentions was so subjective?

Little money. No critical support. Gaudí was dead, his style was dead, the building had no future. Only the city's deep identification with the Sagrada Família eked out resources sufficient to keeping the construction alive. The chief architect, Francesc de Paula Quintana, continued his work until he died in 1966, aged seventy-four. But then slowly the outlook changed. After the death of Franco, Spain began to open up to tourism. Gaudí's unexpected motifs of trees, flowers, foliage, fruits, turtles, birds, and signs of the zodiac thrilled visitors. When the Olympics came to Barcelona in 1992, more than a hundred nationalities visited the basilica and went home exclaiming over the crazed, hallucinogenic use of color and geometry. Charging for admission meant that, for the first time, it wasn't just the citizens of Barcelona who would pay for the church to be built. Now the whole world did. The original guiding ambition of the project had expanded. What had once been a local expression of devotion to the Holy Family as a symbol of shared humanity was now seen around the world as a potent articulation of the universal capacity to endure and adapt.

Gaudí's designs were not just visually startling. They depended on extreme manipulations of geometry: paraboloids, hyperboloids, and helicoids, often combined at a level of complexity that can't be seen by the naked eye. It's hard to imagine how, in the nineteenth century, the building could ever have been finished. But by 1980, a miracle arrived in the shape of computer-aided design. This new technology—of a kind Gaudí could never have foreseen—made the 3-D mapping of each part of the building easier and faster. Laser cutting, computing, and automation all accelerated the work of growing teams of engineers and builders. Money, resources, technology: for the first time in its history, the Sagrada Família started to make the transition from chimera to reality and in 2010, the basilica was finally consecrated.

At the beginning of the twenty-first century, more than two million people visited the cathedral, attracted in part by the unique opportunity to see a cathedral taking shape before their eyes. With income of 50 million euro a year, the project also became a company with a staff of a thousand people led by Chief Executive Xavier Martinez I Perez. But still new, unimagined problems arose. While annual tourist revenue provided the project with ample funding, the sixteen thousand visitors a day meant that construction couldn't continue safely. Stop the tourists—no money for the construction. Stop the building work—the building is never finished and tourists dry up. Stopping the weekly mass wasn't an option; worship was what the building was for. Once again, the Sagrada Família seemed impossible.

But Martinez, like CERN's Marzio Nessi, takes impossibility in his stride. Driven by his passionate commitment to the power of this church, he scoured the world looking for answers and identified one firm capable of solving his problem. In the City of London, a site for a new skyscraper nicknamed "The Cheesegrater" had been so tightly hemmed in by existing buildings that the building had to be constructed off-site, then disassembled, trucked in piece by piece overnight, and reassembled. The engineers who had pioneered this form of construction worked for Arup, a company famous for its stated ambition of only working on projects that matter. After a hundred years of dogged devotion, there was no doubt in anyone's mind that the Sagrada Família mattered.

The business operation that manages the project is housed in a conventional office that is far from Gaudíesque: stark white walls, modern steel furniture, rows of desks and computers. Martinez's office is ordinary, too, except, perhaps, for the crucifix on his wall. To him has fallen the challenge and, in his eyes, the rare gift of finally being able to promise a completion date for the church: 2026, one hundred years after Gaudí's death. After all the vicissitudes of its constructions, was he confident that now it can finally be finished?

"Oh sure," he said, putting quote marks around his words and laughing. "Sure" is not a word readily associated with this project. Completing the building by 2026 will require a few more miracles. The foundations of Villar's original church were designed for a building 70 meters high—but Gaudí's design called for a height of 172.5 metres. Reinforcing the foundations will help but won't solve the problem entirely. Instead, the towers have to be much lighter, their thickness reduced from two meters to just 300 millimeters, using materials that didn't exist when Gaudí was alive. Out of town, the construction site, where the new pieces of the cathedral are made, looks more like a car production line than a church. It is here that workmen rehearse assembling the additions so that, when the parts are trucked into the city, adding them to the cathedral is quick and safe. Mixing modern materials with traditional craftsmanship has demanded huge flexibility in everyone's thinking. For the most part, the crew is optimistic that the building will be completed by 2026. But one sandy-haired engineer, Esteve Umbert, acknowledged that after such a long and troubled past, nothing is guaranteed.

"It is really a challenge but you never know," he said, smiling. "The story can always change. But you fall in love with the challenge. There's meaning in the work. My work will be there for hundreds of years. . . ."

As 2026 approaches, uncertainty recedes but doesn't disappear completely; Catalonian politics or world events could still throw the work off schedule. What happens after the building is complete? The cathedral lives on and CEO Martinez will be fifty-seven. But most of his workforce won't be needed anymore and Martinez will have to manage the winding down of the organization he created.

"To do well the things that matter, that is my job. That is enough," Martinez said. "You know, our local business school, IESE, ran an executive program, spending a week in the U.S., visiting Amazon, Google, Microsoft. And then they visited this. There was a lot more to explain here! Values. Sticking to Gaudí's values. At Microsoft, it is the bottom line that pushes things. If I were a manager there or Google, my main preoccupation would be my salary. At Sagrada Família, that isn't important. What is important for us is a higher idea. We need self-discipline. We need self-criticism. We need to do whatever we do better always. That's what we worry about."

Cathedral projects start big and grow in the face of uncertainty and complexity. Their huge ambition keeps people humble, eager to measure up to the guiding principles that inspire them. For everyone building the Sagrada Família, that humility includes accepting that, eventually, they won't be needed. After 2026, Martinez will no longer decide how the cathedral's funds are spent; that job will transfer to the bishop. Restoration will always absorb a lot—but where will the rest go? The people of Barcelona and the people of the world feel that they own this church, that they have sustained it all this time. This will be another test for the project: whether it can maintain its legitimacy into the future, when it is no longer the work of the people. There are no guarantees.

Nobody I met who runs a modern cathedral project takes their longevity for granted. They have never attempted to "future-proof" them and most find the idea absurd. Instead, they've had the courage to contemplate how, if, or when their project might end. When CERN announced that the new Collider will cost $28 billion, many asked whether that money would be better spent on the more immediate threat of climate change. Chris Llewellyn Smith, who even in retirement still loves CERN, doesn't believe it has an indefinite right to exist. It should last, he thought, only as long as there are big questions it could answer. He'd often debated with his colleagues when they would know if high-energy physics was finished as a worthwhile field to work in. He believed that would be only when it ceased to attract first-class minds, but his colleague Murray Gell-Mann thought it would be when the science became predictable. The two were really agreeing with each other: that the field will no longer matter when it isn't complex, ambiguous, uncertain, or difficult enough.

At the Sanger Institute, Julia Wilson and her colleagues contemplate sequencing the genome of every living thing on the planet, a scientific odyssey that may hold the key to life on earth. But that will only be feasible if man's life on the planet becomes sustainable and if the public retains its faith in the institute's research as a public good. If the public grows cynical or angry about the uses to which genetic research is put, the institute could die. The Sagrada Família will always be an exciting architectural novelty but for it to remain meaningful to people around the world requires that it find a new role for itself that garners as much public devotion and support as when it was an unfinished freak.

Cathedral projects are all voyages of discovery in uncharted territory. What they find, in the people who make them and the distance they cover, is unpredictable at the outset. They conform to Popper's concept of what makes the future: new knowledge. Not just the intellectual discoveries of CERN and Sanger, but the engineering and social discoveries that propel the Sagrada Família toward completion. What keeps them on course is shared, passionate commitment to the guiding ambition that demands that the best be allowed to emerge and be improved, by anyone, from anywhere. Starting with ambition, they regard outcomes only as landmarks showing how far they've come. They map the future not by trying to preempt or co-opt it, but by believing in it, being ready to explore and map whatever awaits finding. With aspirations too great for an end date, they sustain people by making them feel big, important, doing work that lasts. In all of this, they stand in startling contrast to many conventional institutions.

It has been fashionable in recent years to talk of the need to adopt a purpose: something akin to a guiding ambition, which defines what an organization does and stands for. The speed with which the word "purpose" has been adopted speaks volumes about just how purposeless much work feels now. When 181 business leaders, representing 30 percent of the U.S. market's capitalization, signed a statement asserting that the purpose of all companies was to "promote an economy that serves all Americans," many applauded a broader and longer-term vision for business.[3] A deliberate departure from Milton Friedman's belief that companies serve shareholders alone, the statement challenged business leaders to articulate their purpose and their means of serving it. Harvard business academics rushed to demonstrate that serving a broader purpose was great for growth and profits, too; shareholders could have their cake and eat it. But even the proponents of the statement were wary, wondering whether, a year hence, any company would have made meaningful changes. In the same week that the chairman and CEO of Johnson & Johnson, Alex Gorsky, signed the statement, his company was ordered to pay a $572 million fine for the company's role in opiate addiction in Oklahoma, suggesting that serving all Americans remained a distant goal, rather than an active guiding principle. And in an era of climate change, that the purpose served only Americans seemed out of sync with globalization, epidemics, and the world's weather systems. Will purpose statements turn into another vague management fad? Most are meaningless, lathered on top of old values statements and mission statements without any substantive change in power structures or decision-making. What the debate around corporate purpose most clearly articulates is how far organizations struggle to define or articulate a meaningful role for themselves in the larger world that they inhabit, and on which they depend.

The success and endurance of cathedral projects contain provocative lessons for more conventional organizations. These seem to shrink in the face of uncertainty and ambiguity, where cathedral projects expand their range and domain. Where companies typically plan from where they are, cathedrals are driven and defined by an ambitious end goal that may never be reached. Moving toward that goal is always experimental. That they are wildly long term from the outset gives them coherence even through turbulence; however much day-to-day decisions may change, everyone knows what they stand for, year after year. This lends them a legitimacy that must be preserved, but not originated, by each successive generation. Stability isn't achieved by short-term promises but long-term, unwavering vision. That the goals aren't designed to be achieved in a quarter, a year, a lifetime gives the work meaning over time, in stark contrast to the ever-receding lifetime of a public corporation. By contrast with corporations that struggle with low levels of employee engagement, cathedral projects attract brilliant minds by refusing to constrain their ambition and by the sheer difficulty of the work. The scale of their aspiration ensures that, instead of being passive victims of the future, they are actively involved in making it.

True cathedral projects can sustain such ambition because they are so broad: in their base of support, in the number and diversity of people and ideas that they bring together, in the number of experiments they contain. In doing that, they create and sustain the legitimacy that allows them to endure. Lose that and they're finished: anachronisms or pariahs that will dwindle and die. They remain public goods only as long as the public says so. In this, they are profoundly democratic.

Does that imply that democracy, too, is a cathedral project, one in which all of us are involved? Constructed over centuries, radical in conception, daring in ambition, sustained only by those who continue to believe in it. What we know of such projects is that, to endure, they require enormous openness to new ideas, a broad base of support, the ability to adapt and to change, a willingness to experiment, and to be febrile in their responsiveness to the unforeseen and unpredictable. Without that, they have no future. But with it, they may last for millennia.

PART III

LIFE HAPPENS

CHAPTER EIGHT

SIMPLE, NOT EASY

If you dare nothing, you can change nothing.

—Olga Neuwirth

When the future arrives without warning, we are shocked into a crisis: of identity or endurance or survival. Such moments are, by definition, unpredictable—but what does it take to survive them? What resources—ways of thinking, of seeing, of connecting—provide robustness, the better chance of survival? In the middle of such crises, what do we see that we *should* have done, the resources we could have developed, the observations we wish we had made time for: these emerge with clarity. We might accumulate many of those advantages ahead of time, if we knew what they were.

Existential crises occur in private agonies of choice, in the volatility of large corporations, in the tragedy of global pandemics. If we're lucky, we watch from the sidelines, hoping that these won't be our future. But when the future collides with the present, what will we want and what will we need to endure?

Zeitgeist

Most funerals double as family reunions. This one was no different: three generations, in London to pay respects to Aunt Nonie, who'd always been a little difficult. Afterward, we gathered in her home to eat, drink, and gossip. As usual, Father John was the center of attention: such a privilege having a handsome young priest in the family, providing a personal sendoff.

As the attention died down, John sought me out. "Have you got a minute? Let's step outside." We went out onto the street, a mild day. The same generation, he had officiated at my wedding when I married his cousin. He conducted my husband's funeral, too. Fond of each other, it seemed that John and I met only at life-changing events.

"When are you heading back to Waterford?" I asked.

But John hadn't traveled, as I'd thought, from Ireland. He had come from Stroud, a Catholic retreat house in the English country-side, mostly used to patch up alcoholics and pedophiles. Ostensibly he was there to rest and recuperate from stress and overwork. In fact, he'd been sent to Stroud because he had fallen in love and now had to choose: the church or Mary.

In theory, John was married to the church. When he had been ordained, his mother had cut the cake with him. For a poor Tipperary family to produce a graduate from the leading seminary in Ireland was a triumph. It wasn't just his doting mother who thought so. Everyone recognized John's talents: capable of organizing anything, good with finances, wonderful with people. The Catholic Church was on the lookout for men with his finesse and authority. He was sure to make bishop. "I don't even remember it being a choice," he told me later. "It just seemed my life was sorted. I was idealistic, it felt like I could contribute to society, but what really drew me in was the certainty."

Celibacy hadn't seemed like a big deal at the time, not compared to the opportunities that would open up for him. In seminary at Maynooth, it had felt like the church was changing, losing its old rigidity, flattening the hierarchy, embracing community and the poor. Liberation theology, a new church for the poor, gave the church a fresh dynamism; that the institution was changing was a big part of its attraction. As a student, John had been sent to live in a rural village, with instructions to learn everything about the hopes and needs of the people he would serve. Education, homelessness, marriage: as social servant, the church was central to all the issues of the day and John was inspired at Maynooth by the intellectual, social, and spiritual challenges he would face.

By the age of twenty-five, he was running a parish and life was heady; living in a freezing old rambling house, serving Mass, teaching science and religion, he had two full-time jobs but more than enough energy for both. Working with groups of young people, or with isolated rural families, John developed a passion for conversation, exploration, the bonding needed to be helpful. He had no real interest in power or status; the daily pomp of ritual wasn't what excited him. Where his more conservative colleagues defined their job as the dispensation of sacraments, John was fired up by helping his community find in their lives something that deserved celebration.

By 1982, John was in another big old, cold house, this time in the center of Waterford. As youth director for the diocese, he was seen as a radical: meeting young people in coffee shops, talking to them about what they wanted from the world and from their church. He was popular, unstuffy, accessible. If asked, he'd talk about birth control, about inevitable stresses in married life. Local radio and newspapers adored the charismatic priest while young people found him easy to talk to because, well, he was young, too. He was changing—but now the church was not.

Over the next few years, advising couples preparing for marriage, he started to wonder: What did he know about relationships, having never had one? Talking about contraception, he felt a fraud: What did he know about sex? It was grand hanging out with his contemporaries, going to parties, and blending in at dances but the job inserted distance between them: he was expected to have authority in areas where he felt he had none. He took to going around town in mufti, uncomfortable in the clerical dress that seemed to flaunt power. One of his colleagues told him he was a disgrace and he was stopped from doing youth work. He made it his business to visit the rougher parts of town, to get to know who lived there and how. When a girl was raped and he went straight over, eyebrows were raised—eyebrows, John felt, that would have remained unperturbed had she been a middle-class girl.

"I had nothing to offer apart from human kindness," John later recalled. "But just my being there, people were amazed: the church would do that for us? *That* was our job: to challenge the comfortable, to comfort the challenged. They had everything to say to the church but the church had absolutely nothing to say to them. I started to feel I didn't want to represent an old, oppressive institution."

People came from miles around to hear his sermons and he wanted to bring his struggles to walk alongside them. But that wasn't what the church mandated. With no institutional support, and no personal allies, the work became exhausting, lonely, and confusing. He was getting burned out.

What support John got didn't come from the church but from the people he supposed himself to be helping. He was learning more from his contemporaries than from his colleagues, from doctrine or liturgy. As the group started to divide into pairs, John spent more and more time with Mary. She'd heard about John—"the cool priest in the next parish"—and, together with friends, they went to dances, parties, out on walks together. Mary worked thirty miles away, in a jewelry store in Dungarvon. She hated her job, despised her bully boss, but the economy was rotten and there was nowhere else to go. Today Mary says that she had a reputation for being so sensible and down-to-earth that nobody imagined anything could be going on—although soon something was.

In a village where everyone knew everything about John, including what he ate for breakfast, privacy was impossible. He and Mary could be seen in the company of friends, but never alone. Living thirty miles apart in an age before mobile phones, every meeting was difficult and risky. They had to be, John said, "unbelievably covert."

"We had a few holidays together," Mary recalled. "The Isle of Man for two weeks—*nobody* goes there for that long!" It sounded funny but it was agonizing: the sense that everyone was watching, ready to judge. The strain was so great on Mary that she quit her job and became unemployed. Neither had any support because no one knew. John had given his life, his faith, his identity to the church. If he wasn't a priest, who was he?

"Towards the end, I couldn't preach," John recalled. "I couldn't stand physically at the altar. I just rattled off a few words and collapsed. I couldn't do the job anymore."

After John told his bishop about Mary, he was dispatched to Stroud. The time was supposed to be for healing but for six months, surrounded by alcoholics and pedophiles, never allowed out alone, and forbidden any communication, it was clear that the church hoped to brainwash him into returning. Before going, he and Mary had made no promises to one another. Both were adamant that whatever choices each made had to be freely on his or her own terms, not burdening the other with baggage. So, at this point in their young lives, John and Mary had nothing. They didn't have each other; they had no jobs, little money, no home of their own.

Mary says she did a lot of what she describes as "angst walking" in the Irish countryside; thinking, alone, in silence. She had faith in John but did not know what he would decide. All she could do was wait. No one to talk to, no comfort, full of doubt and questions, nothing about Mary's life felt romantic. John knew something had

to give—but what? For both, pain, exhaustion, and loneliness con-
verged on a single question: What would you do if you were free?

Staying in the church offered John certainty: a secure career, a
home, the solid backing of the institution, and the adoration and
support of his family. But the price would be high. He would have
to move far from Mary; it would be unbearable to live in the same
town, seeing her every day. He had seen such priests: adrift, their
surrender looked a kind of death. On the other hand, if he left the
church, he would lose everything: career, financial security, public
respect, the love of his own family, his identity.

"At Stroud, they asked me when I would stop celebrating Mass,"
John said. "The question startled me; I had been thinking about
moving away from the church but I hadn't begun to think about
becoming a layperson." He was starting to ask himself who he was,
independent of the institution of the church. Never mind John the
priest, who was John?

When news of Nonie's death came through, the church refused
John permission to attend her funeral. But John replied: either you
let me go or I'm out altogether. He was starting to act like a free
man and, by the time they conceded, his mind was made up. The
mass I witnessed was the last John would ever celebrate.

Standing in the London street, leaning against a parked car as he
told me the story, John became self-conscious, aware that we had
been talking for a long time. Would people inside start to notice?
Hyperalert to gossip, his new self was so new, so raw, he didn't know
how to wear it. What would he do now? He'd need somewhere to
stay, somewhere he and Mary could be together. I said they could
come and stay with me for as long as they liked. Recently widowed,
I had a big empty house and more than a little sympathy for people
trying to forge new lives.

In the end, John said, it all became clear: if he looked for guarantees, he'd be lost. With Mary he had the chance of his own life,
with the church he had none. If the church wouldn't let go of the

past, he had to: to act for himself, not as the agent of an institution. However risky that future looked, it offered more possibility than the certainty that trapped him now.

The worst part, he told me later, was telling his mother. "Her whole edifice collapsed." Her identity, her status in her village, her entire life were absorbed in John's identity as a priest in the diocese. She became suicidal and refused ever to see Mary.

John and Mary spent days talking and walking the streets of London. They decided to move to Dublin, live apart, and see what became of their relationship. But even with just a few pounds and nowhere to stay but a friend's couch, John felt liberated. When he and Mary finally decided to get married, he was unemployed and penniless. A church wedding was forbidden and, though invitations were sent, neither John's parents nor his sister replied; only his brother-in-law risked family opprobrium by attending. It would be twenty-five years before they were all reconciled.

Working as a counselor with women who had been victims of domestic violence, John's role was to ease them back into being able to talk to men. He came to see that having been excluded from society was what made the women trust him. He didn't need the church to make an impact. As he built a new life for himself, the church was losing everything: respect, decency, power. Celibacy came to be seen as a problem, not a virtue. The scandal of pedophilia, of buried babies and punitive orphanages, along with the growing number of priests leaving the institution meant that the church came to be seen as John had seen it: remote, out of touch, too caught up in its rituals and status to serve its community. Over time, John came to be seen not as a rebel but as a trailblazer. Many now saw what he had felt: that the church was mired in the past, unable to adapt to a future it refused to see or comprehend.

"I'm so thrilled you got out of that old dungeon you'd been in" is how one parishioner put it. Old friends were delighted for them—for the escape they'd made, the freedom they found, the joy they radiated. John found many ways to be useful, in social work and, after the banking collapse in 2008, deploying his financial skills to guide the poor and debt-laden through a grueling crisis. After many years, even his mother forgave him. Today he is working on a PhD about artificial intelligence and ethics, concerned as ever by the difficulty of independent thought.

What was it that allowed John to survive his crisis? He liked change and was good at it. The dynamism of the church had attracted him to it; when it stopped changing he withdrew. Exposure to so many young lives and difficult questions kept him in touch with how his world was changing, and its institutions failing. Picking up weak signals made him ask hard questions about what he saw, becoming uncomfortable when the answers proved inadequate. Thinking like an artist, he kept sifting through all his conversations and conflicts, trying to glean what was happening around him and what it might mean. He might have, as so many did, delegated responsibility to the church, trusting it to know what was best for him. But he didn't let the most powerful institution in the country, its power, or its promises distract him from thinking like a free man.

This might seem easy, even inevitable, but it isn't. Sherron Watkins, famed as the whistleblower of Enron, once said that she knew many of her colleagues were uncomfortable with the accelerating fiction of the company's business model. They all started drinking too much, overeating, their humor becoming disquietingly unfunny. They all knew, she concluded, that something was wrong. But the company was so rich, the rewards so great, they didn't want to listen to the nagging voices in their heads. It's such a common story: that sense that something is badly wrong, but it is so much easier to ignore all the weak signals, leaving it to others to determine your future.

But John paid attention. In doing so, he refused to inhabit a role that had been defined for him by others. Instead he insisted that he alone—not his family or any institution—had the right to determine who he was and what he should do. Existential crises are intense experiences of free will, the possibility of choice. The way John puts it is simple: action is how you search. Giving up the need for certainty gave him the freedom to discover. John and Mary's story bears an uncanny resemblance to the narratives of abused women, runaway slaves, refugees, of anyone forced to flee for their lives: the absolute certainty that the only possibility of safety lies in choosing danger. Only if you concede that someone else owns your future are you truly trapped.

More than Money

Companies have existential crises, too: defining moments when, if they aren't to die, they must forge a new future for themselves. The mythology of this moment follows a hyperbolic narrative: long-term willful blindness to creeping failure puts the organization in jeopardy. It teeters on the brink until a heroic guy (almost invariably, a guy) rides into town and single-handedly saves the day. Heads roll, weaklings are thrown overboard, ruthless cost cutting and savage deal-making deliver victory. The hackneyed simplicity of the story implicitly casts the old guard as idiots and the hero as a genius technocrat, slaying bureaucratic dragons with inspirational bravura.

The reality is more complex and subtle. It is also more emotional. When great old companies fail, grown men weep: at their folly and weakness, at the loss of reputation and legacy, at the end of an institution's history. Their tears acknowledge that companies are more than buildings and balance sheets; they are living organisms containing personal dreams. When businesses die, personal hopes go with them.

One of the most radical corporate reinventions in recent times has been the reincarnation of Nokia. Once the world's dominant designer and producer of mobile phones, in the 1990s and early

2000s, the company had transformed what had been a luxury item for high-paid executives into a must-have for every consumer in the world. The first company to put cameras into phones, a pioneer of tablets and mobile games, for many Nokia was all anyone knew about Finland, where the company's revenues represented 4 percent of the nation's GDP. The company made as much money as all the country's other companies combined.

Contrary to Silicon Valley mythology, the launch of the iPhone in 2007 did not spell an inevitable end for Nokia. Comparing Apple's invention with the Nokia smartphone N95, reviewers dissed the newcomer, lauding the incumbent. In the first quarter of 2008 Nokia shipped 115 million phones, compared to a mere 1.7 million devices from Apple. It didn't even look like a contest. But when the Android operating system launched later that year, the market changed and accelerated. Endemic demons started to surface: weaknesses in Nokia's Symbian operating system made it too hard and slow to update, the phones were so rugged that the touch screen almost needed a hammer. These problems weren't secrets, but the company's culture was so polite and hierarchical that nobody talked about them. The huge global coverage of Nokia—in 140 countries—became a burden, as it made design permutations too complex. What had been assets became liabilities: the technology, the culture, the management structure. Each new product came to the market too late and it began to look as though the company was caught in a death spiral.

Toward the end of 2009, McKinsey's Organizational Health Index—comparing Nokia to thousands of other companies—placed it in the bottom 25th percentile. McKinsey predicted that any company at this level would cease trading within two years. In desperation, the board did what so many businesses do: prayed for a savior CEO. In 2010, they appointed Stephen Elop, an executive from Microsoft who became the first non-Finn to run the 150-year-old company. His famous memo made it clear where the company now stood: "We've poured gasoline on our own burning platform. We have lacked accountability and leadership to align and direct the company through these disruptive times. We haven't been delivering innovation fast enough. We're not collaborating internally. . . ."[1]

Knowing you are in a crisis is essential to surviving one. But it's rarely enough. Plenty of companies (Sharper Image, Washington Mutual, Lehman Brothers, Toys "R" Us) have been incinerated on their platforms. Routine responses—layoffs, cost cutting, exhortations to work harder—breed cynicism, division, and contempt. To define a future no one can see yet requires radical imagination. When time is tight and money is running out, a company can't afford binary choices; it needs lots of options. But under pressure, thinking typically becomes even more constrained and hackneyed, rigid with fear. In its new chairman, Nokia got lucky. Risto Siilasmaa was, by background and mind-set, an entrepreneur, accustomed to risk and to thinking freely for himself. As a board member, he had chafed for four years at the company's formality and complacency. Now he had a license to challenge.

What distinguished his approach was that, at a time when focus typically narrows, Siilasmaa was prepared to go broad. Instead of trying to cut his way to prosperity, Siilasmaa cajoled, encouraged, nagged, and berated board members and employees to question everything. No sacred cows. No hostages to fortune. No deference. He conducted what now looks like scenario planning on speed: multiple plans, diverse configurations of a new Nokia. When you know you can't afford to stop, he said, it's much easier to keep going.

The idea of constructing and testing out a variety of scenarios seems obvious, but in a crisis, most companies work frantically to construct a single, perfect plan. (Governments often do likewise.) Overwhelmed by complexity, they shrink their options just when they need to expand them.

What surprised Siilasmaa was that thinking together helped everyone trust each other more. When you feel you are being listened to, he observed, you appreciate your listener. It was a great way for executives and the board to learn and to search, a fast and transformative way to get a deeper, richer contribution from everyone. Refusing to trust that any one plan would prove perfect, they kept recombining different pieces of the puzzle until, by 2013, the company found a first step: selling the handset business to Microsoft would buy the company time. Siilasmaa's quiet, consultative style even persuaded Microsoft's famously incandescent Steve Ballmer to negotiate in good faith.

At no point did Siilasmaa think about Nokia as just a financial entity. The company contained huge meaning for employees, business partners, customers, and the Finnish nation as a whole, all proud of a business that had pioneered one of the coolest technologies of their lifetime. Nokia's crisis could not be solved by compromising standards, only by rising to them. The company's "Bridge program" wasn't a typical corporate euphemism for laying people off; it offered training for new jobs, money for a new education, backing for entrepreneurial ventures, or help finding work with a new company. The way in which their colleagues had been treated built trust and energy among those who remained.

When the Microsoft deal was done, many in the company cried. But the crisis wasn't over. What was to become of the company's remaining, strategically incoherent assets? Again, Siilasmaa and his team searched for multiple configurations for a new company until finally in 2016, with the acquisition of Alcatel-Lucent, Nokia emerged as one of the top three telecom infrastructure businesses in the world. Today, whenever you send a bit into the Internet, it goes through Nokia equipment or software somewhere along the way.[2] As such, it is one of the very few non-Chinese makers of Internet infrastructure.

The Nokia story isn't a neat melodrama of death and resurrection. As perhaps befits a nation famous for taciturn stoicism, it is a story of hard grind and nerdy negotiation delivered with patience and trepidation by thousands of individuals for whom the company is more than a job and their colleagues more than economic units of production. That the company had a tradition of reinvention may have helped: it had started as a lumber mill in 1865, became a power generator, then a manufacturer of electrical cables, rubber boots, and power supplies. The company's legacy is all around change, adaptation, and reinvention. Looking for an image to represent the company's future, it's no wonder Siilasmaa points to a blank whiteboard.

Wildly creative strategic thinking, being prepared to consider anything, was essential to Nokia's survival. But it wasn't sufficient. As important in generating that open exchange of ideas was the relationship between company leaders. Although Siilasmaa had been critical of Nokia's board in the beginning, over time he came to see how much they cared about the business. And as they labored together to save it, what had been formal relationships deepened. On one level, what enabled Nokia to survive was the emotional commitment its leaders made to each other. "In business," Siilasmaa said, "we forget that we are human. Many strong leaders think they should not be friends with their colleagues. I disagree. Business is emotional. I like to be friends with my colleagues. You get through a crisis because you care so much."

"The way I used to think was: hc who cares wins," Paul Matthews said. He was working at Standard Life when, overnight, the deputy CEO learned that what had appeared to be the insurance company's £9 billion surplus was, in fact, a £1 billion shortfall. Millions of insurance policies—on lives, houses, and pensions—were underfunded. Once the CEO had been fired, everything about the business had to change. The crisis was exacerbated by the Standard Life business model, which paid high commissions to financial advisors who acted as their agents, selling its policies to consumers. To save the business required ending those commissions and persuading the advisors to earn their income from fees paid by clients—something that, at the time, nobody in the industry did.

Matthews and his team needed to go to every financial advisor and explain what had happened and why the business model had to change. This could have a devastating impact on the advisors' own business: anyone who had sold SL products to a thousand clients could find all their income wiped out at a stroke. It was, Matthews said, a horrible experience.

Everyone in the industry insisted that selling products without commission was impossible, but Matthews and his team took years proving it could be done. The work was emotionally and physically taxing: absorbing the stress and anguish of his workforce, who were themselves absorbing anxiety and rage from their customers. Matthews was clearly great at motivating his team—but through a marathon of abuse and apology, what kept him going?

"Longevity matters," Matthews reflected. "I was inspired by the people around me. When people have worked with you for a long time, they know you and trust you—and when you're in a crisis, you've got that!" It was, he added, "pretty much the opposite of the gig economy."

Forced to be creative, the company found a way to sell insurance without commission via financial advisors who charged for their work, just as any lawyer, dentist, or accountant would. When, in 2008, the banking crises revealed just how corrupt and perverse commission structures had become, financial regulators insisted that the entire industry move to this new way of working. Standard Life was already there.

Everyone I've spoken to about this period describes it with amazing energy. In such moments, leadership can get simpler, the sense of urgency shared and pervasive. But more than a few companies dissolve at this point, too, when low levels of social capital surface all the lurking demons of rivalry, fear, blame, suspicion. Matthews is right; longevity does count, because teams grow stronger over time, more loyal to one another, more open, more trustworthy, and more robust. Gig economies, by contrast, make complex systems more fragile; their very efficiency means there is nothing—no trust, no solidarity—to fall back on. But going into a crisis with high levels of trust and solidarity provides an advantage that can't be manufactured in the moment.[3]

History can be an asset, too, not because it repeats itself but because it sets standards and makes people feel that they belong to something more meaningful than a temporary gig. Like cathedrals, old firms have meaning, if they can articulate it. Alan Mulally found this when heading up Ford during the financial crisis. Spending weekends in company archives, he sought out imagery and stories connecting the resilience of the company's past with the demands of the future. During the banking crisis, Joe Garner, then CEO of HSBC UK, drew inspiration from the bank's wartime history when the bank's general manager set up supply lines to get money and food to prison camps. Similarly, when a rogue trader brought down Barings Bank in 1995, the history of survival was the first note of the crisis.

"Eighteen ninety. It's happened again."

This might sound like code but to the corporate lawyer, Nicholas Gold, the meaning was clear. The Barings Bank Panic of 1890, a moment when Argentinian debt had nearly triggered a global financial meltdown, was legendary. That such a thing could have happened again seemed inconceivable, but when Gold joined the meeting of directors, he learned that the bank had lost all but £10,000. The chairman, Peter Baring, sat in disbelief repeating: "This cannot be happening. This cannot be happening."

Gold says that crises are what he's good at. His entire career had been spent advising executives under pressure: pursuing a takeover or under threat from one. The previous year, his part of the business—Barings Corporate Finance—had been rated the best advisory business in the city of London: ahead of Goldman Sachs, ahead of Warburg. Gold was proud of the team's reputation and determined to protect it. He was instantly pragmatic. At work on Glaxo's hostile bid for Wellcome, he knew his client's work, on completion, would bring the bank £10.5 million. Whatever else happened, that money could buy time. The trading division of the bank might be in disarray but corporate finance would stay productive.

Over a weekend, ideas came in from everywhere. Barings was a venerable name in the industry and bankers hoped to save it. Would the Bank of England step in, as it had done before? What about the Bank of Japan? Could the other banks chip in to cover Barings's losses and keep it afloat? Could the charitable Barings Foundation take over the commercial bank? Tommy Suharto, the son of the president of Indonesia, owned $17 billion worth of platinum; perhaps that could be used as collateral to recapitalize the bank. The most promising scenario proposed a former customer, the Sultan of Brunei, might be able to help, but the Bank of England would still need to guarantee the deal.

By the end of a long weekend, all the ideas had failed. The Bank of England wouldn't step in; the other banks couldn't contribute enough. Suharto wasn't up for the challenge. To put a charity in charge of a bank would make it impossible to operate. At 8:36 p.m., news came that the Sultan of Brunei had decided not to proceed. At 9 p.m. the news echoed across the trading floor: Barings had collapsed. CEO Peter Norris wept.

Only two options remained: to go into administration or to sell the bank. But laden with debt, what was there to buy? All the debt was on the trading side of the bank; all the value lay in corporate finance—but only if the team stayed. They could all have gotten jobs elsewhere but Gold says there wasn't a moment's hesitation, because the way they had worked at Barings was so different. "It was human and humane. And we wanted to keep it that way."

In the end, Barings was sold to a small, unknown Dutch bank called ING, for £1 and a billion pounds of debt. The trading side of Barings fell apart but corporate finance survived. The following year, they were, once more, named the top advisory business in the city. Gold remained until his retirement fourteen years later.

When asked how had he managed to weather such an immense crisis and stay so cool, he laughed, always uncomfortable with praise, demurring to the quality of his colleagues. Having lunch together every day, he thought, kept them united. And he identified another source of strength: he had always operated on the basis that anything could end tomorrow. So he lived on his salary, never spending his bonus. Not depending on the bank kept him clearheaded about what was at stake—the bank itself, not his own personal financial security. It's the only way, he said, not to muddle what might be best for the institution with what might be advantageous for you. But headhunters are notorious for circling the minute news of any crisis breaks. What had kept the team together? Gold laughed again, remembering how everyone had run rings around recruiters. "We wanted to work together. We loved Barings. We just loved it. . . ."

Nokia, Standard Life, and Barings survived because they meant something to the people who worked in them. They stood for something—innovation, endurance, fair honesty—that mattered enough to draw from their workforce qualities of endurance, creativity, and determination. With a real passion for the place and the people in it, they worked for more than money.

It's often said of business that, in a crisis, cash is king. There's a brutal truth there: money buys time to craft a survival strategy. What it won't buy is the motivation people need to keep going, to endure humiliation, recrimination, anger, and grief. Only deep bonds, of trust and concern, built over time, will supply that. At Barings, Gold found that in the colleagues with whom he lunched every day. He also had one further resource. The day the news broke, after the strategizing, after the management meeting, his head reeling with work, he phoned his best friend. "I just had to talk to someone who would understand," he said. "Understand what it meant to me, this old place that had dignity, that had always been so careful. . . . It was the most shattering and emotional experience of my life."

Friendship is a topic rarely talked about in the upper echelons of business, but it should be. Nobody survives these crises alone. Survivors have friends: people not necessarily in the business but who know what it's like, what it means, people who have only their best interests at heart. Every successful business leader I've known or worked with has such friends and every one can describe the crises through which they've sustained each other. These relationships aren't transactional, they're not networking; some leaders refer to their friends as their "north star," others as the bridge between intellect and character. What gets people through crises and into the future is each other.

Yet recently, working with rising leaders of important organizations—high achievers from both public and private sectors—all conceded that they had few, or no, friends. They had had them. But now they were too busy. Lunch together? It was inefficient. Friendships had faded and time to think was rare. It left me wondering: Who will give us stamina and solidarity when the storms come?

Try Everything

In 1981, the CDC reported the occurrence of a rare cancer in otherwise healthy gay men and, even though just 180 cases were seen that year, the center declared the disease an epidemic. On July 4, 1982, Terrence Higgins was one of the first British men to die of the mysterious disease. He was just thirty-seven at the time. His friend Rupert Whitaker was also sick and had moved to London for treatment of what was assumed to be a weird form of cancer. He couldn't climb more than a flight of stairs and doctors didn't expect him to live more than a year. Higgins's death left him traumatized, puzzled, and angry. He didn't understand why Higgins had died in an isolation unit, or why the clinicians treating him wore full barrier clothing. Whitaker decided to become a doctor at least in part because, he says, "I couldn't get my head around the bizarreness of this disease. We just had no idea what had happened. . . . We just kept thinking: This is going to kill us. We are going to lose all the people we love. . . ."

Together with friends, Whitaker set up the Terrence Higgins Trust to support people dying from the mysterious disease. But how? The battle had too many fronts. The disease itself, which was unknown, undefined, and might be untreatable. Homophobia and public ignorance. Government prejudice and apathy. A scientific research establishment that was arrogant, remote, and slow. A health care system that was expensive and exclusive. Hospitals that turned away the dying and undertakers that turned away the dead. Politicians saw no advantage in helping a marginalized community and drug companies did nothing to respond to a disease nobody understood. The AIDS epidemic was so complex, its uncertainties so perfuse and so frightening, that it vividly illustrates the energy, creativity, and capacity to break barriers that crises demand. Such moments draw from people and institutions the most and the best that they offer, even when everyone wishes that these weren't required.

Crises are often said to provoke solidarity. But the gay community was not homogeneous. Some homosexuals believed in coming out; others stayed in the closet. Many aspired to conventional acceptance while others condemned assimilation as selling out. What consti- tuted normative sexual behavior became an incandescent, divisive question. Even in the face of death, such burning issues of identity defied unity. Add to them issues of race, class, and gender and the complexity of the community became paralyzing. The one thing everyone had in common was a sense of doom. "In all the history of homosexuality we have never before been so close to death and extinction," the playwright Larry Kramer declaimed.

The AIDS epidemic became a global existential crisis of a kind, and on a scale, that defied planning and prediction. No models showed how to attack such a vast, ambiguous, and diffuse enemy, no way even to map out a plan. Many activists were inspired by the anti-apartheid movement in South Africa. But that fight for the future had had structure: a single mission (dismantling apartheid), leaders (Mandela, Mbeki, Tambo), and a big, clear enemy (the all-white government). When companies face existential crises, at least their choices are stark: find the cash to keep going or find a buyer. But in the AIDS crisis, the gay community had no such clarity, no precedents, no plan.

In the second year of the epidemic, Kramer and five colleagues founded Gay Men's Health Crisis to raise money for research, disseminate information about the disease, and man a help line. In the United Kingdom, the Terrence Higgins Trust did similar work, building a buddy network to support people suffering from a disease that still had no name. The most these organizations could do was to share information and help people die well. "We had no road map at the beginning, no plan," Whitaker recalled. "We just had fear and love, grief—and the losses that were starting to happen very fast." In an existential crisis, you have no choice but to start where you are. Time is too precious to wait.

When Jonathan Blake, a young London actor, checked into the Middlesex Hospital, a biopsy revealed that he had HTLV3, which is what the disease was called at the time. It was a terminal diagnosis and he was sent home, not yet ill enough for palliative care. By December 1982, he'd decided to commit suicide. All that stopped him was his mother's mantra: you shouldn't leave others to clean up your mess. Isolated and afraid, any thought of his future remained paralyzed.

By the end of 1983, Luc Montagnier had isolated the HIV virus but still couldn't prove that it caused AIDS. No diagnostic test existed. And no treatment. In New York, Kramer grew increasingly frustrated by Gay Men's Health Crisis, thinking it had become too bureaucratic, too friendly with power, playing it safe in a dangerous world. The crisis was too urgent for conventional planning. ACT

UP was created in a deliberately different mold: no leadership, no bureaucracy, just ferocity. Its weekly meetings called for ideas to ratchet up demands for a cure. Anybody could join, there were no leaders, nothing was off-limits. The structurelessness of ACT UP was a strength, because it welcomed everyone with ideas. But it was a weakness, too, because those ideas represented no battle plan but outrage. "I often describe it as democratic to a fault," Larry Kramer recalled. "We were making it up as we went along. There were no rules."[4]

"ACT UP! FIGHT BACK! FIGHT AIDS!" Energy focused on massive, public provocations: an invasion of the New York Stock Exchange, obstruction of the post office on the day citizens filed their tax returns, a die-in at St. Patrick's Cathedral where activists played dead in the aisles to protest the church's perverse stance on condoms. These were brilliant, crazy, unforgettable public events that forced the public to pay attention to the young and old dying around them. As a young journalist, David France reported the rise of gay activism as he lived through the AIDS crisis, and as his partner was dying. "If we did nothing, we knew we'd die. That much was certain," France recalled. "ACT UP used to brag about saving lives—but they were just casting about like the rest of us. We had no idea what would work so we had to try anything. Everything. . . ."

Between 1983 and 1984, the number of AIDS cases and deaths in the United States more than doubled. In 1985, a test for the infection was finally available and the CDC estimated that more than a million people worldwide were infected. By 1986, just five years after the first reported death, Anthony Fauci at the National Institute of Allergy and Infectious Diseases estimated that a million Americans were infected and that, within five or ten years, the number would rise to three million. Meanwhile, the Reagan administration urged people not to worry since the disease was confined to gay men and intravenous drug users. Willful blindness prevailed.

Gay Men's Health Crisis and ACT UP fought over hard cop/soft cop tactics: Should they collaborate to get the establishment onside, or attack? Doctors couldn't agree about how or whether to treat people with AIDS. Scientists debated the most promising avenues of research; politicians fought over funding. Drug companies havered between hoping their existing drugs would find a new market and trying to decide whether to invest in new drug research. Every one of these communities needed to work together—but nobody had the power or authority to bring them together. This was complexity at its most lethal.

Developing new drugs could take decades—and still fail. At the time, drug approval, regulated by the Food and Drug Administration, took an average of seven to ten years. That was too long, so ACT UP invaded and shut down the FDA. This shamed them but it didn't produce any drugs. In desperation, members of the community started to experiment with their own treatments, some crazy, some dangerous, but none a cure. Chinese watermelon enemas, AL721 extracted from egg yolks, swallowing hydrogen peroxide. In London, thinking he'd be dead within a year, Rupert Whitaker tried injecting himself with proteins; with no treatment, why not experiment? The germ of an idea emerged: people with AIDS had to take an active role in finding a cure.

Into the tragic chaos walked Iris Long, a chemist and housewife. She wasn't gay, she was just interested in AIDS. That she would prove a linchpin in the fight against AIDS was completely unexpected. "This woman just shows up one day," Larry Kramer recalled, "this straight woman—and after a few meetings, she gets up and she says, 'You guys don't know shit.' And that's—in her nice way. And, 'I'll teach you.' And she did."

Long recognized that accelerating drug development would require that the activists force the FDA and the whole, complex ecosystem of science and medicine to involve people with AIDS in every level of their decision-making. That meant a radical institutional fight with bureaucrats and scientists. For the battle to be won required expertise; people with AIDS had to learn what drugs were being developed, how clinical trials operated, and how to get drugs into bodies fast. If people with AIDS didn't become as expert as the experts, they could always be patronized and marginalized and they would all die. An organization, a strategy of sorts, began to emerge. Attending one of his first ACT UP meetings, film archivist Mark Harrington listened as Long delivered a long, complex presentation about current treatments. He understood almost none of it. He wrote down every word he didn't know, looked it up, created a glossary, and distributed it to ACT UP. He became, in essence, a cultural translator for the group, enabling it to communicate with anyone about anything connected to AIDS.

By 1987, with nearly twenty thousand deaths in the United States, the new drug AZT became available for the first time. After five terrifying years, this was the first glimmer of wild, incredulous hope. ACT UP made it a principle never to recommend any treatment, merely to disseminate information, but they now had the expertise to provide a considered assessment. "One of our early successful actions was to force the NIH and the FDA to lower the dose of AZT," Harrington recalled."[5] For the first time, the medical establishment had taken activists seriously.

But academic researchers were fascinated by molecules, not suffering. Pharmaceutical companies weren't used to meeting the dying. Government institutions were authoritarian, arrogant, and unaccustomed to being held directly accountable to citizens. All were hostile: How dare these crazy, sick, gay people challenge their authority? A pattern started to emerge, too inchoate to call a plan: public actions of civil disobedience kept in the public mind that more than a hundred people a day were dying horribly of AIDS. Demonstrations in Washington, at the FDA, at scientific conferences, and in pharma companies hoped to shame medical institutions into change. And the citizen-scientists were learning where to intervene.

ACT UP collected data showing that there were more than forty new drugs ready for clinical trials. That seemed like good news. But, incredibly, thirty-nine of them had no people with AIDS enrolled in them. Only AZT, with its known problems, was being meaningfully tested, to refine dosages and identify when in the disease it was most effective. For people with AIDS, like Silvia Petretti, the pace was surreal, as though there were no crisis at all.

"I thought I had one, maybe two years left to live," Petretti recalled. A self-described "party girl," she had contracted AIDS in London. Diagnosed days before her thirtieth birthday, she had been told she might not get any medication because only good girls got drugs. She felt lonely, tainted, dirty, and scared. When she saw a doctor, all she could do was cry.

In the absence of drugs, only the companionship of others provided comfort. "My doctor told me about Positively Women: a room full of women and kids," Petretti said. "I thought they would all be dying—but they were knitting! Knitting to make money. It was only here I felt safe and not judged. And we kept each other going, because we were the only ones who knew what it was like."

"It was like the trenches in World War One: this decimation," Jonathan Blake said. "It was so lonely." What brought Blake out of his isolation was helping others. In the British coal miners, Blake saw another group being persecuted and marginalized. He joined Lesbians and Gays Support the Miners (LGSM) out of solidarity and because, as he says, if he was going to die anyway, why not help someone? LGSM raised money to support miners' families, organized what became the legendary "Pits and Perverts" benefit ball, and visited mining towns to show solidarity. A distraction from hospital visits and funerals, the work was creative, collective, and generous.

But by 1989, the number of AIDS deaths in the United States had passed the million mark. Government-funded AIDS research was described as corrupt, secretive, ethically barren. There was no plan. By 1990, one person died from AIDS every minute in America.

In cities, it had become the leading cause of death for women aged fifteen to forty-four. Promising drugs remained untested. Congress voted $800 million for treatment—but none of the money was ever released. Rumors of deportations, mass incarceration, and suicides swirled around the community. Activists were dying; they were also burning out. But as they retired from the field, others replaced them, fired by the certainty that if silence meant death, acting up at least meant possibility. Faith defies uncertainty, is how David France put it. Without optimism, there was nothing.

Glimmers of hope began to emerge. With AZT still the only available treatment, and too toxic for many, it had proved profitable. That encouraged other drug companies to tackle AIDS, too. A few medical researchers were spotted at conferences, secretly carrying away "Silence=Death" posters; that signaled a shift in attitude. When Merck entered the field, the company created the first-ever formal community advisory board with ACT UP. For Merck, this was a risk—drug companies are paranoid about leaked trade secrets—but the company recognized that involving self-educated people with AIDS could drive research that was better, faster, cheaper, and more likely to succeed.

But the 1990s seemed to reprise the '80s: a lethal roller coaster of hope, activism, and expertise, followed by crushing disappointment with millions more dead. Ten years after the first reported case, in 1991 2.4 million people died of AIDS; 1992: 3.3 million; 1993: 4.7 million.[6] Bereaved lovers, children, and parents carried their loved ones' cremated ashes to hurl them onto the White House lawn, whispering the words "I love you."

The mood became apocalyptic. In 1994: 6.2 million. An ACT UP member was now on the approvals board of the FDA. But in 1995, in the year that 8.2 million people died of AIDS, the disease had become the leading cause of death for Americans aged twenty-five to forty-four. When a promising drug at Merck failed, scientists despaired, questioning whether a solution could ever be found. They considered giving up but it was the activists who kept them going. At Merck, Emilio Emini took the moral challenge personally: "I have no right," he said, "to say I can't do this."

A new category of drug, protease inhibitors, triggered the same excitement and fear that had greeted AZT. Another false dawn? Arguments broke out again over how fast they should be tested and approved: too fast and they could prove lethal, too slow and lives would be lost. The caution wasn't ill-placed; the first protease inhibitor, saquinavir, proved to be effective for just sixteen weeks. But if no single drug worked long enough, would combinations of them do better?

In 1996, at an annual medical conference in Washington, D.C., Merck and Abbott presented their data on combination therapies. The results made the audience gasp. A single trial had kept very sick people with AIDS alive for two years. A few days later, a New York press conference convened by all three major drug companies announced their results. They couldn't fully explain why or for how long the combination of drugs worked, but they knew they'd made a breakthrough. Not for the first time, technical jargon got in the way and one scientist, sensing confusion, interrupted to translate.

"Maybe you are not understanding what I am saying. . . . This is the biggest news ever in this epidemic. This stuff is actually clearing virus out of people's bodies. People are getting better! We don't know for sure yet, but we think these drugs—this whole class of drugs—might allow people to live a normal life. . . ."[7]

The triple drug therapy received FDA approval in just six months.

In London, Jonathan Blake counted himself lucky that he had refused to enroll in trials of AZT. His doctors had helped him manage opportunistic infections but over time, he lost weight, got shingles and neuralgia, and reached a point where he could scarcely move. Though Blake was still reluctant to trust the medical establishment, his doctor persuaded him that he had run out of options.

"He works out this combo for me. A week goes by: nothing. Second week: same thing. Third week: I still have to take all these pills and—nothing. Fourth week: I wake up one morning and I have such energy I can't believe it. Like Lazarus rising from the dead! I go outside and lay a patio in my garden. Phenomenal. Extraordinary. . . ."

Nothing about this triumph was inevitable or foreseeable. Many diseases today remain incurable one hundred years after their discovery; the extinction so feared by the gay community could have been its history. So what made the difference? It wasn't just one thing: No one action. No one plan. No one organization. No one leader. Not even one drug. It had taken everything and everyone: men, women, activists, scientists, bureaucrats and radicals, healthy and sick, the living and the many, many dead, and years of failure.

David France said the sheer scale of the tragedy ultimately made it impossible to ignore, a bitter advantage. Rupert Whitaker thought it came down to two things: shame and expertise. Shaming the medical establishment, he believes, was the only way to get their attention—and expertise made it productive. Silvia Petretti says that nobody could have survived without peer support, the only protection against stigma. Everyone pays tribute to allies and friends, many now dead, who stood shoulder to shoulder, bringing food or comfort, knowledge or ideas, all breaking through the isolation of fear, discrimination, and despair. What kept the movement going was a passionate faith in a better future. The thing about courage, Whitaker told me, is that seeing courage instills courage.

There are many lessons to be taken from a terrifying crisis that was met with unbridled conviction, daring, imagination, and courage. Talking to AIDS activists and historians, I was wary of suggesting parallels; I didn't want to belittle their immense suffering and achievement. But they were bolder and had already seen similarities between AIDS and the physical, present dangers we face today.

"Those Parkland kids," David France said with a smile, thinking about the Florida students who had seen their friends shot down in school and had taken to the streets and to politics to fight for gun control. March for Our Lives, France said, stages actions against the National Rifle Association that come straight from the legacy of ACT UP. "These kids feel their personal peril, they were mowed down! Their die-in at a grocery store chain where the executive had a role in the NRA: their technique and strategy are lifted straight from this. These kids are fighting for their lives."

These kids have also learned the lesson of finding allies. In the 2018 U.S. midterm elections, working alongside OurLivesOurVote and shooting victim Gabrielle Giffords, they raised money to support gun control candidates across America and to encourage young people to vote. Where, between 1994 and 2014, just 20 percent of the vote came from the young, in 2018 it was 30 percent. These kids, France said, don't just know what to fight for, but also who to fight against. For everyone, it's personal.

"I see real comparisons with climate change, especially in terms of not knowing what to do, having no plan," Ian Green said. Diagnosed as HIV positive at the age of twenty, he is amazed to find himself alive, thirty years later, running the Terrence Higgins Trust. "The story of HIV and AIDS is all about people taking action and not sitting back. It was hell but we had a real community, we all knew each other, and we came together in adversity. It was personal; we felt each other's pain, going to funerals all the time. And it was a multi-factoral response: government, activists, families, scientists. The real lesson: sit back at your peril; what you can't be is patient or passive. . . ."

All the hallmarks of the AIDS epidemic can be seen in the fight to address climate change, albeit on an even bigger scale. Frustrating years of inaction and denial. Uncertainty about where to start. Ambiguity around where solutions will be found: in technology, in lifestyle, in corporations, in experiments. Arguments about whether to fight for a solution or adapt to tragedy. Widespread disagreement about tactics and priorities. Extinction Rebellion takes many of its cues from ACT UP, its decentralized activism launching huge public actions to accelerate action. The growing public desire to do something—anything—even if that means sacrificing time, effort, personal reputations, and physical safety. Emergent, unexpected leadership in Iris Long and Greta Thunberg. All of this is amid a crisis so large and terrifying that many institutions and individuals watch paralyzed or overwhelmed, preferring to turn a blind eye or hope that a miracle will somehow save the day.

But there are further lessons to be taken from the AIDS crisis, lessons that apply to any existential crisis. Progress in these fights is lumpy, advancing, stalling, accelerating, and disappointing. They rarely end neatly or conclusively, but solutions emerge—and continue to emerge. Despite generations of new treatments and prophylactics, AIDS remains a live issue as social stigma remains and new therapies are expensive and often, inexplicably, withheld.[8] Even after decades of research, there is still no AIDS vaccine. Crises on this scale defy tidy management structures and strategic plans because good ideas do and must come from everywhere. Efficiency and hierarchy are lethal because they constrain energy and ideas at a time when you need those most of all; only the extravagant oversupply of creative thinking is equal to the challenge. Allies are essential—especially alliances with presumed enemies. It's when AIDS activists sat down with medical researchers—the same ones they'd attacked for stalling progress—that real advances were made. Cultural translators like Mark Harrington were critical to enabling that; being able to explain in easy, accessible language brings in more people and answers can come from anywhere. Shame and expertise, as Rupert Whitaker saw, are both needed to keep the daily reality of immediate physical danger alive and real to everyone. But as important as the fight is caring for the injured and traumatized.

Crises are always personal. John and Mary fought for a future they could share and that would allow them both to change. Companies are saved by individuals who care about each other. Adults change their minds about the climate crisis when the arguments come from their children, especially teenaged daughters.[9] It can be tempting to sentimentalize crises, looking back with nostalgia to the sense of solidarity and meaning that they provoke. The deeper, harder truth is that going *into* a crisis, with years of generosity, reciprocity, and trust deeply established, provides resilience and stamina. The efficiency of the gig economy, the splintering of communities into competitive individuals, our dependence on technology undermine this, eroding the lifesaving power of loyalty and friendship that these crises demand. Staying human, being more than a user or a consumer, is the first way to address an unpredictable future. Existential crises are long and painful and what keeps people going is each other.

Drawing in so many people, from all walks of life, accelerates options, too. Today, a vast array of technologies are emerging, all of which address climate change. None is the perfect solution; what matters is that so many of them could work. These engineering solutions, however, are powerless without political, social, and economic support, which in turn requires the capacity for opponents to work together for a future that benefits them all. No one idea or one leader will be sufficient; as complex as the problem must be the response.

We have wasted thirty years, hoping or waiting for a master plan or superhero capable of fixing the environmental catastrophe that we perpetuated. During that time, being passive has made the problem worse. We have seen slowly what AIDS activists saw so fast: we sit back at our peril. In this new decade, we will find out whether we have enough capacity for shame and expertise, courage and complexity, imagination and exploration, to keep trying everything. If we do, we will make one kind of future; if we don't, we will make another. Neither is inevitable. It's up to us.

Along the way: expect surprises. When Jonathan Blake supported the coal miners, he did so because he just wanted to help another group under threat. No longer feeling helpless was reward enough. He never imagined that it would result in the National Union of Mineworkers pushing gay marriage onto the Labor Party platform. It's in the nature of complex systems that such weird, unforeseen events will emerge. As David France said, faith defies uncertainty.

CHAPTER NINE

WHO WANTS TO LIVE FOREVER?

It seems to me that one ought to rejoice in the fact of death—
ought to decide, indeed, to earn one's death by confronting
with passion the conundrum of life. One is responsible for
life: It is the small beacon in that terrifying darkness from
which we come and to which we shall return.

—James Baldwin, *The Fire Next Time*

Even people who didn't know her looked up. As Olivia crossed
the club's dining room, heads turned. Age ninety-two, she had
shrunk to under five feet and no longer wore the high heels of her
debutante days. But even as she approached the end of life, her
glamour and presence commanded attention.

Anytime my work takes me to Texas, I try to make extra time
to visit my godmother. She's been a wise support all my life, funny
and stylish. Now that she is in her nineties, it takes her longer to get
dressed—she wouldn't be caught dead looking anything less than
gorgeous—but this morning, we will still talk for hours, catching
up on her life and mine. She laughs about the fact that her social
life these days mostly revolves around funerals and bridge, adding
that her biggest fear is that she might soon run out of friends to

lose. Her late husband, a rigid and conservative man, might have felt her comment to be in poor taste, but one of the delights of her old age has been watching her grow bolder, in what she thinks and dares to say. Who's going to stop her now?

At lunch, she still eats like a bird and relishes the fact that I don't. Tonight she will give me the keys to her car and I will drive us to dinner. She will enjoy the fact that now I am looking after her, and I'm proud to do it. When we were both younger, we might visit museums or go shopping, but now it's enough to be together. In the last two decades, her life has steadily shrunk: not just her physical height, but the reach of her social life. Ten years ago, she gave up the trips to Europe she adored. Then she stopped going to New York. A few years later, eye problems meant she gave up driving. She still plays bridge twice a week and her children and grandchildren are good at staying in touch. But there are many days now when she just stays home, looked after by friends and helpers she's known most of her life. My visit is precious for both of us.

Olivia may be ninety-two but she's more daring than when she was at the height of her beauty and social success. I wish, she told me, I hadn't been such a conformist when I was younger; I wish I'd known that I was more than just pretty. Her political views have changed (she swore me to secrecy); her wicked confidence is now more assertive. So it would be wrong to see her old age as nothing but loss. At an age where most people might expect to stop changing, Olivia is still becoming. And she is happy. When I come to visit, we always have plenty to talk about. She's curious about my work, my family, and is such an acute social observer that it is still fun to hear her acerbic take on the local gossip. Each time I come, we both know but neither of us says: this could be the last time.

In an unpredictable world, one glaring exception confronts us from an early age: we know we will die, just not when or where. We may go through most of life desperate to know the future, but this is one sphere in which we do not. Knowing when we were going to die would turn all of life into a long, dreary countdown. So when we think about death, it's easy to see how uncertainty gives us a sense of freedom that absolute certainty never would. Even here, as the end of life approaches and the certainty of death becomes tangible, we continue to have choices. How we approach the end of life articulates much about us that will resonate for years to come. We still have an indelible impact on the future, even if we aren't there to see it.

My godmother, Olivia, elegantly reflects our current understanding of aging: that as we grow older, we get happier. This takes many forms. Across a lifetime, negative feelings tend to decline but positive ones stay fairly stable; toward the end of life, that leaves most people pretty cheerful. Older people are drawn more to positive images and remember them longer than young people given the same choices. Much of this research has been pioneered by Stanford's Laura Carstensen, and what it reveals is a picture of aging around the world quite different from the standard gloomy narrative of decline and failure. When she and her colleagues followed a group aged between eighteen and ninety-four, they asked the group to carry pagers over a ten-year study. Each member was regularly interrogated about their emotional state: were they happy, sad, frustrated, anxious. What they found was not that one generation was universally more contented than the rest, but that each individual became happier over time. So those who started adulthood grumpy became less so; those who were cheerful to begin with got even more so. Carstensen says, laughing, that when they hear of her research, many young people ask her how they can get old faster.[1]

In addition, the elderly retrieve happy memories more easily and frequently than sad ones—and these memories may be more positive than when they were first made. Diaries kept during the Blitz, for example, are replete with intense negative emotions—fear, anger, loneliness—that decades later were supplanted by memories of solidarity and purpose. We call this nostalgia but it isn't just a rewriting of history. Rather, our experiences teach us emotional coping skills and we get better at managing our own feelings.[2]

A second explanation for greater happiness in older people is simpler: time is short and what is scarce becomes valuable. Younger adults have longer futures to consider and may be more keenly aware of what they lack. That may encourage them to go out with people they don't really like, or take jobs they don't enjoy. But the opposite is true for older adults: with shorter futures, they prioritize emotional goals, searching for meaning in what they have. They know better what they like and dislike and don't want to waste time. This makes them better—at times, quite ruthless—at moving toward the positive and negotiating their way out of the negative. So while Olivia may have fewer friends, those whom she still sees are rich in the memories and support that they bring. The future is easier to navigate when there is less of it.

More meaningful than how long we have been around is how long we have left. So HIV-positive patients who are symptomatic care about the same things as the very old, no matter how young in years they might be. HIV-positive patients who are *not* symptomatic behave more like the middle-aged, while the young share priorities with the completely uninfected.[3] Age alone, it turns out, is a poor indicator of progress along the course of life. What's clear is that, regardless of chronological age, as life shortens, emotional ties deepen and strengthen, sometimes to a point of almost unbearable intensity. This could be seen tragically throughout the AIDS crisis and is a deep and recurring theme in much art. *La Traviata*'s Violetta, *La Bohème*'s Mimi, Munch's *Sick Child,* Strauss's *Four Last Songs*: all attempt to capture the ineffable value of life as it runs out. I think now that it might also explain the crystalline gaiety of my first husband, who understood, far better than I, the true implications of a congenital heart defect.

"Here is something real" was how a friend commented on his cancer diagnosis. In sharp contrast to the ephemeral urgency of daily life—the missed train, the lost promotion—here was an experience undeniable, nonnegotiable, and surprisingly rich. "Such clarity," he recalled. "Small moments of intense domestic delight. Such awareness of life all around me. Noticing all the time . . ." He wasn't alone. Ulla-Carin Lindquist, a Swedish TV presenter, wrote toward the end of her life, "It is now for the first time that I feel myself to be living in the present. Death brings me closer to life."[4]

Every moment human beings are alive, they continue to change and to grow. This is what fuels the drama of *King Lear:* that this old, flawed man can gain wisdom. At the beginning of the play he is foolish and self-satisfied, thinking himself wise, but the fact that he won't meekly submit testifies to his ferocious appetite for life. That his wisdom comes so late is Lear's tragedy, but that he does learn, right to the bitter end, is his redemption and it is why we weep with him. *Lear* challenges us: How much can we still learn? And it challenges its actors, typically toward the end of their careers, to excavate their talent and capacity—physical, intellectual, emotional—to move us. Taking on *Lear* requires every kind of stamina and courage, never more so than when, at the age of eighty, Glenda Jackson chose the role for her return to the stage after twenty years service as a member of Parliament. This was an actor not meekly retiring from politics but storming back into the theater with a whole new level of performance.

When the idea was first suggested to Jackson, she'd dismissed it, thinking she'd been away from the stage too long—and that the British would never accept a woman in the role. But when she proposed it to the Old Vic Theatre and they agreed, her first thought was that she'd been mad to suggest it. "My big fear," she said, "was that I wouldn't have the physical or vocal strength to do it." She went into training—swimming and walking, condemned to solitary confinement with the script. Only after the first read-through of the whole play did it start to feel possible. "I actually got through to the end and I didn't feel as though I was going to die," she said with relief.

An exercise regime, a hugely supportive cast, cutting down smoking (every day but Sundays), and the sheer energy inside what Jackson calls the greatest play Shakespeare ever wrote: these got her through the fear and challenge of the role. But what made her performance so ferocious was more than the professional risk she was taking. After twenty years in Parliament, Jackson's King Lear scintillated with political shrewdness and acumen. There was nothing about politics this actor couldn't sense, know, and show. Those who had seen Jackson onstage at the beginning of her career saw an actor now working at a level beyond anything she had done before. To demand so much of herself and so triumphantly succeed at the age of eighty revealed to the world just how much age has to say.

Far from winding down or petering out, it is not unusual for artists toward the end of their lives to unleash a final period of exuberant creativity and invention. That paradox—that the less of life that remains, the more we treasure it—fuels the energy and daring of what has become known as Late Style. Beethoven's late quartets, Rembrandt's self-portraits, the late plays of Ibsen, Schubert's *Winterreise,* Matisse's cutouts, the radical simplicity of Peter Brook's *The Prisoner*: these aren't easy, consoling works. They lack serenity, bristling with exorbitant life and radical originality.

The idea of the Late Style originated with Theodor Adorno, who recognized it as distinctive, even if he struggled to define what it was. Writing about Beethoven's late works, he describes them as "relegated to the outer reaches of art . . . as if, confronted with the dignity of human death, the theory of art were to divest itself of its rights and abdicate in favour of reality." How much artists ever concern themselves with theory seems debatable, but Adorno is not alone in sensing in these works an explosive quality of liberation: from convention, from expectation, from what *ought* to be. Beethoven's late quartets, written two years before his death, summon up all of his genius, providing to a mere four players a powerful distillation of everything his life's music has given him.

"Touched by death," Adorno writes, "the hand of the master sets free the masses of material that he used to form" and such is the energy and urgency of the work that it can feel unfinished as it breaks through to new territory.

The excruciating, raw honesty of Rembrandt's self-portraits, painted in the year he died, when all hope of success and love were gone, go straight to the question of what it means to be human. Ibsen's last plays, written ten years before his death, remain relentless, ambiguous, anxious, and unsettled in their quest to understand failure and transfiguration. Goya's last paintings scream across the centuries, rejecting placatory platitudes. Schubert, dying at the age of thirty-one, created in *Winterreise* images and sounds of agonizing beauty, exquisite despair. In the last ten years of his life, Matisse took up scissors, using only color, shape, and composition to change the way we think about art; many consider these the greatest of all his works. What Late Style artists have in common is that they refuse to decline, instead distilling their past to accelerate beyond it. With nothing to fear or hope for, these late works explode with questions, doubts, and new ideas that remain to inspire and terrify future generations.

Though such achievement falls to few, the Late Style and Carstensen's research point to a creative experience of old age. Anthropologists and psychologists have argued for more than a century that death is so terrifying that we have had to invent religions, or devise complex systems of deep denial, in order to be able to go on living. But the analysis of blogs written by the terminally ill, or poetry by inmates on death row, suggest that the approach of death does not deprive life of its meaning. This late stage in life, with time so precious, can become a period of rich achievement, continued exploration, and deep satisfaction.[5] This is not to belittle the pain of illness, fear, and suffering in dementia, or what can be the brutal consequences of mistakes, bad luck, poor decisions. It would be naïve and unjust to imagine that a different way of thinking about old age automatically alleviates pain and suffering. But it is equally incorrect to overlook how vivid life becomes when in short supply. What psychologists like Carstensen or any of the Late Style artists show us is that the certainty of life ending offers much that is powerful, inspiring, hopeful, and vividly alive. They do not see death as a problem.

In that, they are unusual. Death is frequently portrayed as a technical challenge or a failure. The education of doctors focuses overwhelmingly on improving and saving lives; in all their medical training, doctors spend roughly just twenty hours with the dying. The physician Atul Gawande has written poignantly about his own, well-intended, but misguided attempts excessively to prolong life. He had never spent much time looking at how old people actually live, but when he did, he came to a startlingly simple conclusion: that making their lives better often required *reducing* purely medical imperatives. Death isn't an error for doctors to correct, or a bug for software engineers to fix: it is a natural process that can be honored and dignified.

But when my ninety-one-year-old neighbor was diagnosed with breast cancer, she felt the full force of medical mechanics. A jolly and understated woman, Alison had led a quietly heroic life. Working in a London hospital during World War II, during bombing raids she would go and sit with patients whose wounds made it impossible for them to be moved to shelters. She made no fuss about the courage this required; it was just a happy memory of being useful. When, in her late eighties, she fell ill and received her diagnosis, she refused treatment. But so irate was her doctor that he stormed out of the room, leaving her on her own.

Casting death as failure denies the dying the opportunity to die well. So, too, does the rhetoric that casts disease as an enemy and the patient as a soldier. When Raj Thamotheram was diagnosed with cancer, he revolted against the cancer-as-war metaphor. A long-time peace campaigner and climate activist, he knew, all his friends knew, that he was a fighter. But as a physician, he also knew that however his disease progressed, whatever happened next wasn't a moral judgment on him. The disease was bad enough; the idea that he had to prove himself by defeating it belittled him. This attitude was implicit at its most self-righteous during the AIDS crisis, when millions, suffering a terrifying, unknown disease, also had to endure the vicious opprobrium of an ignorant public. Positioning death as punishment or failure, and those who escape it as superior, is just a self-serving form of denial. Worst of all, it hijacks the possibility of a good death.

But in Silicon Valley and, to the transhumanist movement as a whole, death is a bug in the software, a problem to be solved. Where recent academic research has concluded that longevity plateaus at around 115 years, they insist that we will soon be able to eliminate death altogether. (Predictions for when they will achieve this vary from twenty to one hundred years, a safe margin for error.) The vision is perpetuated by a strange cast of doctors, scientists, engineers, billionaires, and crackpots, each with varying concepts of what eternal life will look like. Of these, one of the least crazed is Aubrey de Grey. He foresees what he calls the "Methusalarity," according to which we can get ahead of aging by fixing failing parts of our body before they become seriously impaired. He concedes that this is tantamount to kicking the can down the road, and could mean spending a large proportion of life undergoing expensive medical procedures. But the rewards would be that "we can stay as young adults, both physically and mentally, absolutely as long as we live. The only risks of death that we will have will be risks faced by young adults—being hit by a truck or the planet being hit by an asteroid."

Acknowledging that pioneering technologies are notoriously difficult to predict, de Grey gives his vision a 50-50 chance of arriving in the next twenty years (as long as his fund-raising is successful) but an 80 to 90 percent chance in the next one hundred years. Born in 1963, he might just make it himself if he doesn't meet a truck. His premise is breathtakingly simple: more life must mean a better life. Although he claims to be working to save the lives of millions—"thirty September 11s every week!"—he seems strangely uninterested and ignorant about how those lives are lived. He takes it as a given that anyone not young should have a lot to complain about, that their lives must be worthless, detritus unworthy of attention, fatally flawed by age and mortality. So when asked how much time he spent with older people, he was flummoxed. Why would he want to do that? He wanted to *save* people from old age, not talk to them about it! Nor did he have any idea of how they might want to use the decades of life he labored to achieve. What would they do with all this extra health and extra time? He hadn't asked them but seemed certain he knew what they ought to want. Didn't everyone yearn to be a perpetually young adult? "It is a reasonable supposition," he rallied, "that people who still have physical and mental vitality that young adults have would do whatever it takes to get the most out of life, to not get bored."

That was the best vision he could offer: an infinite life of not getting bored. What de Grey couldn't imagine was that an endless life might be filled with infinite losses: habits, mores, rituals, language, fashions, old civilities that one might have embraced, invented, loved—and then lost as the world changed and life moved on. He couldn't grasp that individuals might feel burdened (even bored) by how much past they would be doomed to accumulate forever. We might no longer feel at home in a world where everything we were born with had vanished, to be replaced by new experiences and habits that would also vanish, to be endlessly rendered obsolete by a continuous and furious future that left us with more loss than we could handle.

The more obvious, practical question is where this immortal population might live. De Grey, acknowledging that he's not an economist, sociologist, politician, or environmental scientist, sneered at the question. Obviously, he insisted, as societies become more affluent, the birth rate falls, so the population will inevitably stabilize or decline. Wouldn't that mean that, eventually, there would be few genuinely young people left? How would the planet cope? Well that was simple, too: newer technologies such as renewable energy, desalination, and artificial meat would mean that the average person would create "less pollution." The tone of boredom with which he stalwartly swatted away such petty questions suggested that how the earth could supply the raw materials for immortality was clearly a question for lesser minds.

The logic of de Grey's vision is itself pretty simple. The increase in life expectancy over the last 150 years has derived primarily (but not exclusively) from prevention, so he is merely extrapolating that into the future. At a pinch, it's arguable that he might be doing us all a favor by forcing us to confront the dangers inherent to infinitely increasing life spans. But what was, for him, a thrilling prospect, seemed so dreary. He cherished no great project that he craved more time to complete: no symphonies, no inventions, no permanent solution for climate change, nothing but just more time. To what purpose would these long lives devote themselves? He had no ideas. What makes him think that anyone will endlessly strive to get more out of life when there's an unlimited supply of it? Why do today what can be put off to the next century?

Combating aging is big business. Not just the facelifts and the gym memberships. If, instead of a natural process, aging is defined as a disease, then every person in the world becomes a potential customer with an infinite lifetime value (and data). Calico is Alphabet's (Google's) subsidiary that aims to "devise interventions that enable people to lead longer and healthier lives."[6] The company is one in a crowded network of academic medicine, big pharma, and high tech that is doing with messianic hype what such organizations have always done: searching for medical problems whose treatment will be profitable and, in some cases, beneficial. Disparaging age while idolizing youth has always been the pitch. At one end of the spectrum, this is puffed-up business as usual; at the further end—and it isn't clear where Calico sits—are more radical outfits, with flavors of transhumanism that make de Grey's ambitions look pedestrian.

Google's director of engineering, Ray Kurzweil, declares that his strategy for life is never to die.[7] He hopes to attain this goal with a healthy lifestyle; strict low-fat, low-carb, low-calorie, no-sugar diet; and the regular consumption of a very large number of vitamins and supplements. (These products, newly branded as "Transcend," can be bought online.) But he has also committed to having his body preserved in liquid nitrogen until such time as he can be "reanimated." Several companies provide this service, catering to the band of biohackers determined to discover, and sell, ways to perpetuate their existence. If whole-body cryogenics is too pricey, the cheaper option is to have your head cut off and frozen, awaiting the day when it might be possible to take a comprehensive scan of the brain (neurons, connections, processes) that becomes a blueprint for reconstruction in some kind of supercomputer or substrate. This assumes that we are merely brains, that we learn nothing through the rest of our physical experience of life. Even Kurzweil has acknowledged misgivings—the technology might not work, his legal status would be unclear, he might lose control over the process.

But his goal here is not just defeating death. Over the last decade, he has written extensively about the point at which artificial intelligence and human intelligence merge. By the 2030s, he argues, computers will be so powerful that we won't be able to keep up unless we enhance ourselves with their capabilities. (You could argue we are already doing that with the deep integration of smartphones into all aspects of our lives.) But Kurzweil goes further, imagining our brains uploaded into computers (or computers becoming embedded inside our brains), at which point distinctions between machine and human become moot. By 2045, when Kurzweil will be ninety-seven, he believes that technology will surpass human intelligence and be capable of solving every problem. His so-called

Law of Accelerating Returns argues that because human evolution and technological advances are exponential, we will finally be able to transcend physical and mental limitations to become pure intelligence. What seems to thrill him most about this vision is not so much the prospect of immortality—though he is deeply invested in that—but the opportunity to cast physical biology aside in exchange for engineering perfection. Is that the same as life?

From one perspective, this is just a modern rewriting of ancient myths around death and transfiguration. Where once we believed in gods, some now believe in technology. Investing in cryogenic storage is not that different from the medieval kings and barons who endowed chantry chapels in which sung masses for their souls would resound throughout eternity. (Most are silent now.) Religion and technology both ring with the rhetoric of inevitability, in which the voice of individuals is drowned out by the overweening powers that only a few enlightened (and powerful) prophets understand. It's a curious thought, to imagine Silicon Valley replacing in power and arrogance the dominance of the medieval church. In both, the glory of tomorrow always absolves responsibility for pain and suffering today.[8]

Intellectually, Kurzweil's vision might be dazzling to technophiles but it isn't without its risks. All computer systems develop bugs, at the rate of about one per thousand lines of code, and even the most sophisticated engineers acknowledge that they often don't know why. He can have no idea where these digital mutations will lead, but entrusting all life to a single platform means it's also potentially a single point of failure. Hardly robust. But what is striking about transhumanists isn't their enthusiasm for machines so much as their dismal dreariness when it comes to describing life. I can admire the intellectual dazzle of Kurzweil's analogies between biology, technology, and the stock market; I'm just puzzled by a mind that can't see that the stock market is already an inadequate model of economics and an even poorer one for life. Why is he, like fellow transhumanists

Peter Thiel and Sam Altman, so uninterested in real problems, like
the *fall* in life expectancy, even in rich countries like the United
States? Or the immediate climate crisis, which could make eternal
life pretty miserable and scupper hopes for resurrection? The vision
feels literally disembodied and strangely *in*human. Was it these
technologists that Apple CEO Tim Cook had in mind when he
said "you cannot possibly be the greatest cause on the earth, because
you aren't built to last"?[9]

These men seem incapable of imagining a world being any good
without them. Is that the bug they're trying to fix? The transhumanist world is largely white, male, middle-aged, and middle-class.
It isn't apparently optimized for women, who might anyway be
redundant with the advent of compliant sexbots. And the disabled
disappear completely in a future that "fixes" people. These ideas of
abstract perfection are all about power—computing power, super-
intelligence—whose aim is domination: the colonization of space
and eternity. They are authoritarian and amoral, with seemingly
little concern for anyone who can't afford such longevity. Kurzweil
acknowledges that things could go badly wrong and thinks that
somebody (not he) needs to spend a lot of effort inculcating lib-
eral values of tolerance, diversity, and liberty. But those tasks feel
secondary, requiring moral maids or nannies to clean up the mess
after the master has departed on a higher mission. We are back in
the land of prophecy as propaganda, where technology promises to
relieve us of the burden of thinking for ourselves.

Much transhumanism comes across as merely adolescent.
Having grown up in an era that celebrates youth, these men feel
entitled to hang on to it forever. Would they ever bother to have
children, or would their future be permanently populated by the
same un-old people? Sacrifice is certainly not their game. Nor do
they appreciate the value and purpose of death. All humans throw
off mutations throughout their lives. These produce variation, and
the natural selection of varieties is evolution. The accumulation

of mutations, well past reproductive age, is ultimately what kills us—but no mutations, no evolution. So death is necessary, an essential part of life.

On a more mundane basis, imagine the despair of a nation under the spell of a demagogue, dictator, or sociopath who will never die: Franco forever, a permanent Pol Pot. Do we really want everyone to live forever? It is a gross failure of understanding and imagination not to see that death, however fearful, confers benefits. In de Grey's case this seems particularly obtuse and ungrateful, as the money that funded his research came to him when his own mother died, leaving him a small fortune. Where would he be without her? Instead of trying to eliminate mortality, we do better to see it as a final gift to the future.

"I remember feeling an immense sense of relief when my father died," Lucy told me. She spoke on condition of anonymity, so profoundly did she feel that her emotions at her parents' deaths were taboo. "I know I was loved and cherished, and when that's gone, it's a shock. But after a few months, I had a feeling of freedom. Wow! I have thirty, forty years of active life left, maybe more, and this is my FIRST chance to live my life as I want! It was an incredible realization: you used to think you were free but now, you really are."

Many people feel just as Lucy does: not that they did not love their parents but that their deaths inaugurated a new phase of adulthood. Looking back, she could see how dutiful she'd been—going home at Christmas, getting married where her parents could attend. These weren't big regrets, but the sense that such compromises were over came as a liberation. After their parents' deaths, many loving children discover subtly that a mother's or father's opinion has limited their choices, decisions, self-image. Love can impart a degree of compliance, a desire to please, at least to avoid conflict. When those psychological constraints are lifted, the world looks different.

Lucy was glad she had been a good and loving daughter. But she is also exhilarated by this new phase in her life, when she feels free to make different choices that are fully her own. I am reminded of the CERN scientists working on experiments the results of which they won't live to see. When I asked them how they felt about this, they said that it was important to make way for the next generation, who will have their own ideas. It would be selfish to stand in their way. Thinking of my own children, I can appreciate that leaving them can be my final contribution to the future.

Nobody understands this better than hospice workers, who spend their working lives helping the dying to find a good death. "In so many cases, a good death is the last great gift that parents can give their children," Penny Moorcraft said. "When you are dealing with the dying, it isn't helpful to think only about them—you have to think about the ones left behind."

Moorcraft works as a family support therapist at St. Margaret's Hospice Care in Taunton, England. Where better to explore how people think about their final future than in a setting where it is the daily focus of everyone's attention? The hospice movement began in the 1960s when Cicely Saunders, an English doctor, opened the first purpose-built center to provide for the physical, social, psychological, and spiritual needs of the dying, as well as their friends and families. Original to Saunders was the idea that the whole life of the patient, not the disease, should be the focus of attention. This was a radical thought at a time when the industrialization of medicine was gaining momentum. It remains a challenging proposition in many circles today: that death is part of life and should be treated as an equal part of human experience. Saunders also believed that the dying couldn't and shouldn't be considered in isolation, that their mental and physical states depended profoundly on a broader community of loved ones. How a death occurs resonates for a very long time.[10]

For hospice workers, dying well is not a matter of biology but of biography, connecting the past with the future. What happens when a parent, partner, brother, or sister dies echoes for years afterward. So Moorcraft and her colleagues work with the whole family, and much of their work involves children. They strive to create positive memories of parents and grandparents that the children take into the future. But they also have to consider the needs of the dying, their desire to cuddle children, but not frighten them. This has led them to think about transitional objects.

"The idea is to help with separation anxiety," Moorcraft explained. "We had an admin who does fantastic crochet, so we asked her to make two animals: a big one and a small one. The parent/patient gets the smaller one and the child gets the big one. It's a bond. It helps them walk through what each is feeling. When we had one patient with brain metastases we could see her, cradling and hugging the little animal. As she got worse, the children moved away from her, but she still had her animal and they had theirs—and the kids saw that. It allowed them both to withdraw very gently. And that family has been very resilient." At St. Margaret's, every child and dying parent now gets their own set of animals.

Those who work in the hospice movement see themselves as endlessly researching what is required for a good death. Most people who think about it concentrate on paperwork, drawing up wills and detailed funeral plans, but such administration too often becomes a displacement activity, avoiding deeper conversations. But the failure to think this through explains why people often don't get the death they want. At St. Margaret's, the staff suggests that we talk early to loved ones about where we want to die, who we want to be with us (and who not), how much pain relief we want, what activities or objects should be part of our life to the very end. To achieve a good death requires being willing to think about and discuss such things in the period between becoming aware of disease and the time we die. Fear of what will happen is common to everyone, they said. Not many people drop down dead; very few deaths are sudden. Most die slowly but not painfully. Cancer is more manageable than heart disease. Most, but not all, death is quiet, a gentle winding down—and hospices have become renowned for their skill in providing this. St. Margaret's is surrounded by gardens, fresh flowers are everywhere. It is full of friendly faces and fresh air. Staff, visitors, and volunteers work together as a community to support each other. In fact, most of St. Margaret's work isn't done in their building at all but in private houses and nursing homes where most people prefer to die.

Complex cases come into the hospice itself, but those, too, are managed so that the dying remain in control. Sally Reader, the palliative care consultant, described one long, difficult death of a man with an eleven-year-old son. Suffering from a head and neck tumor, he chose every form of treatment to stay alive as long as he could. He came into the hospice one day, bleeding. He wouldn't go to bed, he wouldn't take any pain relief, and he continued to bleed. It looked, Reader recalled, like a bloodbath, but it was a good death because the patient knew the kind of end he wanted and got it. Doctors and nurses might have wanted him in bed, but he wanted to sit and hold his wife. That's what they wanted and that's what they got.

Everyone at St. Margaret's can describe in detail the many good deaths that they have witnessed. Even as we lie dying, they said, we remain ourselves. Penny Moorcraft told me of two children who carried to university the hospice blankets they'd held as their mother died: not because it was a terrible memory but because it was a treasured one. Patients and their families aren't easily forgotten. Many family members return to the hospice, to stay in touch, volunteer, or just to sit quietly in the place where their loved one died and to talk to people who aren't afraid of the subject.

Why are such conversations rare? In part it is because we don't see death in our daily lives. In the last century, world wars made death a shared experience: public, visible, and honored through ritual. Tony Whitehead, a survivor of the AIDS crisis, says now that one of the strengths that the epidemic experience gave him was an appreciation of the privilege of helping loved ones through the end. "Sitting with my mother as she died, I thought: I have been here before. Maybe I'm better able to deal with these things. Because I've seen it so many times, I can be useful. That's very empowering, not being afraid."

Such respect for death is unusual today. When my first husband died, I remember driving down Irish roads behind his casket, strangely moved as strangers on the street stood silently and removed their hats. They didn't know Michael or me; honoring the dead was an old ritual that paid respect to a common humanity. Returning to London, I sometimes noticed the exact opposite: acquaintances avoiding me because they didn't know how to be.

It's so hurtful when, told of a colleague's fatal illness, many at work say nothing, unable to do the right thing because they are so fearful of saying the wrong thing. All the staff at St. Margaret's had stories like this to share, feeling that in our avoidance of death we injure the living and the dead alike.

Yet increasingly, all over the world, a good death is coming to be seen as a human right. There is even a "Quality of Death" index, one area in which Britain leads the world. While definitions are heavily influenced by cultural and personal values, globally they share two fundamental elements that cleave closely to Cecily Saunders's original work: a good death requires respect for patient judgment and the alleviation of all forms of pain. Death need not be associated with suffering—that's why hospice workers have become so expert in palliative care and why many regard the need for euthanasia as a failure.

I don't think I have ever visited a workplace that was more joyful than St. Margaret's Hospice. This is not because the people who work there—doctors, nurses, psychologists, social workers, and yes, accountants and HR executives, too—feel themselves immortal. It is because they know that they are not. They appreciate that these last, precious moments of life influence the future: how those who remain feel about themselves and their loved ones. The work done in hospices is driven by the desire to make this experience not merely untraumatic but one saturated with beauty, meaning, and love that will live on for years to come.

"People think hospices are all about death and dying," St. Margaret's CEO, Ann Lee, said with a laugh. "But ironically we are all about living, making the end of life a comfortable experience. Most people think they will die a painful death. They always ask: What's going to happen? And we tell them that at some point over the last few hours, breathing will stop. They ask: Is that it? And the answer is yes, most deaths are that simple. We try to get dying understood—it is going to happen but it needn't be scary."

Unsurprisingly, everyone working at St. Margaret's uses their experience to inform their own plans for their death, talking to their families, considering what matters most, and sharing those intentions. Sitting around the table, discussing what they did and didn't want at the end of life, proved a surprisingly fun conversation. The plans are, they said, somewhat akin to the plans that mothers make during pregnancy: a list of hopes and principles made in order to feel involved and in control of the process. Death plans are designed to give the dying power over what happens to them, in part because this leaves survivors better able to carry positive memories into the future. Hospice workers often become involved in these plans well in advance, ensuring that the dying and their family can preserve their relationships and not get sucked into the overzealous medicalization of death. St. Margaret's has even developed its own funeral service, so that the families they have worked with needn't, so abruptly, have to confide in strangers at a moment of intimacy. Even at the very end of life, when contingencies and choices contract, we still touch the future.

"When they're dying, people don't cease to be themselves; they often are more themselves than ever," Ann Lee said. "And people like to say good-bye." She recalled one patient who threw a huge garden party, like a funeral that he got to attend. Raj Thamotheram did something similar: an evening of talk, discussion, food, and drink, full of all the people and ideas that sustained him throughout his life. The community that came to support him poured huge amounts of time into planning it: How could they say they didn't have the time? When else might they get the opportunity to be so explicit about their love and respect?

At the end of life, it's easy to feel that such events are a waste of time. But they aren't. Ann Lee explains to patients that it is important to show your family how to die. "How you do that and how you demonstrate how to cope is one of the best lessons you can give. It will make such a difference to them, to the rest of their lives. And when they can do it, as they wish to do it, there's a great sense of power and calm. It's a final gift."

When it comes, the moment of death is both obvious and indescribable. In an instant, a person becomes a body. For survivors, this feels impossible: that it is real, that it is now, and that it is forever. Many hope that all the grief they've already experienced will soften the blow; that's rarely true. However fully we allow ourselves to know, with absolute certainty, that someone we love will die, the difference between the idea and the reality is everything.

Death is transition. For the religious, this is codified and ritualized. For the rest of us, it is internalized. The people I have loved and lost remain with me forever. They continue to shape who I am and how I think. I don't remember when Michael told me that he thought second marriages, after bereavement, were proof of a good first marriage—but the memory of that conversation was permission to have a full life after he'd gone. Memories of my father's dirt-poor hometown have forever informed the way I think about poverty. My complex feelings about my mother become wonderfully simple when I go to the opera that she taught me to love. I frequently recall a conversation with Alan that stopped me in my tracks and changed the way I thought. I will never forget driving with John on Riverside Drive. And any mention of Texas will always remind me of Olivia: her glamour, her laughter, her refusal to be simplified, and I will remember her not at one age but for all the time I knew her. These people are immortal in me, trace elements of a future that my children will inherit, often not knowing where they come from. I will never be certain where they go. The best I can do is set them free.

CHAPTER TEN

BE PREPARED

Can I get there?
Where the deer pounces on the lion,
Where the one I'm after's
After me?

—Rumi, "The Blocked Road"

On September 11, 2001, Richard Hatchett was on a bus heading to work at the Sloan Kettering Cancer Center in New York City. He was reading about self-organizing systems and thinking about the role that narrative plays in decision-making. Like most New Yorkers that day, what he chiefly remembers is how ordinary it was at the beginning and how extraordinary by the end. In a matter of hours, Hatchett found himself engulfed in a self-organizing system that emerged as he and his colleagues scrambled to establish a triage area. Out of the measured pace of a cancer treatment center, a four-story field hospital suddenly appeared, and it left Hatchett thinking about the contours of order required by unpredictable events.

Hatchett, an English major, had wanted to be a writer. But that day's experience left him with an abiding curiosity about medical policy. What could have prepared New York's hospitals better? Was there any kind of infrastructure that might have made the city able to respond faster? He began to move from the traditional management focus on efficient planning to a more expansive, imaginative concept of preparation. In a world punctuated by events that are generally certain but specifically ambiguous, preparedness offers a more robust and optimistic approach to the future than prediction provides.

Today, Hatchett is the chief executive of the Coalition for Epidemic Preparedness Innovation (CEPI) that was founded in 2017 as "a global insurance policy to defend against future epidemics." Its creation, led by the Wellcome Trust and the Gates Foundation, was provoked by the recognition that epidemics are always with us, but that few institutions or governments want to take account of them or feel any urgency to do so.[1] In some cases, the risk seems too distant or uncertain; preparing for an epidemic doesn't speak to short-term political agendas. The idea of investing billions in the development of new vaccines against possible pandemic threats flew in the face of efficient planning. And while many governments are highly attuned to economic security, few are equally alert to biological threats. CEPI's strategy grew out of four key insights: First, that epidemics come without warning; they are inherently unpredictable. In a world of global travel, they move fast: an outbreak could spread to all major capital cities within sixty days. Since the 1970s, new pathogens have been emerging at the unprecedented rate of one or more a year. Finally, no two epidemics are the same; they don't repeat themselves. There is no profile of an epidemic, because new strains of a wide array of diseases constantly evolve; because separate geographies with distinct medical, education, and transportation systems require a variety of logistics and supplies; because diverse cultures respond to different messages and authorities in specific ways; and because successful approaches are both medical and non-medical, albeit in different proportions.

CEPI's idea of preparedness brings together multiple ways of thinking about an uncertain, unpredictable future. It commissions a wide range of experiments and works through multiple scenarios. Hatchett's work depends on an artist's imagination to craft stories of an optimistic future, one in which epidemics are managed or controlled. As a coalition, public understanding and support is vital to the work that, like cathedrals, stretches indefinitely into the future. But that doesn't make it a distant dream: epidemics emerge at imperfect times, putting the organization to the test. But preparedness demonstrates how far, and how much better, we can think about the long term when we abandon dependency on prediction and accept uncertainty.

Much of this thinking grew out of the Ebola crisis of 2015–16, which had presented a paradox: the response had been successful— for the first time in history, an effective vaccine was developed in the midst of an epidemic—but it had also failed: doing so had taken too long, costing more than twelve thousand lives.[2] The question for CEPI, and for Hatchett, was: What could be put in place ahead of an epidemic to accelerate an effective response whenever, wherever it was needed? At the very heart of CEPI was an acknowledgment that prediction would not be the answer—but preparedness could be.

Vaccines, says Hatchett, are the be-all and end-all of epidemic responsiveness. But developing candidates is expensive and slow. The fastest vaccine took four years to develop; the average time required is closer to ten years. The first Ebola vaccine was in development in 2003, tested in monkeys in 2005, but then stalled because, with outbreaks so sporadic, it was impossible to test it. But the fact that the process hadn't had to be started from scratch accounted for the signal success of ending the 2015–16 epidemic. It would be prohibitively expensive to develop vaccines for every possible disease, so CEPI chose to focus on three kinds of diseases that pose the biggest risk and where a successful vaccine is most likely: MERS, Lassa, and Nipah.

"We are playing roulette," Hatchett acknowledged. "But we have to put our money down somewhere. Lassa is endemic in Africa and has three hundred thousand cases a year. Nipah is just a very scary disease, with a very wide geographic dispersion spread by bats. And we feel like the world has put us on notice that we have to deal with beta coronaviruses, like MERS and SARS, because they have pandemic potential."

Each disease requires three to six vaccine candidates, because some will fail. Researchers don't know which part of the immune response is critical to controlling the disease, or what the antibody needs to be, or how fast the disease will change in response to the vaccine. So these are "just in case" candidates: in case the disease breaks out, in case one of them works. They are all experimental. The failure of some will look inefficient but having several options makes it more likely that CEPI will have vaccines ready at an advanced stage of development when the next outbreaks occur. The organization isn't banking on a single theory of vaccines but is making bets on categories of disease—those with high likelihood and big impact—because these provide more robust options.

But when the time comes for the mass production of a successful vaccine candidate, then efficiency must be a priority. The second prong of CEPI preparedness adopts a just-in-time approach. (Just-in-time management systems, developed in Japan during the 1970s, aim at maximum efficiency by buying and shipping everything at the last minute, when uncertainty is minimal.) That means that Hatchett is developing systems now that will be able to mass-produce vaccines fast.

"Mainstream pharmaceutical markets don't care about manufacturing speed, but we do: the time it takes to produce the vaccine, the time it takes from injection to immunity, and the time it takes to manufacture at scale. These aren't market imperatives so we have to work with all kinds of companies and technologies that offer us the greatest utility and speed against a future we can't predict." In practice, that means that CEPI invests in and facilitates manufacturing processes that are specifically designed for emergencies.

The third prong of CEPI's preparedness requires an appreciation of what it is that vaccines *don't* do best. Before coming to CEPI,

Hatchett spent a decade exploring different models of responsiveness. After 9/11, he worked in Washington, D.C., setting up a medical reserve corps and writing a national food plan for the United States in the face of chemical, biological, and nuclear threats. Fifteen years of thinking about how to prepare for unquantifiable threats has made him alert to how flexible any response to complexity must be.

He had been tempted to look at models as a way of simulating experiments. Science has often turned to mathematical simulations where data is scarce and, in epidemics, it is always scarce because each one is different—or, as data scientists put it, n=1. But the more that Hatchett dug into simulations, the more he came to see their shortfalls. As an English major, he sensed that they were poor at capturing subtle, contextual, and cultural information that was too hard to quantify: "The danger arises when you turn to models to make decisions," he says. "It's too easy to mistake the simulation for the real thing, to believe they're more precise than they can be."

For policy makers with little firsthand knowledge, the danger of computer simulations is that the model looks so much like reality that it is tempting to think that the right answer for the model will produce success in the real world. Models, says Hatchett, "are not designed to give answers; they're at their best when they help you to think and to ask questions. So we think about everything we can relating to vaccines—but we can't leave out our understanding of all the other components, the social aspects of a successful response to an epidemic."

In the 1918 flu pandemic, for example, some urban populations proved more resilient because they implemented social interventions earlier: closing schools or banning massed gatherings. The earlier the social interventions, the stronger the reduction of the peak of the epidemic. The same was found during the bird flu epidemic in Mexico in 2009.[3] However crucial vaccines are, they have to be part of a wider system that takes into account all of the social, political, economic, and geographic complexities of context. These are resistant to mathematical modeling—quantifying them is difficult, if not impossible, because it's hard to gain consensus around what matters, why, and how. What CEPI can't do is conceive of epidemics as purely medical problems. So the third prong of its preparedness is its participation in a global ecosystem of epidemic responsiveness. That means thinking through the scenarios in which people, relationships, customs, and beliefs play an important role. "All of this is less about prediction and more about understanding the terrain," Hatchett says. "There is no entity in the world, not even in the U.S., that could do this alone. We have to own it collectively and find a collective solution."

Epidemics are always crises, so everything depends on speed. Just-in-case vaccines, manufactured just-in-time, work only if accepted by the culture and people that need them. That means relationships have to be carefully nurtured and negotiated *before* an outbreak—or, as Hatchett puts it, "Don't exchange business cards in a crisis." But an epidemic is always a crisis. So just as important to CEPI as the vaccines and manufacturing platforms are human relationships: between researchers, physicians, local doctors, health professionals, and governments in countries where outbreaks are most likely. During the 2015 Ebola outbreak, for example, a big chunk of the five months that it took to set up clinical trials was spent building relationships that hadn't been done in advance. That cost lives. Many Ebola victims died because of a suspicion of vaccines—were they poison?—and the invasion of foreigners in SUVs who might, or might not, have come to help.[4] Changing such attitudes takes time; fostering public engagement, behavioral understanding, and cultural awareness can be harder than the pure science. In Nigeria, for example, CEPI works with the head of Nigeria's Center for Disease Control and other Nigerian scientists to make decisions together about advancing vaccines at an early stage. Hatchett hopes to do that with every vaccine, in each country at risk, so that when the time comes, everyone will have spent years creating a shared approach. Building the necessary trust, generosity, and reciprocal relationships—some of which (like the vaccines) may never be used—takes time. Investment today is the only way to guarantee speed tomorrow.

How much can you do before you need it? That was the question Hatchett had asked on 9/11 and that continues to drive him to understand the whole system involved in epidemics. Negotiating partnership agreements that may need to last for years requires careful judgment about what details to nail down now and what to leave for later, when there's less uncertainty but also less time. CEPI is trying to streamline the due diligence needed for contractual relationships in order to accelerate them. Hatchett and his colleagues are educating and enlisting the global financial system to be informed, ready to provide capital the minute an epidemic breaks out. The whole organization has to consider the ecosystem of intellectual, political, financial, medical, and social capital so that, when they're needed, they're available.

Hatchett isn't working from the present incrementally or trying to define what is intrinsically unknowable. Instead, much of his work could be described as backcasting: imagining the optimal system of response and working backward to understand what that would require. This has distinct advantages: it doesn't mask or deny uncertainty but it does position the work as inherently positive. What could be frightening, disheartening work is recast optimistically. This provides psychological resilience without falling into the trap of promising miracles.

Preparing for events, some of which may never happen, might sound like a leisurely activity. It is exactly the opposite—Hatchett feels he is in a race to get ahead of events. That need for speed is real: in 2018, there were outbreaks of six out of the eight diseases designated "priority" by the World Health Organization: Ebola, MERS, Zika, Nipah virus, Lassa fever, and Rift Valley fever. He's discovered that you can't prepare for speed; the whole organization has to get used to working fast all the time.

I first met with Hatchett when he was six months into his job. Just one year later, it was obvious that operating at speed is how CEPI itself functions. The standing start was the hardest and slowest; with each year, CEPI gains momentum. In the time since we'd met, nine partnerships had been established, nine vaccines were in development, two rapid response partnerships were each working on three vaccines, and total funding had increased to $750 million for the first five years. With so much progress, CEPI has added two more vaccines to its portfolio: Rift Valley fever and chikungunya. But most important of all, they have demonstrated the value of preparedness: the 2018 Ebola outbreak in Équateur, in the Congo, did not develop into an epidemic. Within eleven days of the first case, everyone who had been in contact with the disease had been vaccinated. That was faster than the disease's incubation period—so the disease had no time to spread.

Much of Hatchett's work resembles that of Chris Llewellyn Smith's at CERN: ambition driven by diplomacy and negotiation, creating a coalition of disciplines, institutions, individuals, and industries rich enough in understanding and perspectives to address extreme complexity. Beyond expertise, the job also demands a significant capacity for cultural translation. Hatchett's earlier desire to be a writer has not gone to waste. "I get more mileage out of stories than out of arguments," he said, laughing. "Being able to tell real stories, like what happened to Ebola in Équateur province, completely changes the dynamics. And the stories illustrate how you can't think that this is just one thing—it's not just the vaccine. It requires the whole system."

Strictly linear, command-and-control stories won't work. Hatchett has to be able to tell a story in which everyone has a role and a contribution to make. "We need Citibank to help with currency exchanges, we need companies like Inovio, Profectus, Emergent to develop vaccines. We need to work with my Nigerian colleagues to receive and test vaccines. We don't have control over *any* of these people—yet they're all eager to play their parts. Here is something that has tortured humanity for as long as humanity has existed and being able to talk about what this means, and to whom . . . well, I'm better served by my understanding of narrative than by all my scientific expertise."

Preparedness has come to comprise four components. Just-in-case thinking means making significant, informed bets that accept uncertainty. This requires experiments that produce vaccines. Just-in-time thinking maximizes the efficiency of any aspect of the work that can be standardized, measured, and predicted, such as manufacturing. Becoming trusted participants and investing in a dynamic ecosystem accelerates the effectiveness of vaccines within stricken communities. Cultural translation requires artistry to articulate, reinforce, and adapt insight and experience. These four mark the contours of control that Hatchett so dimly glimpsed on 9/11. This approach is both efficient, where processes are predictable, and robust, where outcomes are uncertain. Collective human intelligence and the sense-making of stories underpins the resilience and legitimacy of the whole system.

Preparedness here is specifically nonideological. Trusting the market during epidemics has already been shown to be inadequate. An efficient mind-set would try to force-fit a predictable model of disease onto unpredictable environments. That would fail because the diseases can't be commanded. But a completely robust mind-set would fail, too, because it would prove exorbitantly expensive. Expertise alone won't work without the glue of social capital. Like a human body, where specific organs play defined roles but all are connected and interdependent, preparedness generates the levels of adaptation and responsiveness that the problem demands.

This approach accepts complexity and change from the outset. There is no overheated rhetoric about eliminating epidemics, no war against nature, no slogans of heroism and triumph. As you might expect from biologists, there's a humble, human response to the complex environment in which our species has always learned to adapt and thrive. Confidence doesn't derive from imposing a determined model but from a quiet belief in the human ability to keep asking better questions, to find and build better answers. Models might speak to this as a means of exploration, but not as an engine of solutionism.

It may be easier to prepare for events whose horror has been visceral for centuries. But that doesn't mean it's impossible to prepare for events that have never happened; it just takes an act of imagination to extrapolate from early warning signs. After both 9/11 and Hurricane Katrina, the American agriculturist Cary Fowler started to wonder about what he called "sooner or later thinking." Experts had said a Category 5 hurricane would hit New Orleans sooner or later; intelligence agents had expected another terrorist attack on the World Trade Center. Why, Fowler wondered, instead of talking about it, hadn't people done anything? But then he turned that question on himself: What was *he* doing about threats to the world's agricultural diversity?

On his computer, Fowler kept a file of gene bank horror stories. In 2002, looting had wrecked Afghanistan's seed bank. In 2005, the Iraqi seed collection at Abu Ghraib was destroyed and in 2006, the national seed bank in the Philippines had been wiped out by a typhoon. Seed banks encompass millions of unique regional varieties, dating back to the beginning of agriculture. As such, they represent a compendium of successful evolutionary responses to every known environment. Some may be very useful, sooner or later, but we can't predict which. Because nature and climate keep changing, it's impossible to know what varieties could suddenly become lifesaving. So the robust solution is to protect our entire genetic inheritance. That's why he started to search for what he called "a fail-safe way to protect the world's stockpile of diversity." What it required, he thought, was the safest place on earth. Just in case.

Svalbard is now home to the world's largest seed bank. It's an archipelago a thousand miles north of Norway, as far north as it's possible to fly in a commercial plane, and it is naturally very, very cold—so the seed bank doesn't depend on refrigeration. Those natural advantages, however, aren't enough. Fowler needed to gain the trust of countries around the world in order to persuade them to donate seeds and find someone to manage the facility properly. So he went to talk to the Norwegian deputy foreign minister.

"If I get you correctly, this seed diversity that you want to conserve, this is the most important natural resource on earth?" the minister had asked. Fowler said yes. "And you are also saying that this territory that Norway had sovereignty over, is the best place in the world to conserve it?" the minister continued. Fowler said yes again, at which point the minister just threw his hands up in the air, saying, "How can we say no?" The scale of the project might seem huge—but it was trivial when compared to the risk.

Today, the Svalbard seed vault is a long tunnel, running some 425 feet into a mountain. Its construction, in a windy environment regularly visited by polar bears and where the temperature runs at -40°C, stretched engineering limits. Because it is designed to function for thousands of years, Fowler's team had to contemplate climate change scenarios in which all the earth's ice melts, sea levels rise, and the vault is hit by the largest tsunami in history. When it was ready, Fowler had to persuade countries to entrust him with every seed known to man, passed down through the generations for the last thirteen thousand years. A few people asked him what he'd been drinking, but Fowler is well known within his professional ecosystem; fellow agriculturists liked the idea and trusted him. Visiting the site is, for some of them, almost a religious experience.

"I've seen people go out of that room with tears in their eyes," Fowler says. "This is not just a living history of human beings on earth, but it is also everything that our agricultural crops, and thus we, can be in the future."[5]

In 2017, global warming caused the seed vault to leak; the

permafrost that guarded its entrance had started to melt. That the project had been started well in advance of it being needed meant that there was time for a redesign that made the tunnel waterproof. In February 2020, the Cherokee nation made the one millionth donation, which may still be only the beginning. It is estimated that, in time, the vault will contain more than two million seeds.

Svalbard is a huge just-in-case project, which, like CEPI, is humble in the face of global complexity—wars, disease, ecological disaster—that can't be controlled or predicted. It tells an optimistic story about the future—we were prepared—without sugarcoating danger. Both projects are designed to be adaptable and robust enough for events that will occur—even where there's wild uncertainty about when, or where or how. Just because there is no single source of control over events doesn't preclude action now.

But it's become a truism that governments don't work that way, that they are short-term in their thinking and unwilling to take responsibility for anything beyond the election cycle. That endemic short-termism of government was precisely what the National Assembly for Wales attempted to address in 2015, when it passed the Well-being of Future Generations Act.

The idea for the act had been initiated by Jane Davidson, when, as a minister in the Welsh government, she became fed up with all the lofty talk about sustainability—and the absolute dearth of action. The United Nations' Sustainable Development Goals gave status, structure, and urgency to her rage; the country had committed to the SDGs but made little progress toward attaining them. She was supported by a new generation of bright young civil servants eager to turn her idea into action.

After the legislation passed, the first future generations commissioner for Wales, Sophie Howe, set to work in 2016. The guiding principle of the work is sustainable development applied to seven areas: making the country more prosperous, resilient, equal, healthy, cohesive, globally responsible, and culturally vibrant. Each of these aims has its own convenor, who is expected to integrate long-term thinking into public bodies, collaborate with a broad cross-section of the population, and stop existing problems from getting worse. The convenors are nonpartisan and expected to focus on "the art of the possible."[6]

The first test came when Howe challenged a twenty-five-year-old plan to expand the M4 motorway past Newport, Wales, a notorious congestion point. The plan, she argued, did not take into account the rise in rail passengers and changes in working patterns, with fewer people commuting to work. It overlooked the fact that fewer young people had cars, and those who did drove less. No one had considered poor air quality or that an extended motorway would make it harder for Wales to meet its carbon reduction targets. But the huge borrowing requirement for the project meant that future generations would be stuck with the bill for years to come.

"I asked the people backing this project to explain to me how it met our goals for a healthier Wales, how, when twenty-five percent of people don't have a car, it addressed the goal of a more equal Wales—and they couldn't!" She laughs. "I definitely put my neck on the block coming out against it, but if I'd gone along with it, the act would have meant nothing." At the end of the public inquiry, the inspector recommended that the extension go ahead, but when the final decision went to the first minister, the scheme was canceled. "That's when people really started talking about the Future Generations Act," Howe said. "They thought the first minister had made the right decision. And the BBC said that in the next five or ten years, my job would be the most powerful in Wales!"

Howe has only soft power: to commission research, review the way that public bodies make decisions, make recommendations about how those bodies can better take the long term into consideration, and to assess, every year, how well they are doing so. But that means she can shape the debate and encourage different modes of decision-making. Previous efforts along similar lines in other countries have been killed off by politics, so Howe thinks it's an advantage that the role is not held by a party politician. But she's canny. Howe served as a local councilor for nine years but left government in frustration. She then worked at reforming public services in policing, local government, housing, and equalities policy. "I know," she said, "how the system works, and how to have influence. I know where the bodies are buried, so I'm not afraid of calling things out. So this is my dream job."

Looking at policies through the lens of future generations upends ancient assumptions. In public health, Howe found that just 10 percent of life expectancy depends on health care services. By contrast, 29 percent depends on housing conditions (clean air, houses, green space), 18 to 19 percent on social capital, and 30 percent on jobs and welfare. But, traditionally, medical health care has always dominated the national budget and, prior to the Future Generations Act, there was no mechanism to address health holistically. But Howe is now challenging health, housing, environment, and welfare bodies to work together to craft a more coherent, proactive health strategy.

Similarly, she's shaken up industrial policy, asking why the government should subsidize old, dirty industries like car manufacturing, when a country so rich in wind and waves could invest in and lead the modern, renewable energy industry instead.

It was fine for the Education Department to restructure the school curriculum, but the commission is now inquiring what is being done to retrain the staff who have to teach it. "People may need to do less work in the future and we'll have more old people," Howe added. "We might go on a pathway of saying we want to have a four-day working week, because on the fifth day, we want you to look after your neighbor. I know it's utopian but how else are we going to think about these trends? We have to set out a vision for the Wales we want."

Howe has a team of only twenty people. But she's resourceful, getting civil servants on loan from other departments for six or twelve months. That way, when they go back to their permanent positions, they've absorbed a way of thinking about the future that she hopes will inform their home department. A practical, political understanding that "everything has a consequence for everything else" can, she believes, lead to better integrated policy-making. Like Richard Hatchett, she is backcasting: working from a future that Welsh citizens have endorsed to define what can be done immediately. "The legal definition of 'a prosperous Wales' nowhere mentions GDP," she says. "So we can escape the trap of thinking that prosperity is only about economic growth. It has to encompass far more than that. We have a legal and a moral obligation to leave the world better than we found it."

The dream job is intense, not least because Howe is also on a mission to take the Welsh blueprint to the rest of the world. Canada has just amended legislation to reflect responsibility for future generations. In the United Arab Emirates, much of the well-being strategy is being taken from the Welsh experience. Gibraltar is trying to pass legislation that is, she says, virtually identical, and she is in discussion with the New Zealand government, too. "I could," she says, "be in a different country every week because their governments are getting to know about what we're doing here and want to know more." When we spoke, she was just back from the United Nations, whose director general had seen in the Future Generations Act a mechanism to smash some of the siloes forming around the Sustainable Development Goals. "They're treated as single issues," she said, "but they are all interconnected. Sustainable needs have to be taken laterally."[7]

Wales is serious about preparing for its future. This is typical of small countries. Unlike rich, powerful nations, the Welsh know they have to be nimble, creative, and collaborative because they don't have the luxury of natural resources or economic clout to call the shots. Being small may make it easier to get things done, but being clear-eyed about their vulnerability is a real prompt to action. The speed with which the idea has spread is testament to the power of small things—ideas, individuals, countries—to make a big impact on complex environments. One of the key requirements in navigating the future is to notice these, share them, and copy them prodigiously.

A mixture of the pragmatic and the utopian, the act implicitly recognizes that any five- or ten-year plan for the future would be an absurdly simplistic response to the complexity of the real world. But it also rejects the view that passivity or predictions provide the only alternatives. Instead, it galvanizes all parts of the population to participate in their future, to feel powerful and responsible, regardless of age or status. The seven guiding principles help to shape experiments and design scenarios for possibilities that they can start exploring today. Howe would be the first person to say the act isn't perfect. But it's a start. The only way the Welsh can prepare a better future for their children and grandchildren is by defining it for themselves. In accepting both their power and their vulnerability, we can see ourselves.

Most of us grew up as planners. We started from the present and worked forward, with reasonable confidence that we knew where we were going and how to get there. That confidence is now gone. In a world where the time scale for accurate prediction shrinks, preparedness is a vital antidote to passivity and pessimism. Instead of incrementalizing from the present, being prepared requires a clear understanding of risk and uncertainty in order to craft positive and robust counter-weights. This means starting, just as cathedral builders do, with an optimistic ambition—what is the very best we can do?—that defines direction. The optimism is no guarantee, but the best way to navigate uncharted territory is to have an energetic, future-facing and long-term ambition in mind. Where a planning mind-set today proliferates dystopias, a preparedness mind-set does the opposite. You can't build a better future until you imagine it.

All creative thinking about the future starts with experiments, feeling our way through a changing landscape, finding boundaries and contours. Bumping up against dead ends or discovering unexpected momentum, detail emerges and alternative scenarios start to coalesce: what else could be, what might be. More experiments reveal opportunity, advantages. All of this work shows us where we are, but still requires resilience because the route itself is uneven.

The biggest unknown in the work is time, which may be on our side—or not. When the future announces itself before we're ready, then having prepared provides vital rewards: resources, fellowship, stories, resilience, and renewed ambition. Along the way, everyone is changed by the work that becomes, in the end, a legacy that others continue.

Navigating the future, whether away from danger or toward opportunity, has to be a collective activity because no one person can see enough. It's impossible to have an adequate argument alone or in an echo chamber. To see people as data is one perspective, but a far from comprehensive one. We may be economic actors, but financial transactions do not fully capture our identity, either. We are also physical beings, subject to biological influences and threats. Creative creatures, too, open to imagination, change, and contradiction. So the capacity to see multiple futures depends on the widest possible range of contributors and collaborators. Leave perspectives out and the future is incomplete or illegitimate. This isn't just a democratic imperative, but a frank acknowledgment that those not involved in making the future will have every motive to upend it.

For decisions to be credible means that they must be developed by more than a few authorities or experts. That this process can be intelligent, meaningful, and productive is demonstrated repeatedly in deliberative polling, citizen juries, and assemblies. Engaging diverse minds is a more robust way of capturing the complexity of the environment in which decisions, policies, and laws succeed or fail. In many ways, CEPI, the Svalbard seed bank, and similar organizations are doing what Mary Warnock did with her fertilization and embryology commission: preparing for uncertain future events and technologies by consolidating understanding and consensus to support positive, early action. As the CEO of Shell commented, leaders now are compelled to think beyond legal requirements and consider their "licence to operate," which is granted only by the public.[8] Imagining that whole swaths of the population and environment can be overlooked in preference to a focus on financial performance might once have been considered operational discipline on the part of both corporations and democratic governments. Now it looks like institutional willful blindness. The only pragmatic protection against surprise is to build public support and understanding along the way. To be prepared requires that, in some shape or form, every organization has its own commissioner for future generations.

This calls for a new kind of leadership. Those who will rise to that challenge will be outstanding convenors, better chosen for their skepticism and curiosity than their confidence. Collecting voices, structuring exploration, keen listening, and synthesizing success and failure will be the focus of their work. They need to be excellent interrogators of the ecosystems in which they reside, aware of where they fit and the impact of their decisions on others. They can't be addicted to prediction or to certainty, but confident and courageous enough to create the conditions in which people can think, and experiment, freely. Being able to reconcile opposites—efficiency and robustness, adaptability and long-term focus, just-in-time and just-in-case—is a hallmark of their adaptive minds. The unborn children who will make great leaders will be able to hold the tension between urgency and integrity, to stiffen resolve for what is confusing, frustrating, and frightening, and to resist simplifying what is innately complex.

Like the director general at CERN, or the leaders of backbone organizations, like Richard Hatchett or Sophie Howe, Oliver Burrows or Fiona Wilson, an effective leader's principal asset isn't power but the ability to make a better future feel urgent, possible, practical, and meaningful. They need the moral authority to be honest about sacrifices and they will have to resist the rhetorical allure of simplistic daydreams. Where will these people come from? From everywhere, identified by courage and energy, or, like Iris Long in the AIDS fight or Greta Thunberg in the climate crisis, they may emerge unpredictably, living evidence of the huge impact of small surprises. Such leaders have rational optimism, a grounded belief in human capacity. They haven't given up on human beings and won't accept that, as a leading psychologist put it, "We've seen the enemy and it's us." They scoff at the goal, proposed by a science technologist, "to defeat mother nature."[9] Instead, they find in people and in nature all the strength they need to act. Progress will be indirect, lumpy, and hard to measure, accelerating at times and stalling at others. Those with stamina, who can work together, will fare best.

The need for broad-based legitimacy doesn't make expertise useless or optional. As the astronomer Martin Rees argues, there is no ivory tower or penthouse high or remote enough for scientists and engineers to disown accountability for the uses to which their work is put. This means that the choices we face, of any kind, have to be informed and led by values beyond those that science, engineering, or any single discipline can provide. None of the challenges we face will be solved by expertise alone. But that places on experts the responsibility to explore and communicate humbly the consequences and ramifications of their work. It is only together that legitimate boundaries for technology can be defined.

The future is also personal. Teen daughters are changing attitudes to the climate crisis, just as attitudes to AIDS shifted when parents watched their sons and daughters die or when scientists met patients and activists. Such epiphanies don't happen without love and friendship. That means making time for each other to develop bonds of trust and respect strong enough to weather crises.

Not knowing the future makes us anxious and, in our anxiety, susceptible to binary thinking: either there's one answer or there is none. The belief in solutions, quick fixes makes us give up when we can't find one. Similarly, perfection can be a problem, when it makes people passive, afraid to experiment. Great careers and great cathedrals weren't built following immaculate plans, but evolved through conviction, collaboration, and a stubborn belief in work that mattered. In confronting the existential challenge of climate change, we have work that matters. Many have wasted time, waiting for a simple solution or a perfect plan—but not everyone has been so complacent. The world is now replete with technological solutions, inventions, and experiments made by people who would not wait. What their vast inventory reveals is that the climate crisis is not one of technology, it is one of collaboration. How far are we prepared to act together, on every front, before the last detail is known, to make common cause with those we once considered enemies, to experiment, to make visible the damage being done today, to be honest about sacrifice, and to remember that courage drives courage? We have the freedom to do this; the question is whether we will use it.

Threats to that future come from anyone or anything that diminishes that freedom. Of these, one of the biggest insults to our power to craft a fitting legacy for successive generations comes from technology. The automation paradox is a physical reality. The more we surrender to the authority of devices, the less independent and imaginative our minds become, just when we need them most. Extravagant claims for artificial intelligence don't just denigrate natural intelligence but mask a determination to force the world into predictable patterns. In a complex world, replete with contingency and uncertainty, nothing could be more dangerous than to constrain imagination, freedom, and creativity. When industry leaders acknowledge that "the goal of everything we do is to change people's behaviour at scale," they tacitly acknowledge that we aren't merely data, that we *are* complex and unpredictable and that the only way they can make the world truly predictable is to shackle us to their digital devices with rewards and punishments. But we become digital slaves only when we think of ourselves as only data. Nothing is inevitable, unless or until we surrender the right to use the freedom that we have.[10]

Every time we use technology—to nudge us through decisions or to interpret how other people feel—we outsource to machines what we could and can do ourselves. It's an expensive trade-off. When we surrender our emotional intelligence to parenting apps, we give up on the chance to learn about ourselves and our children. The more we meet people we are programmed to like, the less we can cope with those who are different. And the less compassion we need, the less compassion we have. So the more we let technology think for us and act for us, the less we will be capable of making a future for ourselves.

The companies enforcing this sterile, monoglot view of the world are so few, so homogeneous, and so powerful that they represent a big and obvious threat to the economic and cultural diversity of the world we inhabit. At a time when both humanity and the planet are struggling to preserve the variety that evolution demands, a single, impoverished definition of life's meaning undermines the will and skill needed to build a better future for us all. Imagination, creativity, compassion, generosity, variety, meaning, faith, and courage: what makes the world unpredictable are the same strengths that make each of us unique and human. Accepting uncertainty means embracing these as robust talents to be used, not flaws to be eliminated.

This book began with two questions: What do we need to do, and what do we need to be, to navigate the future? What we need to do is to hold fast to the gifts we have, and to develop them together. What we need to be is human. The future will always be uncharted but it is made by those active enough to explore it, with the stamina and imagination not to give up on themselves or each other. We have no need to be slaves and we have no right to enslave future generations. All we owe to ourselves and to generations to come is to hone the gifts we have to create the best that we can imagine, exercising daily the self-determination that built cathedrals. It doesn't matter where we start, only that we do.

ACKNOWLEDGMENTS

I f I needed a lesson in unpredictability, writing this book was it. Like every other book I've ever written, this one had a schedule. Unlike every other book I've written, this schedule kept being blown up. So I apologize to all the people I didn't see, meetings I didn't make, parties I missed, and the many kindnesses I'm sure I overlooked. Writing this book has been a daily reminder that uncertainty may be full of possibility but it can also be full of shocks and horrors.

In the face of dire predictions that print was doomed, Ben Loeh nen and Natasha Fairweather have been steadfast in their championing of books and writers. I am indebted to them for their support, insight, understanding, and faith.

All of the people in this book contributed far more than appears on the page. In particular, I am indebted to Jonathan Blake, Silvia Petretti, Tony Whitehead, and Ian Green; I shouldn't be surprised that AIDS activists are brave and generous but I am grateful. Likewise I'm indebted to all the staff at St. Margaret's Hospice, who have plenty to do without giving their precious time to me. Alberto Fernandez was a remarkable host and guide to Mexico and I'm indebted to him and his colleagues for their hospitality, insights, and generosity. Similarly Adam Kahane and his team at REOS

Partners could not have been more open in demonstrating the skill and nuance of scenario planning.

Off the page, my colleagues at the Forward Institute, the University of Bath, and at Merryck & Company have been inspirational, provocative, and remarkably patient with the demands this book made on my time. I'd also like to thank Marco Amitrano, Matthew Brockman, Sandy Crosbie, Ben Story, Clare Gilmartin, Dominik Kaiser, and Lisa Myers for sharing with me their daily experience of leading organizations in periods of deep uncertainty. And along the way of this winding book, David Fishkin, Danica Remy, Paul Schoemaker, Chris Worley, and Elsa van der Zee proved very useful guides.

The team at TED has been stalwart in their support of my work and I am indebted to Juliet Blake, Bruno Giussani, Lisa Choy Evans, and Chris Anderson for their encouragement and enthusiasm. I'm also grateful to Hugh Levinson, Adele Armstrong, Sheila Cook, and Jasper Corbett, who've allowed me to explore some of the ideas in this book through the miracle that is BBC radio. Robert Phillips, Ben Page, and Laurence Evans were excellent guides to the wonderful world of polling and its history. I've also been fortunate in many friends and colleagues who have a gift for asking excellent and surprising questions: Jennifer Board, Charlotte Calkin, Lorna Davis, Sarah Gillard, Jonathan Gosling, Thelma Holt, Pico Iyer, Anab Jain, Juliane Jung, Mike Jones, David Kedmey, Brooke Masters, Eve Poole, Massimo Portincaso, Cindy Solomon, Stefan Stern, Christian Wolmar, and many more. It is impossible to think alone and I'm indebted to my many and diverse thinking pals.

Nicki deFago, Jenni Waugh, and Clemency Calkin provided solid research despite often daunting briefs. Stephanie Cooper-Lande somehow kept her cool as my schedules fell apart. But it is always families who bear the burden of books and never more than this one. My children tolerated with grace my endless interrogations into how they saw their future. But it was my husband, Lindsay, above all whose stalwart belief in this project kept it, and me, going.

This book is dedicated to four friends who faced existential crises of their own during the course of its writing. Their creativity and fortitude sharpened my resolve, reminding me that, for all of us, the future is not an abstract idea but a real, often daunting, reality. I will always be grateful for their inspiration and friendship.

Farrington Gurney, England
2019

NOTES

INTRODUCTION

1 M. R. O'Connor, *Wayfinding: The Science and Mystery of How Humans Navigate the World* (New York: St. Martin's Press, 2019).

2 Shoshana Zuboff, *The Age of Surveillance Capitalism* (New York: Public Affairs, 2019).

3 https://www.pewsocialtrends.org/2019/03/21/public-sees-an-america -in-decline-on-many-fronts/ on American pessimism and https://www .investopedia.com/ceo-confidence-plunges-to-lowest-since-2008-crisis-in -warning-sign-4773789 on CEO gloom. Both accessed February 5, 2020.

CHAPTER ONE: FALSE PROFITS

1 Katherine Ott, *Fevered Lives: Tuberculosis in American Culture since 1870* (Cambridge, MA: Harvard University Press, 1996), p 12.

2 Walter A. Friedman, *Fortune Tellers: The Story of America's First Economic Forecasters* (Princeton, NJ: Princeton University Press, 2014), p. 66.

3 Roger W. Babson, *Actions and Reactions: An Autobiography of Roger W. Babson* (New York: Harper & Brothers, 1950), pp. 65–68.

4 Ibid., p. 107.

5 Ibid., p. 111.

6 Irving N. Fisher, *My Father Irving Fisher* (New York: Comet Press Books, 1956), p. 193.

7 Larissa MacFarquhar, "The Deflationist: How Paul Krugman Found Politics," *New Yorker*, March 1, 2010.

8 Testimony before Congress on the Financial Crisis and the Role of Federal Regulators, October 23, 2008, and Government Reform, Washington, DC, p. 37.

9   Friedman, *Fortune Tellers*, p. 146. Keynes to Bullock, February 11, 1925.

10 An elegant description of why this is the case goes as follows:

> No scientific hypothesis is ever confirmed with absolute certainty; there is always a possibility of it being wrong.
>
> The decision whether to accept or reject a hypothesis depends on whether the evidence is sufficiently strong.
>
> Determining sufficient strength is always a value judgment.
>
> Therefore scientists make value judgments.
>
> For more on this, see Eric Winsberg's *Science in the Age of Computer Simulation* (Chicago: University of Chicago Press, 2010).

11 Joseph Engelberg, Caroline Sasseville, and Jared Williams, "Market Madness: The Case of Mad Money," *Management Science* 58, no. 2 (2010): 351–64.

12 This is one reason why Warren Buffett has advised his wife, after his death, to invest in tracker funds. The pollster Nate Silver makes the challenging observation that the rare group that does outperform the market are U.S. senators, raising all kinds of questions about inside information. See Nate Silver, *The Signal and the Noise* (London: Penguin Books, 2013).

13 See *The Economist*, March 17, 2018, p. 39.

14 I'm indebted to David Kedmey for pointing this out.

15 "The Risk of Automation for Jobs in OECD Countries," https://www.oecd-ilibrary.org/social-issues-migration-health/the-risk-of-automation-for-jobs-in-oecd-countries_5jlz9h56dvq7-en, accessed October 14, 2018, and October 27, 2019.

16 https://www.mckinsey.com/~/media/mckinsey/featured%20insights/Digital%20Disruption/Harnessing%20automation%20for%20a%20future%20that%20works/MGI-A-future-that-works-Executive-summary.ashx, accessed June 21, 2019.

17 https://www.weforum.org/agenda/2018/09/future-of-jobs-2018-things-to-know/. The Frey/Osborne paper was still being cited by *The Economist* at the end of 2019, even though one of its authors had since developed a far more nuanced understanding of how workforces change.

18 Privately, investors in this autonomous vehicle technology now acknowledge that it is much harder and much more expensive than originally thought and that the urban environment of existing cities may prove to be irredeemably complex.

19 Christian Wolmar, *Driverless Cars: On a Road to Nowhere* (London: Publishing Partnership, 2018).

20 Xiuzhen Huang et al., "Big data—a 21st Century Science Maginot Line?" *BioData Mining*, 2015, 8:7.

21 For examples here, see Virginia Eubanks, *Automating Inequality* (New York: St. Martin's Press, 2017), as well as Cathy O'Neil, *Weapons of Math Destruction* (London: Allen Lane, 2016) and reports from the AI Now Institute: https://ainowinstitute.org/.

22 S. Freedman and M. Canaan, "Overcoming Speed Bumps on the Road to Telematics," https://www2.deloitte.com/content/dam/insights/us/articles /telematics-in-auto-insurance/DUP-695_Telematics-in-the-Insurance-Industry _vFINAL.pdf, accessed August 20, 2019. Also quoted in Zuboff, *The Age of Surveillance Capitalism.*

23 "Good Judgment Project research found that super-forecasters can anticipate events 400 days ahead that other forecasters can only see 150 days ahead," www .goodjudgment.com, accessed January 29, 2019.

24 https://www.youtube.com/watch?v=mtrOquc4CJc.

25 David Spiegelhalter, "Why Do People Find Probability Unintuitive and Difficult?" https://nrich.maths.org/7326.

CHAPTER TWO: **DOES HISTORY REPEAT ITSELF?**

1 Katherine Woollett and Eleanor A. Maguire, "Acquiring 'the Knowledge' of London's Layout Drives Structural Brain Changes," *Current Biology,* 21, no. 24 (2011): 2109–14.

2 Sinéad L. Mullally and Eleanor A. Maguire, "Memory, Imagination, and Predicting the Future: A Common Brain Mechanism?," *Neuroscientist* 20, no. 3 (2014): 220–34.

3 M. R. O'Connor, "Ditch the GPS. It's Ruining Your Brain," www .washingtonpost.com/opinions/ditch-the-gps-its-ruining-your-brain/2019/06 /05/29a3170e-87af-11e9-98c1-e945ae5db8fb_story.html?noredirect=on&utm _term=.70c11f4d7c07, and M. R. O'Connor, *Wayfinding: The Science and Mystery of How Humans Navigate the World* (London: St. Martin's Press, 2018).

4 Dan T. Gilbert and Timothy D. Wilson, "Prospection: Experiencing the Future," *Science* 317 (September 7, 2007), p. 135.

5 George Santayana, *The Life of Reason,* ch. 12, vol. 1, 1905, available at https:// ia801407.us.archive.org/11/items/lifeofreasonphas01sant/lifeofreasonphas01sant.pdf.

6 Daniel Kahneman and Amos Tversky, "On the Psychology of Prediction," *Psychological Review* 80, no. 4 (July 1973).

7 Nevertheless, it is strikingly difficult to persuade people that the aesthetic similarity between stories isn't meaningful. The most frequent argument for history repeating itself is always the invasion of Russia. Surely Hitler repeated Napoleon's folly. But military historian Michael Clark dismisses the analogy swiftly. Charles XII of Sweden had taken on Russia and won. The military campaigns of Hitler and Napoleon were different in almost every detail. Hitler might have been victorious had he not made many unforced errors: getting distracted by Greece, failing to gain Ukrainian support, failing to find an effective way to work with Japan. The aims of the wars were different, as were the tactics, talents, and circumstances.

8 Richard E. Neustadt and Ernest R. May, *Thinking in Time: The Use of History for Decision Makers* (New York: Free Press, 1988).

9 Macmillan, *The Uses and Abuses of History*. More recently, Boris Johnson tried to puff his own government by drawing an analogy between himself and Churchill (as he is wont to do). The historian Simon Schama blasted back: 'You are not Churchill and the EU is not the Third Reich. You do not have a war cabinet and THERE IS NO WAR. How DARE you invoke the sacrifices of those [who] fought one."

10 More recently, Mervyn King, a former governor of the Bank of England, compared Theresa May's Brexit deal to Chamberlain's appeasement of Hitler in the 1930s, too: "In the 1930s, with appeasement; in the 1970s, when the British economy was the 'sick man' of Europe and the government saw its role as managing decline; and now, in the turmoil that has followed the Brexit referendum. In all three cases, the conventional wisdom of the day was wrong." https://www.bbc.co.uk/news/business-46446105, accessed December 5, 2018.

11 Alex Sardar, "From the Berlin Wall to the Arab Spring," www.counterpart.org/stories/from-the-berlin-wall-to-the-arab-spring/.

12 "Medvedev Compares 'Arab Spring' to Fall of Berlin Wall," http://www.expatica.com/ru/news/country-news/Medvedev-compares-Arab-Spring-to-fall-of-Berlin-Wall_274177.html, accessed November 30, 2018.

13 Remarks by the President on the Middle East and North Africa, obamawhitehouse.archives.gov/the-press-office/2011/05/19/remarks-president-middle-east-and-north-africa, accessed May 2, 2018.

14 In Egypt, even as Tahrir Square filled, analysts started to question the revolutionary thesis. President Mubarak might be in peril but the real threat wasn't posed by students but rather by the army. Throughout modern Egyptian history, the military had always claimed the right to name the president's successor. When Mubarak started to seize that privilege, asserting that his son Gamal would succeed him, the army decided to curb presidential power and reinstate military influence. Three days after Mubarak resigned and many commentators continued to enthuse about a democratic revolution, the geopolitical strategist George Friedman saw something different—and far from inevitable.

"What we see," Friedman wrote, "is that while Mubarak is gone, the military regime in which he served has dramatically increased its power. This isn't incompatible with democratic reform. Organizing elections, political parties and candidates is not something that can be done quickly. If the military is sincere in its intentions, it will have to do these things. The problem is that if the military is insincere, it will do exactly the same things. Six months is a long time, passions can subside and promises can be forgotten. At this point, we simply don't know what will happen."

Tahrir Square wasn't the Berlin Wall or the Boston Tea Party. In 2014, Field Marshal Abdel Fattah el-Sisi retired from his military career to run for president, winning with 96 percent of the votes. In 2018, he was reelected with 92 percent.

15 Lars-Erik Cederman and Nils B. Weidmann, "Predicting Armed Conflict: Time to Adjust Our Expectations?" *Science* 344 (2017): 474–76.

CHAPTER THREE: FLUKES AND MUTATIONS

1 storage.googleapis.com/kindersight/muse.mp4 on the Muse website: https://muse.socoslearning.com, accessed April 9, 2018.

2 Rana Foroohar, "Vivienne Ming: 'The Professional Class Is About to Be Blindsided by AI,'" *Financial Times*, July 27, 2018.

3 https://www.wired.com/2016/05/we-will-literally-predict-their-life-outcomes/, accessed August 24, 2017.

4 See *The Digital Human*, Series 13, *Oracle,* a BBC Radio 4 program by Aleks Krotoski, available at https://www.bbc.co.uk/programmes/b09wrxtw, accessed October 27, 2019.

5 The *Financial Times* reports that McKinsey employees list their MBTI type in the company's internal profile pages. See Murad Ahmed, "Is Myers-Briggs Up to the Job?," *Financial Times*, February 11, 2016, www.ft.com/content/8790ef0a-d040-11e5-831d-09f7778e7377.

6 Merve Emre, *What's Your Type? The Strange History of Myers-Briggs and the Birth of Personality Testing* (London: Fourth Estate, 2018). (The book was published in the United States under the title *The Personality Brokers.*)

7 S. Srivastava, O. P. John, S. D. Gosling, and J. Potter, "Development of Personality in Early and Middle Adulthood: Set Like Plaster or Persistent Change?," *Journal of Personality and Social Psychology* 84, no. 5 (2003).

8 Emre, *What's Your Type?*

9 The Pygmalion effect in the classroom was first written up here: https://www.uni-muenster.de/imperia/md/content/psyifp/aeechterhoff/sommersemester 2012/schluesselstudiendersozialpsychologiea/rosenthal_jacobson_pygmalion classroom_urbrev1968.pdf, but was also written up in a book, *Pygmalion in the Classroom,* by Robert Rosenthal and Lenore Jacobson. The subsequent study of the Israeli army platoons can be found here: http://psycnet.apa.org/?&fa =main.doiLanding&doi=10.1037/0021-9010.75.4.394.

10 In the United States, 95 percent of Fortune 500 companies are reported as doing so: https://www.msn.com/en-gb/money/career/this-genius-method-will -get-your-job-application-into-the-hands-of-a-hiring-manager/ar-BBNJDDk

11 Caroline Criado Perez, *Invisible Women: Data Bias in a World Designed for Men* (London: Chatto & Windus, 2019).

12 Laszlo Bock, formerly head of HR at Google, rejected them for this reason.

13 Of course, old-style recruiting doesn't offer us such a dream of perfection, either. It is slow, expensive, and riddled with bias. But it carries no promise of perfection. How it works is visible; we can call each other on demonstrable bias. And although it's been fashionable to point out how fallible it is, it's hard to find an organization whose leadership believes all of its hiring has been mistaken.

14 The minimal group paradigm in social psychology was explored and defined by the social psychologist Henri Tajfel and later developed by Thomas Gilovich at Yale. See H. Tajfel, "Experiments in Intergroup Discrimination," *Scientific American* 223 (1970) and H. Tajfel, M. G. Billig, R. P. Bundy, and C. Flament, "Social Categorisation and Intergroup Behaviour," *European Journal of Social Psychology* 1 (1971), and M. G. Frank and T. Gilovich, "The Dark Side of Self and Social Perception: Black Uniforms and Aggression in Professional Sports," *Journal of Personality and Social Psychology* 54, no. 1 (1988).

15 Theodor Adorno, *The Authoritarian Personality*, available online: www.ajc archives.org/AJC_DATA/Files/AP22.pdf.

16 A. Clauset, D. B. Larremore, R. Sinatra, "Data-driven predictions in the science of science," *Science* 355, p. 477, no. 480, February 3, 2017.

17 R. Sinatra, D. Wang, P. Deville, C. Song, and A. L. Barabasi, "Quantifying the Evolution of Individual Scientific Impact," *Science* 354, no. 6312 (2016).

18 Nicola Davis, "Scientists Quash Idea of Single 'Gay Gene,'" *Guardian*, August 29, 2019, www.theguardian.com/science/2019/aug/29/scientists-quash-idea -of-single-gay-gene.

19 Wojciech Branicki, Fan Liu, Kate van Duijn, Jolanta Draus-Barini, Ewelina Pośpiech, Susan Walsh, Tomasz Kupiec, Anna Wojas-Pelc, and Manfred Kayse, "Model-Based Prediction of Human Hair Color Using DNA Variants," *Nature Genetics* 129 (2011): 443.

20 Carl Zimmer, *She Has Her Mother's Laugh: The Powers, Perversions, and Potential of Heredity* (London: Picador, 2018).

21 Robert Plomin, *Blueprint: How DNA Makes Us Who We Are* (London: Allen Lane, 2018), p. 8.

22 L. B. Nicholson, "Expect the Unexpected," account of lecture by Sydney Brenner, https://www.bristol.ac.uk/cellmolmed/air/qanda/archive/sydney_brenner .html, accessed April 17, 2018.

23 https://www.ccalliance.org/colorectal-cancer-information/statistics-risk-factors, accessed November 4, 2018.

24 Sanjana Varghese, "Ruha Benjamin: We Definitely Can't Wait for Silicon Valley to Become More Diverse," *Guardian*, June 29, 2019. See also Benjamin's book *Race After Technology* (Medford, MA: Polity Press, 2019).

25 Paul Davies, *The Demon in the Machine* (London: Penguin Books, 2019).

26 Plomin, *Blueprint*, p. 8.

27 Matthew Warren, "The Power of Many," *Nature* 562 (October 11, 2018).

28 Plomin, *Blueprint*, p. 165.

29 "DNA Tests For IQ Are Coming, But It Might Not Be Smart to Take One," http://www.technologyreview.com/s/610339/dna-tests-for-iq-are-coming-but -it-might-not-be-smart-to-take-one, accessed November 4, 2018.

30 Not a hypothesis. In the BBC's outstanding documentary series *The Mighty Redcar*, this is exactly what happens. Or consider the only child persuaded not to attend university because the mother fears living alone.

31 Young rats brought up with stimuli—ladders, tunnels, and toys—developed cerebral cortex volume that was 25 percent larger than the rats left in cages with nothing to do. M. J. Renner and M. R. Rosenzweig, "Social Interactions Among Rats Housed in Groups and Enriched Conditions," *Developmental Psychobiology* 19, no. 4 (July 1986): 303–13.

32 Plomin, *Blueprint*, pp. 43 and 40.

33 Ibid., p. 178.

34 He wrote a novel, *Kantsaywhere*, describing a society driven by determined, designed self-improvement. The novel was never published and just one copy remains, now in the Special Collections of University College London, where Robert Plomin works.

35 Clyde Chitty, *Eugenics, Race and Intelligence in Education* (London: Continuum International, 2007).

36 Victoria Brignell, "The Eugenics Movement Britain Wants to Forget," *New Statesman*, December 9, 2010, www.newstatesman.com/society/2010/12/british -eugenics-disabled#reader-comments, accessed April 17, 2018.

37 Emre, *What's Your Type?*

38 Victoria Brignell, "When America Believed in Eugenics," *New Statesman*, December 10, 2010, https://www.newstatesman.com/society/2010/12/disabled -america-immigration, accessed October 27, 2019.

39 US Supreme Court justice Oliver Wendell Holmes, *Buck v. Bell*, 1927, https:// www.ushmm.org/information/press/press-kits/traveling-exhibitions/deadly -medicine/quotes-from-the-2004-exhibition, accessed April 17, 2018.

40 "Thousands Sterilized, A State Weighs Restitution," *New York Times*, December 9, 2011, https://www.nytimes.com/2011/12/10/us/redress-weighed-for-forced -sterilizations-in-north-carolina.html, accessed October 27, 2019.

41 Toby Young, "Eugenics, IQ, and the Poor (part 1)," blogs.bmj.com/medical -ethics/2018/01/08/toby-young-eugenics-iq-and-the-poor-part-1.

42 Siddhartha Mukherjee, *The Gene: An Intimate History* (New York: Scribner, 2017), p. 274.

43 Ibid., p. 477.

44 "Rogue Chinese Geneticist Jailed for His Creation of Gene-Edited Babies," https://www.chemistryworld.com/news/rogue-chinese-geneticist-jailed-for -his-role-in-creation-of-gene-edited-babies/4010977.article, accessed January 4, 2020.

45 Hannah Kuchler, "Lunch with the FT: Jennifer Doudna," *Financial Times*, February 1, 2020, p. 3.

46 "Amazon Patents 'Anticipatory' Shipping—to Start Sending Stuff Before You've Bought It," techcrunch.com/2014/01/18/amazon-pre-ships, accessed August 21, 2019. The patent can be found at ibid.

47 Of course, the company might make the wrong choices (it forever sends me emails recommending that I buy books I've written), but that's okay, because the first few I'm allowed to keep as a gesture of goodwill.

48 Shoshana Zuboff, *The Age of Surveillance Capitalism: The Fight for a Human Future at the New Frontier of Power* (London: Profile Books, 2019).
49 Strangely this comment appears to have been made without irony or any awareness that our financial systems are imperfect. Alex Pentland, "Society's Nervous System: Building Effective Government, Energy, and Public Health Systems," hd.media.mit.edu/tech-reports/TR-664.pdf, accessed August 20, 2019.

CHAPTER FOUR: **NO AVAILABLE DATASETS**

1 For more detail, see John Kania and Mark Kramer, "Embracing Emergence: How Collective Impact Addresses Complexity," *Stanford Social Innovation Review,* January 21, 2013. See also John Kania and Mark Kramer, "Collective Impact," *Stanford Social Innovation Review*, Winter 2011; Fay Hanleybrown, John Kania, and Mark Kramer, "Channeling Change: Making Collective Impact Work," *Stanford Social Innovation Review*, January 2012.
2 One example of this was an outstanding Somerset initiative to tackle postnatal depression. It proved highly successful and sustainable but the isolation of the organization that designed it meant that it never proliferated. I encountered this when working with the charity, CreativityWorks, that initiated the project.
3 Hilaire Belloc, "Jim."
4 http://fortune.com/2014/11/18/cadillac-brand-director-melody-lee/.
5 Raghu Garud, Joel Gehman, and Arun Kumaraswamy, "Complexity Arrangements for Sustained Innovation: Lessons from 3M Corporation," *Organization Studies* 32, no. 6 (2011): 737–67. This is an excellent study of two products—both Trizact and BEF.
6 Source is a conference of doctors held in Chicago in 2018, hosted by Advisory.
7 In 2012, the University Regents allocated $25 million of annual funding and $40 million to start recruiting for the project. More remarkable still, the citizens of Travis County voted to increase their property taxes specifically to fund improved health care for all of its citizens. In 2013, the Michael and Susan Dell Foundation pledged $50 million to the school.
8 Stacey Chang and Thomas H. Lee, "Beyond Evidence-Based Medicine," *New England Journal of Medicine*, November 22, 2018, DOI:10.1056/NEJMp1806984.
9 This is in striking contrast to medical record systems that are designed without doctors or patients in mind, as described by Atul Gawande: https://www.newyorker.com/magazine/2018/11/12/why-doctors-hate-their-computers.
10 "The Citizens' Assembly Publishes Final Report," http://www.citizensassembly.ie/en/News/The-Citizens-Assembly-Publishes-Final-Report.html.
11 In the United Kingdom in 2020, a citizens' assembly is being used to formulate a coherent national food policy in the face of climate change. There is also talk of convening an assembly to address climate policy overall.

CHAPTER FIVE: GO FAST, GO FAR

1 Crime data from Poligono Edison, OXXO (email).
2 "Fighting Corruption in Mexico: Taking It to the People," www.foreignaffairs .com/articles/mexico/2016-06-22/fighting-corruption-mexico, accessed August 2019. Shell scenario planning videos: https://www.youtube.com /watch?v=nwub4Bhr-aM&frags=wn; https://www.youtube.com/watch?v= GoBvGOmO8KQ&frags=pl%2Cwn; https://www.youtube.com/watch?v= srY-hJuqYTM; and https://www.shell.com/energy-and-innovation/the-energy -future/scenarios/new-lenses-on-the-future.html.
3 See two articles by Pierre Wack on this period: "Scenarios: Uncharted Waters Ahead," *Harvard Business Review*, September 1985, and "Scenarios: Shooting the Rapids," *Harvard Business Review*, November 1985.
4 Wack, "Scenarios: Shooting the Rapids," p. 3.
5 The scenarios and data sets are published here: https://www.shell.com/content /dam/royaldutchshell/documents/corporate/scenarios-newdoc.pdf.
6 Angela Wilkinson, *The Essence of Scenarios* (Amsterdam: Amsterdam University Press, 2014), ch. 8.
7 The Nobel Prize–winning economist Paul Krugman, widely praised for the elegance of his economic models, once wondered whether what got left out of them mattered more than what was left in.
8 Xiuzhen Huang et al., "Big data—a 21st Century Science Maginot Line?" *Biodata Mining* 8, no. 7 (2015).
9 Wilkinson, *The Essence of Scenarios*, chs. 13 and 14.
10 Alenka Smerkolj and Timotej Šooš, *Prototyping the Future: A New Approach to Whole-of-Society Visioning*. Both of the authors worked on the scenario exercise. To my knowledge it has not been published.
11 I wondered how much of this transformation depended on language, how critical that one sentence—"In 2050, Slovenians are a happy people"—had been. So I asked Betty Sue Flowers.

"Language really matters," she said. "I have evolved a style—almost the opposite of a literary style. It has to be so clear and simple and transparent and self-effacing. The language has to get out of the way, so people can imagine themselves on the stage, not a passive audience waiting to be entertained. They need to be able to inhabit it. That means you have to exclude technical language because the stories aren't intended for experts. The more individualistic you make it, the more jargon you let in, the more people you exclude.

"In the headings and titles though, then you need little things, like poetry, to make them vivid and condensed enough so that if someone just memorizes the headings, they can tell the whole story themselves. The headings become a kind of meme and then they really stick. I remember one set of scenarios for Shell because someone quoted the headings to me just yesterday—and that was twenty years later! Sticking inside you is how they become real outside you."

12 Adam Kahane, *Transformative Scenario Planning: Working Together to Change the Future* (Oakland: Berrett-Koehler Publishers, 2012). Accounts of many of the Reos Partner projects can be found at https://reospartners.com/.

CHAPTER SIX: **THINK LIKE AN ARTIST**

1 Frode Helland and Julie Holledge, *Ibsen on Theatre* (London: Nick Hern Books, 2018), p. xiii.
2 What patterns are discernable become so only after the work is made, but that's a very different, more bounded process than creating them from scratch.
3 Joshua Rothman, "Mirror World: How William Gibson Makes His Science Fiction Real," *New Yorker,* December 16, 2019, p. 50.
4 Peter Brook, *The Shifting Point: Forty Years of Theatrical Exploration* (London: Bloomsbury Academic, 1988).
5 The technology writer Jaron Lanier recommends that consumers be more like cats than Pavlov's dogs as a defense against the behaviorism imposed by social media. Jaron Lanier, *Ten Arguments for Deleting Your Social Media Accounts Right Now* (London: Bodley Head, 2019).
6 Interview in *The Paris Review,* no. 226, Fall 2018.
7 Alex Clark, "Family Stories Mean One Thing When You're Six, and a Whole Different Thing When You Are 60," *The Guardian,* March 7, 2020.
8 Michael Meyer, *Henrik Ibsen,* vol. 3 (London: Rupert Hart-Davis, 1967), p. 229.
9 Rainer Maria Rilke, *Letters to a Young Poet* (London: Penguin Classics, 2016).
10 https://www.youtube.com/playlist?list=PLM4S2hGZDSE4645tTLQ-q0C GiR4eSFlBW.
11 "Novelist Sebastian Barry on the Day His Son Told Him He Was Gay," www .heraldscotland.com/news/14817424.Novelist_Sebastian_Barry_on_the_day _his_son_told_him_he_was_gay.
12 Interview with Tracey Emin for the *Financial Times*: http://www.youtube.com /watch?v=nQQTI-X1OOw.
13 https://www.futurelibrary.no.
14 https://www.nytimes.com/2019/08/06/books/toni-morrison-dead.html?cam paign_id=60&instance_id=0&segment_id=15916&user_id=533be8ef03db f051b0bb06e1f1f74ec7&regi_id=3305561ing-news; Margalit Fox, "The Nobel Laureate Toni Morrison, Known for 'Song of Solomon' and 'Beloved' Died at 88," *New York Times,* August 6, 2019.
15 The Auden reference is from his poem "In Memory of W. B. Yeats," written in 1939.
16 I'm grateful to Sheila Hayman for this observation.
17 Joseph Firth et al., "The 'Online Brain': How the Internet May Be Changing Our Cognition," *World Psychiatry* 18, no. 2 (June 2019): 119–29. Published online May 6, 2019.

CHAPTER SEVEN: CATHEDRALS

1 Stephen Hawking, "Our Attitude Towards Wealth Played a Crucial Role in Brexit. We Need a Rethink," *Guardian,* July 29, 2016, http://www.theguardian .com/commentisfree/2016/jul/29/stephen-hawking-brexit-wealth-resources.

2 Gijs van Hensbergen, *The Sagrada Família: Gaudí's Heaven on Earth* (London: Bloomsbury, 2018).

3 "Business Roundtable Redefines the Purpose of a Corporation to Promote 'An Economy That Serves All Americans,'" www.businessroundtable.org/business -roundtable-redefines-the-purpose-of-a-corporation-to-promote-an-economy -that-serves-all-americans, accessed September 1, 2019.

CHAPTER EIGHT: SIMPLE, NOT EASY

1 Risto Siilasmaa, *Transforming Nokia: The Power of Paranoid Optimism to Lead Through Colossal Change* (New York: McGraw-Hill, 2019).

2 https://www.cxotalk.com/episode/nokias-risto-siilasmaa-transformation -lessons-chairman, accessed November 22, 2018.

3 Veronica Hope-Hailey's research into trust shows that organizations that went into the financial crisis with high levels of trust were more successful in coming out of it faster and stronger. Veronica Hope-Hailey, *Experiencing Trustworthy Leadership,* Chartered Institute of Personnel and Development, with the University of Bath, 2014. See also Veronica Hope-Hailey, *Where Has All the Trust Gone,* March 2012, and *Cultivating Trustworthy Leadership,* April 2014.

4 http://www.actuporalhistory.org/index1.html.

5 Ibid.

6 Number of deaths is worldwide. Source is David France, *How to Survive a Plague* (London: Picador, 2016).

7 Ibid., p. 508.

8 The English government's reluctance to make the highly effective PrEP widely available is one example of inexplicable, incoherent policy.

9 https://www.nature.com/articles/s41558-019-0463-3.epdf, accessed August 5, 2019; Danielle F. Lawson et al., "Children Can Foster Climate Change Concern Among Their Parents," *Nature Climate Change* 9 (June 2019): 458–62.

CHAPTER NINE: WHO WANTS TO LIVE FOREVER?

1 See especially Quinn Kennedy, Mara Mather, and Laura L. Carstensen, "The Role of Motivation in the Age-Related Positivity Effect in Autobiographical Memory," *Psychological Science* 15, no. 3 (2004); Helene H. Fung, L. L. Carstensen, and Amy M. Lutz, "Influence of Time on Social Preferences: Implications for Life-span Development," *Psychology and Aging* 14, no. 4 (1999);

Laura L. Carstensen, "The Influence of a Sense of Time on Human Development," *Science* 312, no. 5782 (2006).

2 Laura L. Carstensen, M. Pasupathi, U. Mayr, and J. Nesselroade, "Emotional Experience in Everyday Life Across the Adult Life Span," *Journal of Personality and Social Psychology* 79, no. 4 (2000).

3 L. Carstensen and B. L. Fredrickson, "Influence of HIV Status and Age on Cognitive Representation of Others," *Health Psychology* 17, no. 6 (1998): 494–503.

4 Ulla-Carin Lindquist, *Rowing without Oars* (London: John Murray, 2005).

5 A. Goranson, R. S. Ritter, and A. Waytz, "Dying Is Unexpectedly Positive," *Psychological Science* 28, no 7 (2017): 988–99.

6 https://www.calicolabs.com.

7 "Ray Kurzweil's Plan: Never Die," www.wired.com/2002/11/ray-kurzweils -plan-never-die.

8 It's important to note that Kurzweil is not alone in this nonsense. The founder of Bulletproof Coffee is equally obsessed by the importance of his own life: "The Bulletproof Coffee Founder Has Spent $1 Million in His Quest to Live to 180," www.menshealth.com/health/a25902826/bulletproof-dave-asprey -biohacking/.

9 Two thousand nineteen commencement address by Apple CEO Tim Cook at Stanford University, news.stanford.edu/2019/06/16/remarks-tim-cook-2019 -stanford-commencement, accessed August 8, 2019.

10 The hospice movement proved a tremendous ally to the gay community during the AIDS crisis.

CHAPTER TEN: BE PREPARED

1 Initial funders also included the World Economic Forum and the governments of India and Norway. Subsequent to its launch, the European Commission, and the Governments of Australia, Belgium, Canada, Denmark, Ethiopia, Finland, Germany, Japan, the Kingdom of Saudi Arabia, the Netherlands, Norway, Switzerland, and the UK also became funders.

2 The World Health Organization considers the death toll of 11,310 to be a significant underestimate. See "W.H.O.: New Ebola Cases Could Hit 10,000 Per Week," time.com/3505982/ebola-new-cases-world-health-organisation/, and Martin I. Meltzer, Charisma Y. Atkins, Scott Santibanez, et al., "Estimating the Future Number of Cases in the Ebola Epidemic—Liberia and Sierra Leone, 2014–2015," Morbidity and Mortality Weekly Report, September 26, 2014

3 "Characterizing the Epidemiology of the 2009 Influenza A/H1N1 Pandemic in Mexico," journals.plos.org/plosmedicine/article?id=10.1371/journal .pmed.1000436.

4 "Why Couldn't My Treatment Center Save This Baby?," *New York Times,* January 30, 2019, http://www.nytimes.com/2019/01/30/opinion/ebola-treatment -democratic-republic-of-congo.html.

5 BBC World Service, *Witness: The Doomsday Seed Vault*, https://www.bbc.co.uk /programmes/w3cswsjv, accessed October 29, 2019.

6 See "A Resilient Wales," futuregenerations.wales/a-resilient-wales/.

7 It's important to acknowledge that there have been such initiatives before. In the 1990s, the French government set up a council on the rights of future generations but it proved insufficiently robust to survive controversy around testing nuclear weapons in the Pacific. The Israeli Knesset also had a Commission for Future Generations, but that lasted only six years. The Finnish parliament has a committee of seventeen members who are supposed to represent generations to come.

8 https://time.com/5766188/shell-oil-companies-fossil-fuels-climate-change/, accessed January 20, 2020.

9 The psychologist was Amy Duckworth; the science technologist is Andy Conrad, CEO of Verily, spun out of Google X. The Duckworth quote came from a private conversation; the Conrad quote can be found in "Verily's All Out War on Disease Yet to Signal Healthy Returns for Investors," *Financial Times*, August 31, 2019, p. 15, and https://www.ft.com/content/6a8395f4-caa9-11e9 -af46-b09e8bfe60c0, accessed January 22, 2020.

10 "The goal of everything we do is to change people's actual behaviour at scale. We want to figure out the construction of changing a person's behaviour, and then we want to change how lots of people are making their day-to-day decisions. When people use our app, we can capture their behaviors and identify good and bad [ones]. Then we develop 'treatments' and 'data pellets' that select good behaviors. We can test how actionable our cues are for them and how profitable certain behaviors are for us." Shoshana Zuboff, *The Age of Surveillance Capitalism* (London: Profile Books, 2019). The book is replete with jaw-dropping interviews with Silicon Valley leaders proudly discussing the efficiency of inevitability when it can be forced.

INDEX

ABOUT THE AUTHOR

MARGARET HEFFERNAN is an entrepreneur, chief executive, and author. She was born in Texas, raised in Holland, and educated at Cambridge University. She worked for the BBC and developed interactive multimedia products with Peter Lynch, Tom Peters, Standard & Poor's, and The Learning Company. She has served as CEO for InfoMation Corporation, ZineZone Corporation, and iCAST Corporation. Her previous books include *Beyond Measure*, *A Bigger Prize*, and *Willful Blindness*, and her TED Talks have been seen by more than 12 million people.